Campingly Yours

A Heartwarming Journey
of a Lifetime at Summer Camp

by

Thomas C. Adler

Five Star Publications, Inc.
Chandler, AZ

 Campingly Yours

· · ·

· · ·

In loving memory of Maggie,
15 years at Girls Camp

• • •

• • •

Renee and Lou: "They had a vision."

Linda F. Radke, President
Five Star Publications, Inc.
P.O. Box 6698
Chandler, AZ 85246-6698

www.CampinglyYours.com

Five Star Publications, Inc.
Your Story Begins Here
Since 1985

Adler, Thomas C.
 Campingly yours : a heartwarming journey of a lifetime at summer camp / by
Thomas C. Adler.
    p. cm.
 ISBN-13: 978-1-58985-111-5
 ISBN-10: 1-58985-111-0
 1. Camps. 2. Camps--Juvenile literature. I. Title.

GV192.2.A35 2008
796.54--dc22
                          2008031629

Printed in Canada

Editor: Gary Anderson
Interior Design: Linda Longmire
Cover Design: Kris Taft Miller
Project Manager: Sue DeFabis

Table of contents

Introduction

Several years ago, my mom encouraged me to write a book—she thought I had a story to tell. My wife, Pamela, told me to just start spewing—writing down anything that comes to my mind—but what could I write about? All I've ever really known or cared about has been growing up with my parents and brother, sports, my adulthood spent as a husband and father, and my lifetime spent at summer camp. I never experienced working in the corporate world and had only a brief tenure as a high school teacher. I did have two stints working at Dad's junkyard, which turned out to be an amazing place to learn more about Dad. How many other boys wanted to be just like their dads? I didn't care about the actual number, as long as my dad was reserved only for me.

Okay, Pamela, I spewed. Thanks for your encouragement. I put my camp life and my home life as I remembered it into words. I decided not to ask my friends for help, since I wanted to keep my story solely as I recalled it. Some of the names and nicknames have been changed, and no matter how hard I tried to put events into chronological order, I'm sure I've messed up a date or two.

Writing this memoir has allowed me to recapture many memories of summer camp, Mom, Dad, Flash, dogs, and friends. It became incredible at times as my mind zoned back to events I would have sworn had just happened. Some of them were delightfully clear, while I would have preferred that others hadn't been so clear, and sometimes sadness overtook me and I couldn't get away from it.

I've come to realize that this book isn't just for those who have attended summer camp. It's for anyone who has cherished memories of people and places they love.

My thanks go to Pamela, Abigail, Anne B, Jim (for collecting and arranging all the photos), Aunt Thelma, Aunt Lucille, Beth and Gregg, Jim, Diane, and Tom, Farb, Little Farb, Gary Anderson (my editor), Leb, Moose, Rory, Judy, Marilyn, Rooster (St. Germain), Mobile Photo Service, CC Burns, Linda Radke and Sue DeFabis of Five Star Publications, Inc. (my publishers), and the thousands of boys, girls, counselors, and parents I met at summer camp.

The majority of the proceeds from Campingly Yours will be donated to help children throughout America-and the rest of the world-attend summer camp.

Campingly Yours

Prologue

The Girls Camp Newsletter
Monthly edition #324
The Final Edition

Dear Campers, Counselors, Parents, and Everyone,

I send warm greetings from summer camp and I trust all is well with you and your family. The leaves have turned a multitude of colors and the lake sits tranquil, resting from weeks of campers making waves. There is stillness in the air, an eerie stillness; it is too quiet. I wish all of you could return now.

Normally this camp newsletter has loads of fun facts to offer: Which of your favorite campers and counselors are planning to return next summer; who is celebrating a birthday; when the reunion will be coming to your city; and news bits about your latest adventures. Normalcy is not part of this final newsletter. Memories are what I have to offer: Memories of camp, memories of life, and memories of those who are no longer sharing memories.

At the end of this newsletter I have added a long attachment. Read it at your own speed. Remember to enjoy your friends and those you love. Make something special for your mom; it doesn't have to be Mother's Day. Go visit your dad at his place of work— you might learn a little more about him.

And to the parents, think about getting a dog for your son or daughter.

Some of you have an easy time letting go—I have to hang on. This newsletter is about wanting more. I hope you enjoy my attached memories.

Have a nice winter and spring, and remember to keep those campfires burning.

Campingly Yours,
The Flash

Campingly Yours

1

My Brother is Sent Away

found myself feeling unusually sad as I crouched at second base anticipating the next ground ball. Why did I have that empty feeling pounding in my gut? On that typical hot, muggy Missouri afternoon, my proud parents were in their usual fold-up lawn chairs. They watched my every move, but never interfered with the coach or umpire.

Dad was in the minority when it came to loud confrontation. He wasn't into showing off and carrying the "my son should bat cleanup and wear number 7" attitude (Mickey Mantle was the standard bearer, no matter where one lived).

Mom was joyfully along for the ride, and she always looked sharp. She gradually learned about baseball and every other sport that was brought into her married-with-sons world. My parents brought Bulky the bulldog to each game, and probably more people were enthralled with that dog than with the talent on the field. Bulky had been around all my life and became an identifiable attachment with Dad.

My stomach was churning and I was feeling sad. A tall, burly guy at the plate interrupted my emotions by hitting a screaming one-hopper to my left. All the guys seemed big to me. I was nine, playing with the twelve-year-olds, and all four feet of me weighed in at a whopping fifty-nine pounds. I dove to my left, not minding the thought of dirt and another scar; recovered the ball from the webbing of my glove, not bothering to get up; and flipped the ball from my knees to throw out the lumbering cleanup hitter by two steps. From the corner of my eye I could see Mom clapping and Dad standing with a small grin on his face.

I was still sad, though, even after that big play. The previous winter, a husband and wife had pulled into our driveway in a yellow Pontiac station wagon. Apparently, Mom and Dad had invited them to our home to show a movie about a program for my brother.

The husband seemed big to me—linebacker-like. He introduced himself as Lou as he stumbled into our house carrying a movie projector and screen. I assumed that Lou was smart, since he was carrying all of that high tech stuff, and I thought he was going to show demonstrations of math and science to my brother. But what new things could Lou show my brother? After all, my brother was the smartest kid on the block—and probably in the whole city. He knew more than the teachers. I was sure of it.

Lou set up his movie equipment in our living room as Mom prepared dinner for everyone. Lou's wife, Renee, marveled at Mom's cooking and requested a copy of the noodle kugel recipe. Renee also commented how perfectly proportioned the food sat on each plate and the systematically arranged color combinations. Vegetables, meat, Jell-O mold, kugel, and whatever else was served always were color coordinated on Mom's table.

Lou probably didn't notice the matching food colors, but he did take a second helping of everything. He then excused himself from the table to get his movie equipment ready. Mom held off dessert for a while as everyone gathered in the living room to watch the presentation. Renee had brought her knitting and sat quietly working as Lou began his explanation of the events we were about to see on screen.

As the movie began, I quickly determined that it wasn't a science demonstration after all. I was surprised to see baseball, football, swimming, rafting, and canoeing (my first look at a canoe). Boys were screaming and yelling—not at each other, but in a friendly, spirited way. I only knew about Little League and how everyone screamed and yelled at each other—

Campingly Yours

although it was actually the parents who did most of the screaming. It seemed downright dangerous to be a volunteer umpire, and coaches could never play anyone's son enough or in the right positions, especially their own sons. I think Dad even felt that way, but he never said anything.

As the movie progressed, I was amazed at how deftly Lou explained each event and seemed to know everyone's name as they appeared on screen. Lou also called my dad by name a lot, as he did with my brother, as he pointed out the highlights of the film. Mom was getting dessert ready, but I assumed that her name would have been used often, too, if she'd been in the room.

A few moments later, the picture quality of the movie became noticeably unclear. Dad turned on the lights and my brother discovered that the roll of film had become scattered underneath the projector. Lou acted a bit perturbed, but it appeared that it wasn't an unusual occurrence.

Mom seized the opportunity to invite everyone back into the kitchen to get their dessert. My brother stayed behind to help Lou put his film back in place. It was a pretty easy task for my brother and everyone marveled at how fast he was able to rectify a potential disaster. I wasn't entirely convinced that Lou could have repaired the problem on his own.

A short time later, the film continued as we ate dessert in the living room—Mom's famous ice cream parfaits. Lou did little narrating for a while, but it was actually okay, because Dad said that the images on the film spoke for themselves—and he was correct. The movie showed boys having a great time with seemingly no cares in the world.

My brother focused on the shots of sailing, making photographic prints in a darkroom, and the neat leather billfolds the boys made in crafts, but I only noticed the baseball, basketball, and football shots—and the fact that the normal attire was jeans and a t-shirt. I also saw that boys continued to scream and yell, but not at each other—and that there were no parents around! There only seemed to be some high school or college guys who looked pretty neat as they held kids on their shoulders, threw boys into the lake, and showed guys how to use a fishing rod. There were a few underwear shots, as well (tasteful, of course).

After the film, Lou asked to see my brother's bedroom. Mom no doubt had an immediate panic attack, since our bedrooms seldom were clean, at least not up to the standard of being seen by company. For my brother and me, cleaning simply meant that we closed the door before anyone arrived.

Lou wanted to have a private talk with my brother and to see what types of items were in his room. My brother had *Scientific American* and *National Geographic* magazines, math books, and a vast collection of *Mad* magazines. I was sure Lou related well with the Mad collection, and he used Alfred E. Newman as a way to engage my brother in conversation. Lou learned of my brother's likes and dislikes as he asked which parts of the film looked most interesting.

After a few minutes, my brother and Lou came out of the room, laughing and acting like they were good friends. I began viewing Lou as a pretty smart guy, and he also seemed to be a really nice man. He came across as a bit teacher-like and coach-like—a little intimidating, but still a neat person. In fact, I was convinced that Lou was okay, mainly because I could tell that Dad really liked him.

Lou and Renee talked about how many friends from all over the country and around the world that my brother would make, but I thought making friends outside of our Missouri town sounded odd. I couldn't recall knowing anyone outside of town, except maybe a few relatives, and relatives never seemed like friends—they were just relatives.

My brother asked if it was difficult to sail and said he wanted to learn. Lou said he'd personally show him how to sail and that he took boys out on the lake all the time. It was one of his passions.

That appeared to be a good answer, since my brother lit up, tugged on Mom's sleeve, and said, "I want to go to CAMP!"

I sensed that Lou and Renee actually cared about my brother, and I was pretty sure that Mom and Dad also felt the sincerity of the two visitors. The evening suddenly became a little less confusing to me, and I could tell that something quite different—but potentially scary—was on the horizon.

• • •

Little League season was almost half over by mid-June. For some reason, that summer my brother and I weren't placed on the same team. I think my coach wanted to make sure his team didn't lose, so he'd somehow managed to put an all-star team together. Of course, the coach's son made that team and pitched every other game. I guess that did help make all-stars out of some of us from a defensive standpoint.

Whenever we did something *wrong*, we were scolded and told to run a mile—and a mile to a nine-year-old seemed like a trip from St. Joe to Kansas City. It was right at the time when President Kennedy had inaugurated his national fitness plan. Our country was learning that exercise in all forms was important, and students, as well as all of America's citizens, needed to get into better shape. We learned that push-ups, sit-ups, pull-ups, and daily running were good for us. At the same time, our coach was making us run if we did something wrong. It seemed strange that the coach punished us with something that was supposed to be good for us. When I messed up at home, I don't recall Mom ever taking away my dessert. I think Mom was ahead of her time.

Everyone knew my brother was an outstanding student. He was known as a math and science wizard and he digested those subjects easily, but not as many people knew that he could also hit a baseball with authority. He wore glasses, probably seemed pretty nerdy to other people, and loved math, which was too much for an aggressive Little League coach to comprehend.

Dad used to come home after work and throw countless pitches to us. I hit ground balls; my brother hit line drives. I fielded all of the line drives; my brother missed every ground ball. Dad went to work at seven a.m. and came home after five. He worked half days on

Saturday, but he still managed to toss pitches to us almost every day.

My brother was a member of the opposing team we played that mid-June day, but he wasn't in the lineup, and I was sad. My parents had sent him away to Lou and Renee's summer camp in northern Wisconsin. My brother and I had always done all kinds of fun things together, and for some reason he rarely beat me up. It seemed like all of my friends got beat up by their older brothers from time to time, but not me.

I secretly rooted for my brother to hit a home run every time, and it made me happy to see the others groan when the *math nerd* hit one into the gap. For some reason, the coaches never noticed how he could pull a fastball—not a curveball, but a fastball. He never came within a foot of a curve ball. Maybe his glasses were too thick.

Less than a month earlier, my team had played my brother's team. We were ahead by a run in the last inning, the coach's son was pitching, and their best hitter came to the plate. My coach intentionally walked that hitter to get to my brother. I thought about telling the pitcher to throw only curveballs, but that might have changed the pattern of my not getting beat up, so I just mumbled to myself and asked the Lord not to let the ball come toward me.

Our pitcher threw a fastball and my brother pulled it down the left field line, fair by a couple of feet. By the time the left fielder had retrieved the ball, my brother was rounding third and the lead runner had already scored. I backed up the relay throw that had gotten past the shortstop and fired a perfect strike to the plate. My brother slid more or less headfirst (actually, I think he tripped) and his glasses hit the dirt. He stumbled through the catcher as the umpire signaled *safe*. All the boys on my team threw down their gloves and muttered grade school swear words as the opposing team hoisted my brother onto their shoulders. Our coach said a few adult swear words and immediately ordered us to run a mile.

What a feeling that must have been for a math nerd to suddenly find himself on top of the Little League world. I looked up in the stands and saw Mom clapping and Dad standing, wearing a small grin.

My brother went away to camp shortly after that, which was the reason I was sad. That summer, I often enjoyed daydreaming about my brother's big moment at the plate—and wondered if Lou ever made him run a mile.

• • •

We won the Little League title in our division that summer. Thank goodness! Otherwise, I might have become a long distance track star. Mom and Dad attended every game, Dad threw pitches to me most evenings, and I retrieved my ground balls from the neighbor's yard.

Dad bought me a catcher's glove and a mask that summer. He liked pitching and wanted to break up the routine a bit. He loved throwing roundhouse curves, but I never had the heart to tell him that he hung most of them. I secretly wished I could see pitches like that in a game.

When Dad's friends visited, they all took turns throwing to me. I could catch them for hours; I loved it so much. Two of his friends were very athletic and both had a lot of zip on the ball. I think they sometimes forgot that I was only nine, but I really didn't care. They could throw as hard as they wanted as far as I was concerned.

One of Dad's friends was a lefty and he once threw me a fierce curveball that nailed my left shin—I never got a glove on it. That was the first time I'd ever received a *real* curve ball. Dad had a startled look on his face, but I didn't think he was worried about my shin. After witnessing that wicked curveball, I think Dad realized that his roundhouse curve wasn't so round.

Mom had dinner ready every night when we finished playing ball. She never disappointed us, and gourmet meals kept coming our way. We actually sat at the table and had fun conversations. One meal was especially exciting, since Mom and Dad said my brother was coming home that Saturday. It was mid-August and he'd been at camp for nearly eight weeks. I received one letter from my brother that summer.

Hi, Kid Brother,

I threw up on the long ride to camp, and everyone else threw up several times. The food is okay, and we get to have seconds on beanie weenie. Parts of the beanie weenie are served for the whole week. It's been cold and rainy, and I have forty-one mosquito bites. Once, a mosquito lived in my ear all night.

I got a fishhook stuck in my hand and the nurse had to remove it. No one has beaten me up because I wear glasses. I love camp!

P.S.

Everyone here calls me The Flash because they say I walk and talk slow, don't tie my shoes, and come from Missoura.

• • •

Saturday finally arrived—the day my brother was coming home. The camp had arranged a flight for him into Kansas City, which was about an hour from our St. Joseph home. Mom and Dad planned a big reunion and made reservations at a nice restaurant near the airport. We hadn't seen my brother for eight weeks. The camp had scheduled a visitation weekend after four weeks, but Mom and Dad didn't attend because they thought it would interfere with the program. I assumed they took the same attitude with the camp director as they did with the Little League coach.

My brother trudged off the plane with a few other camp boys from the area. All the parents were hugging their kids, and Mom hugged my brother. Dad shook my brother's hand and displayed his patented small grin. I could tell that Mom and Dad were happy to see my brother and they couldn't wait to hear all about his first adventures at camp.

I shook my brother's hand, but didn't want to let him know how much I'd missed having him around. All the attention that had been focused on me that summer suddenly shifted to my brother. At first it hurt a little, but Mom and Dad had a way of equaling things out.

They stepped aside for a moment to talk, and then Dad made a quick call on a nearby pay phone. He canceled the dinner reservations and announced we were going to grab a bite to eat at a hamburger joint down the road. My brother and I were thrilled that a hamburger and malt had replaced a meal where we would have been required to use napkins and good table manners.

Mom jokingly asked my brother if he'd bothered to shower during the summer.

He seriously answered, "Yes, Mom, five or six times."

It appeared that my brother's layers of dirt weren't going to be appropriate for a nice restaurant, but they were acceptable at a hamburger joint. My brother's dirt made me wonder what else I could get away with by not keeping clean. I hadn't heard a word about camp yet, but already it seemed like a great place.

We wolfed down the meal as my brother dominated the conversation with tales of his camping experience. He said that Lou had taken him sailing, just as promised. He said it was a really big boat and six other campers and a counselor were also on board. Apparently it had been loads of fun until Lou had inadvertently run the mast into some overhead wires on the second lake from camp. The boat partially capsized and Lou went flying into the lake while the campers held on to the sides.

A counselor had then instructed everyone to swim to a nearby resort, where he was able to make a phone call. After an hour or so, a ski boat came to haul the beached sailors back to camp. Lou and my brother had remained at the sailboat's stern to steer with the rudder as the boat was being towed back.

Although my brother told us it was actually a fun experience, I couldn't help asking him if Lou had gotten mad at himself, said some adult swear words, thrown down his life preserver, and swum a mile. To my amazement, my brother said it had actually been quite the opposite. He told me that Lou had laughed at himself because he'd known the wires were there but had just forgotten.

Lou had also warned my brother that when they arrived at camp everyone was going to

poke fun at them. He told everyone else who'd been on board to brace themselves for some serious teasing, but that it would be okay. To my brother's surprise, the whole camp was gathered on shore to greet them with a hero's welcome when they returned. In fact, Lou was hoisted onto the shoulders of several counselors and they paraded him around in circles. The other six sailors, including my brother, were also hoisted up and paraded about. He said it was the neatest feeling he'd ever experienced.

As I listened, I sat thinking what a lucky summer it had been for my brother. He'd been hoisted on shoulders for hitting a home run and then for capsizing a boat. What kind of place would hoist a nerdy eleven-year-old with glasses onto people's shoulders for messing up?

I also wondered about how Lou could have been glorified for capsizing a boat with a bunch of kids aboard. Maybe he'd broken that film on purpose in our living room! Maybe he'd made sure that it was my brother who fixed the film. Regardless, I was looking forward to hearing more stories about camp.

2

I'll Try for You, Dad

Daydreaming always occupied a large portion of my day. I often thought about a big play in baseball, basketball, or football. I also enjoyed thinking about life and wondering why certain things were done the way they were. My brother's camp stories had also entered my daydreaming repertoire.

One day, I remembered my brother telling me about how he and his cabin mates had to pass cabin inspection every day. He said cabin cleanup was pretty tough, since the campers actually had to make their beds. That made the cabin cleanup process a lot harder than just closing a bedroom door.

He told me that a village director would come around and check to see if the cabin was clean, if there was sand in the beds, and if the shelves were neat. The village director, an older guy, but younger than Lou, would pound his hand on all the beds and if sand hit him in the eye, the camper who owned that bed was doomed. It meant shaking out the blanket and remaking the bed.

My brother said that everyone in the cabin relied on each other to do each job well—or the whole cabin was doomed. He said that Lou described it as teamwork, but I told him that teamwork was for a ball team, not a bunch of guys making beds.

Campingly Yours

He just laughed and said, "That's what I thought, too, until I got to camp."

When I asked him what *doomed* meant, he said, "Just imagine cleaning for a whole morning."

In that light, *doomed* began to take on a pretty heavy meaning.

I asked, "How much fun can camp be if the guys have to keep their cabins clean all the time?"

He laughed again and reminded me about how few times he'd taken a shower that summer, which settled my thoughts down a bit.

After a full day of thinking about things, I was happy to welcome Dad home. He brought Bulky out and then Dad and I threw the football around before dinner while my brother studied in his room. Dad told me we were going to have some familiar guests the next week.

I asked, "Do I know them?"

Dad said, "Of course you do. That's the meaning of the word *familiar*."

I mumbled something about not having to think about the meanings of words while playing catch. Mom came to the door and shouted that it was time for dinner, which saved me from trying to figure out what Dad was talking about.

• • •

Mom served another great meal and told me to try everything, since it would help me grow tall, but I thought it was just a ploy, judging from our family tree. Dad and my brother worked on math equations during the meal, but as usual, I had no idea what they were talking about. It wasn't unusual for me to be totally clueless about both the food and the conversation at suppertime. Just to change the subject, I asked Mom about the familiar guests who were due next week.

"You must be talking about Lou and Renee," she said. "They're coming to dinner again, but this time some other boys from the area and their families are also coming."

I asked why Lou and Renee needed to come to town again.

"Well," Mom said, "that's what they do. They travel from town to town and visit with campers and their families and sign up new campers."

Apparently she and Dad had mentioned the camp to a few local families and they had showed enough interest to come to our house to check it out—but I suspected they just wanted to eat Mom's food. Mom said that they'd sent my brother to camp on a recommendation from some close family friends and that those friends had found out about the camp from other friends in Omaha. Then Mom dropped a bombshell.

"This year we're thinking about sending you to camp, too."

Oops! I hadn't been expecting to hear that! Lou and Renee, that big linebacker-like guy and his wife, were coming to see me? Suddenly Mom's gourmet meal took a turn for the worse and I needed to pry Dad away from my brother's math equations to confirm what Mom had just told me. I finally got Dad's attention, but he answered my question before I could ask.

"Your brother had a great time at camp last summer and he wants to go back, so your mother and I thought camp might be good for you, too," he said, looking up from my brother's math textbook.

"What do you mean by *good*?" I asked.

He said he thought that getting away from city life would give me an opportunity that most boys never have.

"It did a world of good for your brother and he made lots of new friends," said Dad. "We won't make you go, but we'd like you to at least keep an open mind about it when Lou and Renee get here."

I wondered if he was implying that going to camp would also help me grow—but at that moment, I was more inclined to vote for Mom's food theory.

After supper, I moped to my room, foregoing my dessert. My stomach felt queasy. The feeling was neither nausea nor pain—it was more like a churning sensation. It felt as if a blender was slowly stirring things up and then switching gears into reverse.

For a long time I just sat pounding a ball into my glove, waiting for the churning to stop—until I heard Mom knock on the door. A moment later, she came in carrying my dessert. When I told her about my stomach, she set the dessert aside.

"You probably don't know it," she said, "but I often experience the same sensation, especially when I think about something new and far away. I felt it the first time when I was twenty and getting ready to transfer from our local junior college to Oklahoma University."

I never knew that Mom had gone to college, but I asked, "How can a twenty-year-old girl have the same stomach problems as a nine-year-old boy?"

She said, "The fear of the unknown has no age limit. It took me a long time to get away and see something other than St. Joe, and for me, I thought Norman, Oklahoma, was like living in another country. I got to experience different people, buildings with no basements, odd food, and the sensation of having no parents guiding my every move. It's not that I had anything against my parents. I just needed to experience the feeling of independence for the first time."

"Is independence a good thing for a kid?" I asked.

"I think so," she said. "I learned that after seeing what camp did for your brother. When he came home from camp, it was the first time I ever heard him talk about friends, being silly, and having nobody care what anyone looked like. He could always do math and science at home, but your brother needed to let loose, and camp gave him the chance to do that."

Seeing the puzzled expression on my face, Mom added, "You can play all the sports you want to at the camp—and you can experience the independence thing at the same time."

"Well, if Oklahoma was so good, why are you still living in your old hometown?" I asked.

Tears welled up in Mom's eyes at that question, and for a few moments I was sorry I had asked.

Then she said softly, "Fear has always played a big role in my life." When she saw that I didn't understand, she added, "I promise to tell you more about it when you get older."

I was going to remind her that she'd just told me that fear and age had no limits, but I could see that she was upset, so I tried to change the subject.

"Well, Mom, one thing I know for sure. It's awfully hard for me to pass up your homemade chocolate cake."

We both laughed as I dug in.

• • •

Lou and Renee were due to arrive the next night. My stomach began to churn again, but it was a unique form of churning. My stomach really hurt, but I didn't tell anyone, because it wasn't about me or Lou and Renee—it was about Dad.

Bulky had died in our backyard early that morning. From my room, I saw him lying still and somehow I just knew he was dead.

My brother was still sleeping, but I was watching as Dad picked up an old gunnysack and wrapped it around Bulky's lifeless body. I saw Dad pick up his bulldog, then set him down again. I saw him take off his glasses and wipe his eyes with his sleeve. I didn't know dads could cry, especially *my* dad.

For as long as I could remember, Bulky had gone everywhere with Dad; they were interwoven into each other's identity. Dad picked Bulky up again and gently laid him in the front seat of the car. He didn't use the trunk or back seat; he used the front seat.

I could see Dad's hand reach out and touch Bulky as he slowly drove away. My stomach was hurting as I wiped the tears from my eyes. I stared out the window waiting for Dad to return. I was in pain—in pain for my dad. I cried for Bulky, but I cried more for Dad.

Later that afternoon, Dad came home, and all of us sat quietly in the living room. Dad told us that he'd taken Bulky to a veterinarian to be cremated. The ashes would come back in a few days, he said, and then he'd spread them outside his place of work.

Dad told us, "Having Bulky has brought me both joy and sadness, but I'll remember the

Campingly Yours

joy."

I didn't tell Dad that I'd watched him from my window that morning. I would always remember the sadness.

• • •

The next day, Mom scurried around the house, preparing for our company. She also managed to get my brother and me to clean our rooms, since she assumed Lou would again be taking a peek at them. My brother was excited to see Lou and Renee again. It was the first time I'd seen my brother excited about seeing older people, except for relatives. My brother said that everyone at camp called Lou and Renee by their first names, so there'd be no *Mr.* and *Mrs.* stuff.

Lou and Renee arrived before the rest of the crowd.

Lou gave my brother a sturdy handshake and said, "Hi, Flash!"

Renee gave my brother a hug.

They did the same with me (except for the Flash part) and my parents. Lou asked my brother and me to help him with his gear, so we helped lug the projector, screen, reel-to-reel film, and a bunch of pictures into the house.

Mom had appetizers ready and told Lou and Renee that the other guests would be there soon. My brother and I helped Lou set up while the two of them reminisced about the previous summer. My brother had a certain glow about him at that moment that hardly ever showed. I couldn't quite place it, but I knew it was a nice kind of different.

Three other families arrived shortly and Mom served one of her powerhouse dinners. Lou talked about camp and then held a question-and-answer period before showing the movie. As the film progressed, my brother constantly interrupted Lou to help explain the events being shown on the screen—but I could tell that Lou was happy with my brother's enthusiasm and didn't mind the interruptions.

I also noticed my brother monitoring the film, making sure it didn't break again. It was cool when my brother's image popped up a couple times on the screen. Everyone cheered and Dad grinned. We had dessert, and then Lou handed out enrollment information and the guests said their goodbyes.

Then it was my turn!

I knew it would happen eventually. Lou asked to see my room—and Mom just offered him good luck. Actually, I had cleaned my room pretty well and was hoping that Lou would check my bed for sand. Instead, he sized up my wall posters, mainly of sports figures, and though he'd been aware of my fondness of sports, he was surprised to also see my collection of Kennedy/Johnson campaign buttons.

Lou told me that he'd once been a boxer and a football player. That seemed really cool to me. He also said that he had voted for JFK and asked me why I liked Kennedy. I said I liked the fact that Kennedy played football on the White House lawn and that he was trying to get Americans to do more exercise. Lou told me that he'd be implementing the president's fitness program at camp next summer. I thought that was pretty cool. He then said that he could tell my brother and I had different interests, but camp had something for everyone.

I asked, "Can I play baseball, basketball, and football?"

"You bet. You can play almost every day. I'll even get in some of the games with you," he replied.

I reminded Lou that he'd promised to take my brother sailing and that I'd heard all about the accident. He cleared his throat, scratched his head, laughed a little, and then let me know that he was happy no one had been injured.

"It must have been neat to be raised on people's shoulders after capsizing a boat," I said.

Changing the subject, he reminded me that there was something at camp for everyone, including the directors.

We finally came out of my room smiling and I tugged on Mom's shirt, proclaiming, "I want to go to camp!"

Campingly Yours

Mom obviously was thrilled with my response and offered extra dessert. We all dug in.

My brother and I hauled Lou's equipment back to the car and said goodbye to Lou and Renee, saying we'd see them next summer. Mom gave some of her recipes to Renee and they hugged goodbye. Lou patted both my brother and me on the back and shook Dad's hand. The camp directors waved from their Pontiac wagon as they headed for the next reunion in Omaha.

Mom and Dad came into my room while I was getting ready for bed. Dad said he was happy I had decided to give camp a try.

"It looks like a great place, at least for now," I said, not knowing if it would still look good the next week, "but I feel bad that you won't have anyone to play catch with next summer."

Dad just grinned and said goodnight.

Before Mom left, I asked, "How was Dad able to act happy in front of everyone after losing Bulky?"

"Your father would never allow the night to be ruined for you and your brother. Is your stomach still hurting?"

When I said no, she kissed me goodnight and left. I stayed awake awhile thinking some about camp, but mainly thinking about Dad and Bulky. I wondered if Lou and Renee had ever lost anything as important as Dad's bulldog.

$$\bullet \ \bullet \ \bullet$$

That winter, I read my name in the monthly camp newsletter, saying that I had enrolled as a new camper. The newsletter also mentioned returning campers and staff and featured several articles about what to expect at camp, about former camp people, and a few poems and sayings. The newsletter was a big deal to my brother and he rushed to the mailbox at the beginning of the month, hoping the latest copy had arrived. I had to admit that it was pretty neat to see my name in print.

When the second week of June arrived, my brother and I were almost halfway through Little League season. Dad brought home a small Army trunk and a green duffel bag, exact duplicates of those my brother had used at camp the summer before. I had breezed through spring without thinking much about going away to summer camp, but reality set in upon the arrival of my luggage.

A swarm of bees began swirling in my stomach when I saw that trunk and duffel. It was really happening to me. I was being sent away for eight weeks! I decided not to tell Mom about my churning—I kept my internal Mixmaster to myself. I'd promised Lou and Renee that I'd see them in the summer and I was determined not to back down.

The day I'd been quietly dreading finally arrived. Dad stuffed the back of his Plymouth station wagon with two duffels and two trunks and we headed for the Kansas City airport. My brother was talking up a storm, really excited, while I sat in the back seat, my stomach quietly churning away.

I'd said goodbye to my ball team earlier in the week, and as we drove along, I rehashed their comments about my going away.

They'd said things like:

"Good luck in prison."

"Have fun at boot camp."

"Your parents must really want to get rid of you. What did you do to them?"

I thought they were kidding me, but I wasn't completely sure. However, I knew that none of them had a clue about summer camp—and I, too, knew very little about camp.

We arrived at the airport and met a few other boys and their families. Apparently Lou and Renee had been pretty convincing at our house. Everyone checked their baggage and headed for the gate to board the jet-prop Braniff plane, headed for Omaha and then to Minneapolis, where we'd be picked up by a staff member from the camp. Then we'd take a three-hour ride to camp.

 Campingly Yours

3

Welcome to Summer Camp, Kid Flash

Parents kissed their sons goodbye at the airport, but not Dad. He shook my brother's hand and then took me aside for a moment. He told me that my brother and I were special.

He said, "You might have a few tough days, but you'll get through it. I believe in Lou and Renee, and they'll also see you as special."

That was all he said, and then he shook my hand. Dad wasn't one to lecture, and I didn't want to disappoint him. I knew I'd try to make him proud, but at that moment I just wanted to stay home. I didn't want to go to camp, but I'd try it for Dad's sake.

As I waved goodbye from the window of the plane, Mom was crying and Dad had a small grin. An incredible tingling feeling shivered through my body every time Dad grinned in my direction.

A moment later, the plane was airborne, on its way toward camp. The jet-prop Braniff leapfrogged every other cloud and it seemed to me that my brother's letter was happening all over again. Everyone got sick, except for me, and all the barf bags were used. At least the horrific ride took my mind off missing Mom and Dad for a while.

I didn't know why I avoided getting sick, but I knew I wanted to land in the worst way. At last, the pilot found the runway and we finally piled off the plane, looking as if we'd invented the flu. We clumped together and headed toward the arrival gate, where a guy wearing a green and white camp t-shirt met us.

He said, "Hi, Flash" to my brother and told all of us his name was Crash.

I didn't remember my brother mentioning anyone named Crash, but we gathered all the baggage and followed him. We loaded everything into a trailer behind a van and took off on a three-hour drive to camp.

I asked Crash how he got his name and he said, "Oh, last year I hit a large cow on the way to pick up the campers at the airport."

Thus began my camping career.

• • •

Crash was a pretty interesting guy and he kept our attention for most of the ride. There were lots of curvy roads, several pit stops for the sick ones, and fortunately, no cows. Finally, we turned onto an old dirt road and saw a sign for the camp.

Crash told us, "Only one more mile to go."

He pounded on the horn during the last full minute of the ride which gave everyone at the camp fair warning of our arrival.

When we pulled into camp, everyone gathered around to greet us. We were the last group to arrive and the mob scene overwhelmed me. Boys were pushing and shoving my brother around, showing their joy at seeing him again while staff members and camp directors greeted all of us. We then formed one large circle and listened as Lou gave a welcome speech.

He said, "In the city, we're boys, but in the North Woods, we become men."

I was feeling more like a baby at that moment, wanting to head straight back to Missouri.

 Campingly Yours

The head counselor shouted out the cabin assignments, and after I had met my counselors and the other boys in my group, we headed toward our cabin.

When we arrived, I found that our cabin had just one entrance, which led through the counselor's quarters into a rectangular room that housed the campers. The interior walls were unfinished and the plywood floors were painted gray. My nose sensed a hint of bleach trying to overtake the musty smell.

There were four bunk beds placed unevenly in the room and several shelves were scattered about. Writing covered the walls and rafters, mostly names and sayings of past lore. I saw dates from the 1940s and I could tell it would take a long time to read the whole cabin. Some of the campers must have been acrobats in order to reach the highest corners of the ceiling, and those who had managed to reach those far corners hadn't bothered to take down the cobwebs. All the writing was clean; no swear words. I found the cobwebs pretty intriguing and wondered if they dated back to the first year of the camp—whenever that was. They just had a look of fine antique quality about them. I started to imagine the countless generations of spiders that had occupied the cabin before me.

I was given the bottom bed of a double bunk, and a huge guy from Milwaukee took the top bed. Nicknamed The Bulk, he had attended camp the previous year. Everyone seemed big compared to me, but The Bulk was definitely high school-size. He requested the top bunk, but I wasn't sure why.

After we'd unloaded our duffels, he jumped onto his bed and—wow! His bed sagged halfway toward mine. I thought about offering to switch to the top, but I kept quiet. There was no sense getting on the wrong side of The Bulk. My brother wore glasses, not me.

Our counselors interrupted our unpacking to lead us on a tour of the camp. I figured it was a required ritual for staff to take the campers on a hike, even though only two of us were new. They told us it was good for initial cabin bonding, and I knew it was a good idea for me, since I had no idea where anything was located—except for The Bulk's bed and mine.

The Bulk stayed by my side as we hiked for a half hour or so. He knew everything about the camp and he described things to me that the counselors hadn't mentioned. The camp seemed huge to me. I was used to my own front yard and a Little League field, but the camp contained large fields, tall pine trees, and gobs of buildings. There were tennis courts, archery targets, a rifle range, two baseball diamonds, and a soccer field—all surrounded by water. At one end of the property was a place for campfires and all the way on the other side was an area marked off for swimming. My cabin was just a few yards from the lake. The counselors told us about the beauty of the camp and the North Woods, but said we were too young to appreciate it. The Bulk never mentioned anything about beauty.

We headed back to the cabin after the tour and finished unpacking. I had three shelves to cram my duffle and trunk belongings onto. Mom had packed everything neatly, so all I had to do was transfer my clothes in five or six swoops. I could tell the hard part would be keeping things in orderly fashion, but at least they were fine at that moment.

The counselors had everyone place their duffels in a trunk and then they stored all the baggage in a partial attic upstairs. A bell rang, indicating that it was time for my first camp meal. The Bulk led me to the dining hall, where each cabin had a designated table.

We stood at the table and listened to Lou make a few announcements before he said grace. It was just a saying, not a formal prayer. Then we sat down to dinner, but no one sat down for long. The dining hall suddenly erupted into a mass chaos of cabin cheers and strange songs—well, they were strange to me, but not to anyone who'd been to camp before.

At first, they shouted some guy's name over and over—John Jacob Jingleheimer Schmidt. Then the counselors and older campers started marching around the dining hall singing about Mrs. O'Leary's cow and screaming, "Fire! Fire! Fire!" Even Lou began marching and yelling "Fire! Fire! Fire!" while he raised his fist in the air.

After ten minutes or so, everyone sat down and the atmosphere regained a little more normalcy. I was scared, homesick, and not feeling like a man at all—in fact, I was feeling vastly overwhelmed by it all. What kind of mess had I gotten myself into? Why had my brother spent a whole year counting the days to the start of camp?

 Campingly Yours

The Bulk interrupted my tortured thoughts, telling me that the cow and fire song was a true story of an incident that had happened in Chicago many years before.

I asked if that was before or after the cobwebs had been formed in our cabin, but he just laughed, shook his head, and said, "I don't know for sure. Nobody at camp sings about cobwebs."

The meal was really good, though it wasn't the beanie weenie my brother had described. It was some kind of pasta with garlic bread and an assortment of vegetables. I was expecting grade school assembly line food with sauerkraut on top. I thought it was a pretty shrewd move for the camp to have such a nice meal the first night.

As the meal progressed, I got to know the other guys and counselors at our table, and then dessert arrived. It was chocolate pudding with whipped cream on top, and though it wasn't up to Mom's quality, it was still a darned good-looking dessert.

One of the guys next to me complained that his pudding had a funny smell. He put his nose close to the whipped cream and made a squishy face. Then several others smelled their desserts, too, and the guy next to me told me to smell mine.

As I brought my face down toward the dessert to take a sniff—bam! My head was suddenly slammed into the whipped cream and pudding. Everyone in the cabin broke up laughing— except me, of course. As I wiped my eyes, I could see boys at several other tables who also had pudding all over their faces.

Before I could cry—and believe me, I wanted to—the counselor explained that it was a tradition to pick on the new campers. He told me that the same thing had happened to him his first year, and there was an unwritten rule that no one was allowed to talk about it to the new campers. Of course, I immediately felt better—not really.

The head counselor made a few announcements and then informed us that the annual staff show would be held that evening, and then dismissed us. Thank goodness my first meal was over. I'd never felt so small in my life. I'd been feeling bad enough as it was, but then the dessert incident had happened. Did Lou and Renee purposely serve pudding during the first meal every year?

I noticed that no one was hoisting me on their shoulders for having pudding on my face, and I wasn't liking camp very much at that moment. What was my brother thinking, and how could Dad have thought that camp would be good for me? Dad had been wrong, and so had Mom. I needed to get out of the place, and I wanted to cry, but somehow, I couldn't. I hurt, I felt queasy, my stomach was tossing in all directions, and I would have thrown up the pudding and whipped cream if I had eaten it. I just wanted out of that place—it wasn't my home.

• • •

We'd been informed that we had thirty minutes until the staff show, so I headed back to the cabin by myself. I could see The Bulk trying to catch up with me, but I was too embarrassed to be with anyone at that moment. Some of the CITs (sixteen-year-old counselors-in-training) were tossing a ball around in a grassy area near the cabin. Several of the older counselors joined them as I watched through the screen window of my cabin.

The Bulk startled me from behind and asked if I played ball.

I nodded, so he said, "Why don't we go out with the counselors and play some catch?"

I grabbed my catcher's mitt and mask and went outside with The Bulk. He asked me about the mask and I told him that my dad had bought it for me. I could tell The Bulk thought my mask was kind of weird.

We threw a few to each other and then I overheard some counselors laughing—at me, it turned out. I was suffering from some form of self-destruction (the common term was homesickness) and then, to make it worse, the older guys laughing at me!

One burly counselor named Snarl came over and asked why I was wearing the silly mask. I blinked away tears and told him that my dad threw pitches to me and had bought me the mask. A couple other counselors strolled my way and picked up on the "fun." How much more could I take?

The Bulk came over, but he wasn't able to be of any help. He was big compared to me, but he wasn't counselor-size. Soon all sorts of counselors and older campers had gathered around. They all seemed curious about my catcher's mask. The pudding incident was beginning to look like a blessing compared to what was happening at that moment. I was being brutally teased, when out of the corner of my eye, through all of the chaos, I spotted my brother talking to a tall staff member who was wearing a baseball glove.

My brother stayed back as that staff member came over. I later learned that the tall staff member was the baseball instructor, nicknamed The Vacuum, and it was obvious that he had everyone's respect. He'd attended camp for years and I could tell he was really popular.

The Vacuum said, "Snarl, what's the problem here?"

It appeared that The Vacuum wasn't very fond of Snarl.

The Vacuum told Snarl and me to stand a few feet apart and crouch down in a catcher's position. Then he paced off sixty-feet-six-inches and announced that he was going to throw a pitch to each of us.

"Whoever misses a pitch will get tossed into the lake," he added.

By that time, it seemed like the whole camp had gathered. The Vacuum was tall and lanky and I overheard someone say that he had pitched for his college team. Snarl had a smirk on his face, and I instantly understood how he'd gotten his nickname. I, on the other hand, was shaking inside.

I thought about the thousands of pitches my dad and his friends had thrown me over the years, and I thought about Dad's roundhouse curve—and his friend's "real" curveball, the one I'd missed. I wished Dad were there, sitting in his lawn chair, always quiet, but always watching me.

A few moments later, The Vacuum wound up and threw a medium-paced ball to Snarl, who caught it easily. The crowd applauded mildly. Then he threw the same-paced pitch my way, and I caught it, too, but the crowd made no noise at all.

The Vacuum then threw a bit harder, first to Snarl, who caught it, but looked a bit shaky I could tell that Snail wasn't a ballplayer, but he was probably twenty years old and I'd just turned ten, so I knew the odds were stacked against me.

The Vacuum then threw a pretty hard one my way, about as hard as Dad always threw. I caught it easily and the crowd rippled with some noise of approval. It was the first time since I'd set foot at the camp that I'd gotten any form of approval, except from The Bulk.

After I'd tossed the ball back to The Vacuum, he announced that he was going to throw his three-quarter-speed fastball, so we should be awake. Then he whipped the ball toward Snarl and it barely stayed in his glove as he fell sideways. The crowd gave him an ovation of laughter and applause while the Snarl showed disdain. The same pitch then came my way and I caught it pretty easily. The crowd began to cheer. The Vacuum's pitch had been harder than Dad ever threw.

Finally, The Vacuum announced that he was about to throw a fast curveball and warned both of us to be careful. He unleashed a wicked curveball toward Snarl and I could see that it moved far more than the one Dad's friend had thrown that had hit me in the shin.

Snarl swiped his glove at the ball, but he never came close. The ball smacked him in the stomach and he crouched over in pain. Luckily, he was too overweight to be hurt very much. The crowd erupted in a combination of sarcastic cheers and laughter—and Snarl snarled.

My fate had been set. If I could catch the curveball, I'd be spared the lake. The Vacuum took a big windup and showed no mercy as he hurled the hardest, meanest, nastiest curveball I'd ever seen in my direction. It was like a comet from Jupiter, starting high from the left center of the sky and suddenly bursting my way—until it landed just below my mask into my catcher's mitt.

I had caught it! I had caught it!

All those days of having Dad and his friends throw me their best stuff had finally paid off. The crowd cheered wildly as the ball landed in the middle of my glove. At first I thought the cheering was all for me, but then I realized that they were actually more excited to see Snarl tossed into the lake.

I took off my mask, let out a sigh of relief, and noticed my brother and Lou standing on a small hill a short distance away. The Vacuum walked over, shook my hand, and gave me a pat on the back.

In a low, confidential voice, he said, "Your brother clued me in on your baseball ability and told me that I could throw the ball as fast as I wanted—and you'd catch it."

I looked over toward my brother, who just smiled. The Vacuum said he expected me to sign up for baseball and would be looking for me. A short distance away, I saw Lou smiling as he put his arm around my brother—and in my mind, I could see Dad's grin.

• • •

A short time later, a bell rang to signify that it was time for the staff show. The Bulk told me that the counselors always put on variety acts for the campers at the beginning and end of camp. He said it was a lot of fun and was a way for the campers to get to know the counselors—and indeed it was a fun show. Some of the counselors sang serious songs, some sang funny songs, some performed silly gags, and they all poked fun at each other. They also poked fun at Lou and Renee, all in good taste, and they made a special point of making fun of the beanie weenie my brother liked so much.

Then three guys went on stage and threw a bunch of baseballs, at a counselor who played Snarl. When he missed a pitch, they picked him up and threw him in a barrel of water. Everyone laughed, including Snarl. How had they put that skit together so fast? I ducked down in my chair, but no one was watching me.

When the show was over, Snarl found me and gave me a playful shove, saying, "You're an OK, kid. I just like picking on new campers with catcher's masks."

At that moment, I could see that even though Snarl was kind of a bumble, he wasn't really such a bad guy.

Campingly Yours

He added, "I just found out that you're Flash's little brother, so I'm gonna call you Kid Flash. I'll see you tomorrow, OK?"

I said, "Thanks, Snarl. See you tomorrow."

I decided that maybe Snarl wasn't so bad after all, and in a strange way, I realized that his bullying had put me on the camp map. I found my brother and thanked him for saving me.

He laughed, playfully hit me on the arm, and said, "No big deal, Kid Flash."

• • •

It was time to head back to the cabin and get ready for my first night of sleeping. So much had taken place since my parents had put me on the plane that morning to be greeted by a guy named Crash.

After we brushed our teeth, the counselors had us form a circle. Our senior counselor lit a candle and as he held the candle in his hands, he told us what he hoped to accomplish during our camp experience. He made serious comments about how he wanted our cabin to become a unified group, but he also told us that his most important goal was to help each of us have a fun and rewarding summer. Our CIT told us he'd been at camp for six summers and each had been better than the one before. His goal was to get us to like camp as much as he did.

The senior counselor then asked each of us to hold the candle and to say anything we wanted to about our camp expectations. One camper said he was tired of all the fighting at his home and hoped our cabin would get along. Another camper said he could tell we had a cool cabin and he wanted us to stick together. When the candle was passed to me, I was nervous. I didn't have many words to offer. I thanked the counselors for making me feel at home, even though I still secretly wanted to go back to Missouri.

When The Bulk received the candle, he said that he'd already made a new best friend. Then he added that he was going to write to his parents and have them send him a catcher's mask. Everyone chuckled, including me. I told him he could use mine any time.

All of us got into our bunks, and then our junior counselor pulled out his guitar and sang two nice folk songs. One of them had a chorus of "this land is your land, this land is my land," but I couldn't remember all of the words. I really liked the tune, but as we listened, I could see the bed above me sagging closer and closer to my head. I kept quiet as The Bulk and I got closer and closer, and I couldn't help but wonder why he'd picked me as his new best friend.

The night grew uncomfortably long. Everyone fell asleep but me. I wanted to fall asleep, but I kept thinking about everything that had happened. I had mixed feelings about my first day at camp, and I missed home. I would have gone home if anyone would have let me—but I already sort of liked camp. I felt better knowing that Snarl wasn't as bad as he had seemed at first, and I felt even better knowing that he seemed to think I was a decent kid.

I knew the cobwebs were looking back down at me as I stared at the ceiling. I wondered how many spiders had contributed to those cobwebs. I wondered how many homesick, lonely boys just like me had slept under those cobwebs. The Vacuum was a pretty neat guy and I looked forward to being in his baseball activity. I wondered if Mom and Dad would visit camp. I needed them to come right away, but parent visitation was still four weeks away and it was only my first night.

"I need to catch some z's…Please, fall asleep, Kid Flash…I need to fall asleep…"

I felt tears rolling down my cheeks. I didn't want anyone to know I was crying. I thought about Dad and his bulldog. Dad never knew that I'd seen him cry.

"I need to fall asleep…Please, give me some z's…Why can't I just fall asleep?"

My stomach was churning. Where was Mom? I needed her.

"My brother really did me a favor, and someday I'll pay him back…zzzzz…I wish Mom was here to tuck me in…zzzzz…Why did she let Dad send me away? What if I had missed that curveball?…zzzzz…What if Crash had hit another cow?…zzzzz…The Vacuum, Snarl, The Bulk, pudding and whipped cream, Mom, Dad…Thanks, Flash, for your help…zzzzz…I owe you one…zzzzz… 'This land is made for you and me'…zzzzz."

Campingly Yours 🌲

4

Get It? Got It? Good!

The sun radiated across the lake, piercing through the window screens. It was five in the morning, and I was wide awake. I put my head under the pillow, but there was no way I could fall back to sleep.

The Bulk rolled around, leaned over the edge of his bunk, and said, "Let's go outside."

He told me that he woke up early last year, too, at least for the first few days. We put on our bathrobes and sneakers and quietly headed outside. My mind was telling me that I could probably plan an escape, and no one would find out I was missing for a couple of hours—except the Bulk.

I mentioned it to him and he said, "Last year two boys decided they were Lewis and Clark and tried to get away. They blazed a trail through the camp woods and ended up at the fire circle on the far west side of camp. They were way past frightened when their counselor finally found them, and that was the end of it."

I asked The Bulk who Lewis and Clark were.

He said, "They were explorers. I learned about them on a canoe trip last summer. They were big on rivers."

At that point, I realized it was too complicated to try to escape.

The Bulk told me that he thought I'd do well at camp. After all, my brother was popular and I was already known for what had happened to me the night before. He said my brother walked slow and talked slow, was from *Missoura*, and never tied his shoes. He also said that for some reason the counselors liked that sort of thing, so they had nicknamed him Flash.

"Yeah," I said, "that was pretty much how my brother explained it to me, too."

I let The Bulk know that I'd had a rough start and that I hoped the camp wouldn't think I was some kind of square—but then I mentioned that it seemed like squares did pretty well at camp.

"Hey," said The Bulk, "anyone who can catch The Vacuum's curveball will do well at camp."

I told him I was lucky it had curved into my glove. Otherwise, I might have been in for more of the same.

"It wouldn't have mattered," said The Bulk.

I asked how he knew that.

Looking at my feet, he said, "I see that your shoes are untied."

With that, we headed back to the cabin.

• • •

The wake up bell sounded. It could be heard across the lake, so the campers rolled out of bed pretty quickly. The counselors grumbled a bit and told us to get out of bed while they rested comfortably under their own covers. The Bulk said the counselors would make it to breakfast just before Lou said grace.

Another bell rang, and it was time for breakfast. We gathered around our cabin table and the counselors indeed made it just in time. Lou also grumbled a bit and said we'd have to wait for the stragglers. He seemed somewhat perturbed. The Bulk said that happened a lot.

I liked the grace.

Campingly Yours

Lou said, "I once felt sorry that I had no shoes, then I met a man who had no feet."

Then he directed us to be seated. I wondered what my brother would have been called if he'd had no shoes…

The food arrived and everyone was pretty quiet—and I saw no signs of pudding and whipped cream. All the guys in the cabin, including me, joined in the conversation. The counselors told us about the upcoming day's events, but I already knew most of what was going to happen, since The Bulk had clued me in.

The meal was really good: pancakes, cereal, juice, and homemade coffee cake named after the cook. I had settled down a bit and my wanting to go home had waned for the moment.

The head counselor made some announcements. All campers had to see the nurse for a general checkup. The Bulk said it was a law, and I asked if it was a national law or just a camp law.

"I'm not sure," he said, "but my dad's a doctor and he told me that we needed to be checked."

That was good enough for The Bulk, so I decided it was good enough for me.

The head counselor then announced we'd have to take a swim test. I knew that was coming, but I wasn't happy about it. The counselors confirmed that all of us, even the returning campers, had to pass the swim test so the waterfront staff could determine what activities we could do in the lake.

Mom had me take lessons in the spring before camp, but for some reason water and I had never gotten along. Land was fine; but water was for drinking. The meal ended and I dreaded what was ahead. I wanted to like camp, but it seemed that my roller coaster ride was about to head back downhill.

When we got back to the cabin, it was time for clean-up. Everyone was given a daily task that was posted on a job wheel. The Bulk and I were assigned to clean the grounds around the cabin and to take the clothes off the line. A couple of boys were given sweep duty, another was on trash detail, one was lucky enough to collect the cabin mail, one was unlucky enough to be commissary (KP, table duty) for all three meals, and one much more fortunate camper was assigned no duty at all.

I looked forward to two of the assignments and figured I'd be quiet and take my lumps with the other duties. The counselors explained all of the cleaning rules to us, but I was suspicious as to their expertise, since their quarters already looked a bit like my room at home. Nonetheless, they showed us how to make a bed, how to shake the blankets to get rid of sand, and how to sweep in the corners, pick up paper outside, keep our shelves neat, and perform all the other tasks to pass inspection.

The Bulk shook his blanket and brushed the sand from his bed, which meant that it all ended up on my bed. I thought maybe he did that on purpose to test my sense of humor. Then The Bulk and I went outside and picked up a little paper; there were no clothes on the line to worry about yet. The Bulk said the village director would be around soon to inspect. He also said that we'd pass that day and most every day. Once in a while, however, the village director would be in a bad mood and make everyone re-clean. When I asked The Bulk who inspected the village director, he just looked puzzled.

To my surprise, we passed with flying colors and the village director praised our first cleaning effort. He pointed out some areas that needed improvement—one being my bed— but he was nice about it. He said we needed to sweep the corners a little more and straighten some of the shelves, but he commented that the grounds looked very neat. I whispered to The Bulk that it was the first time I'd ever received a compliment for cleaning (sorry, Mom). Finally, the village director told us to turn out the lights when leaving the cabin. I noticed that he didn't mention anything about the cobwebs.

A runner came to our cabin to let us know that it was time to go see the nurse. Mom had always made me take a shower before I went to the doctor, but I noticed that no one had showered yet, so I figured the nurse was in for a long day.

We put on our swim trunks and trudged to the infirmary. Everyone was weighed. I guess it didn't bother anyone to announce their weight—in fact, the big guys seemed proud of their heftiness. I think I was only as heavy as one of Snarl's legs. The nurse looked at our ears and throats and checked our heads for lice. She checked everyone's feet, too, but I wasn't sure why. At first I thought it was because of my brother, but The Bulk said it had something to do with athletes.

I passed, along with the rest of my cabin mates, and it was all pretty painless. There was a visiting doctor there, as well. The Bulk said that a different doctor showed up each week to help out, and that many of the doctors currently had sons attending camp.

He said, "The doctors take care of the tough stuff, like mumps, measles, and the boys who get beat up."

"Is your dad going to be a doctor at camp?" I asked.

The Bulk said, "I don't think so. Anyway, I see my dad enough at home."

I mentioned that he probably wouldn't see his dad at camp. No one would have considered beating up The Bulk.

After visiting the infirmary, we were told to head to the swim point, which was a few hundred yards away via a dirt path parallel to the lake. Lou was walking the opposite way on the path and stopped The Bulk and me. He asked The Bulk how his family was doing and said he was glad to see the two of us together. I could tell he liked The Bulk.

When he spoke to me, he called me Kid Flash and smiled. He said he was quite impressed with how I had caught The Vacuum's curveball. Then he took me aside and quietly told me that he knew I needed help with swimming. My mom had written on the camp form that I'd be embarrassed to swim in front of the others.

Finally, Lou told me, "See the Pumpkin twins at the swim point. They'll be expecting you."

As Lou walked away, The Bulk (who had overheard my conversation with Lou), told me that the Pumpkins could teach anyone to swim. They had really improved his swimming the summer before.

"Lou really likes you," said The Bulk.

I was momentarily on cloud nine. It was such a cool feeling to know that Lou already

knew my new name, and for a brief moment, I forgot I was about to take a swim test.

We finally arrived at the swim point. It was a distinct area with two long piers about twenty-five yards apart marking the swim area on each side. In the deep end, maybe seventy-five yards out on the right side, sat a diving board. Across from the diving board was a large floating raft. Swim buoys stretched from the end of the piers to the board and raft. Several counselors, including Snarl, were leaning on one end of the raft, trying to tip it over. Snarl was the first to fall in, and then down went the rest of the staff. I could tell they were having a blast.

The Bulk said everyone wanted to go out there during free swim. He told me that the staff was out there on purpose to encourage all of us to pass our swim test. When our cabin was announced, everyone lined up on the pier. All the boys dove in, and I jumped in, since I didn't know how to dive. Yikes, it sure was cold water! I could barely see the bottom, since the lake water was much darker than a swimming pool, and waves rippled—sometimes big waves—when a motorboat passed by.

The Pumpkins immediately greeted me in the water; one was my cabin counselor. He hadn't told me that he taught swimming and that he had an identical twin brother. The Bulk hadn't said anything about that either. I guessed he wanted me to be surprised.

I already liked my Pumpkin counselor and was relieved to find out that he was going to help me swim. The Pumpkins spread me across the water and helped me work on my arm and leg technique long after the rest of my cabin mates had left. However, I noticed that The Bulk stayed on the beach to watch.

My Pumpkin said he and his brother were on their school's swim team. Their coach said they always carved out their team's victories, so they were given the nickname Pumpkins. He told me that he'd trade me a swimming lesson for a baseball lesson, but I told him it would take more than one lesson for me to learn to swim. He didn't mind, though. In fact, he said he could never play baseball with the rest of his friends, but he could beat anyone in the backstroke.

Both Pumpkins devoted their full attention to me and as miraculous as it seemed, they soon had me doing a fairly good crawl and breaststroke. I even swam a full length, from pier to pier. My Pumpkin counselor said that if I could teach him to catch a ball as fast as I learned to swim, he'd relieve me of my cabin cleanup duties. With that incentive, I swam another stretch from pier to pier. The Pumpkins said I still needed a lot of practice, but they'd work with me all week during third activity period.

· · ·

The bell rang and we all headed to lunch. I was getting the routine down of sitting at our cabin table, waiting for grace, and having conversations with everyone during mealtime. I liked mealtime, since it presented a great opportunity to get to know the others. I looked around at some of the other tables and saw a few boys crying with their heads down on their table. I still felt sad and missed home, but not as much as those boys. It was then that I knew just how lucky I'd been to catch that curveball.

Activity sign-up came after lunch. Most activities lasted four days. The new campers were required to take canoeing and camp craft. Some, including me, had to take swimming lessons until our skills were adequately developed. There were four periods, and I was able to take baseball second period. I wasn't thrilled about the other three activities, but I was excited about baseball.

In the afternoon our cabin played another cabin in basketball. The other cabin was a year older, but that didn't matter much. We had a pretty athletic—and tall—group, except for me. We won pretty easily, and after the game the other cabin did a cheer for us. I didn't recall Little League teams cheering for us at home after we had beaten them.

It was pretty neat as the other guys talked to us after the game. Some of them welcomed me to camp and were quite friendly. They said I was a good basketball player, and I could tell that I was going to make several friends out of that group. The counselor from their cabin introduced himself to me and said he'd see me second period for baseball, since he assisted with that activity.

I wasn't sure how he knew that I was in the baseball activity—I just supposed that news traveled fast at camp. I thought The Bulk knew a lot, but it seemed that everyone knew everything about everyone at camp. I was making quite a few friends, both campers and staff, in a pretty short time. It was kind of overwhelming, but exciting.

That night, we had an all-camp campfire at the council ring on the other side of camp on a separate lake, facing west. It was the area where the two boys who had tried to escape had eventually been found. There was a semicircle of benches, enough to accommodate the entire camp.

Lou and Renee wore matching wool plaid shirts and sat in the front. Everyone else sat with his cabin mates and counselors. The program consisted of humor, songs, stories, and a "key log" ceremony at the end. Lou explained that years ago logging had been the main industry in the area. If logs became jammed, a key log would be released to allow the core of the logs to float downriver. It was kind of confusing to me, but campers and staff could throw a small piece of wood (key log) into the fire to give thanks for anything. It was a pretty neat ceremony, and there was a long line of boys with nice things to say.

When Snarl took his turn, he embarrassed the heck out of me. He said he was sorry he'd made fun of me and said he was looking forward to being my friend. It was dead quiet as he sat down. I just looked toward the ground and stayed silent. I didn't want that attention and wished he hadn't made anything of it. On the other hand, I thought it must have been tough for him to stand up in front of everyone and say what was on his mind.

I went up to Snarl after the campfire and thanked him.

He said, "Sometimes I act like a jerk. Everyone knows that, and a lot of people don't like me. You looked pretty silly wearing that catcher's mask, so I decided to pick on you."

"Well," I said, "I like you, Snarl. I'll see you tomorrow—and thanks for picking on me."

At the end of each campfire Lou had us repeat after him, in segments, "And now, may the

Master of All Campers be with us until we meet again. And the trails that we follow, though they be of different paths, lead straight unto him. Night, you all."

As everyone headed for their cabins, I glanced back at the campfire. I became mesmerized with the flames and how, together with the smoke, they combined to make a scenic picture by the lake. The sun had just finished its descent. It was all new to me, and I knew that I didn't need to be older to appreciate the beauty.

· · ·

The counselors turned out the lights and then read us a story. The Pumpkin sat on my bed and told me not to worry about swimming; he'd help me until I felt comfortable. He was an easy person to get to know and made me feel comfortable. It felt nice having a teenage friend.

I remained awake for a long time, or at least it seemed like a long time. Some of the boys were goofing around with their flashlights as the counselors asked them to settle down. I stared through the darkness at the cobwebs and caught a glimpse of them as the flashlight beams streaked across the ceiling. Their tangled webs were trying to tell me something, but I wasn't sure exactly what.

I was feeling lonely again. I thought about how my grandfather loved taking the family out for ice cream. One would have thought he'd given us the key to his basement vault as he handed us our cones.

Mom's sister Lucille would go, as well. She never married and was always like a second mom to us. My brother and I could do absolutely no wrong as far as Lucille and my grandparents were concerned. My dad also liked taking us out for ice cream, but he always stepped into the background and let my grandfather bask in the glory. My dad always mumbled a complaint about how ice cream kept going up in price, but Mom never cared; she just liked ice cream.

Tears were rolling down my cheeks and I hoped the boys darting the flashlights wouldn't see me. I wanted ice cream at all costs (sorry, Dad). I stared at the cobwebs and envisioned Aunt Lucille laughing at me as ice cream melted down my shirt. It wasn't a mean, teasing laugh, just a fun laugh. She'd never make fun of me. No one at home ever teased or made fun of me. Nothing like what had happened at camp.

I was sad and needed to fall asleep. No one was coming to rescue me, and I couldn't escape. I liked Snarl and really liked my Pumpkin counselor. My brother wasn't helping me at that moment. I had to do it on my own.

All the flashlights finally went out and I wiped my cheeks.

"Help me, Mom, Dad, Lucille, someone, anyone…zzzzz…So much has happened to me in a day and a half at camp. I swam a lap for the first time ever and made friends with a guy many don't like…zzzzz…Boys gave us a cheer after we beat them in basketball…Dad, don't complain if the ice cream was too high—it was worth the price…zzzzz…"

• • •

It was my second full day of camp. I had just finished making a fire and handing a hatchet to a counselor, who showed us the proper way to receive and hand a hatchet.

He asked, "Get it?"

I replied, "Got it."

Then he said, "Good."

Get it? Got it. Good. It was a catchy phrase. He told us that we had to make a log cabin fire that day and then we'd learn the teepee and slop fire techniques. He said that to pass the class, we had to make a fire with just one match. We also had to learn to handle an ax and to chop wood properly. I wasn't too worried about the hatchet and ax, but I couldn't remember ever lighting a match. My brother and I were told not to play with matches, so I never messed with them.

Actually, I had tried smoking in third grade, but I got caught. Some fifth-graders down the street were savvy smokers and tried to get me involved. I never lit the cigarette and blew outward when it was handed to me. It turned out that the smoke from the cigarettes trailed upward toward my bedroom window where Mom was standing. I was never interested in smoking after that—I'm not sure if that was because of my mother's wrath or just the lousy taste. At some point, I needed to locate my brother to find out how he passed the fire test.

Next I headed for baseball wearing my Spalding glove, blue jeans, a t-shirt, Keds tennis shoes, and a Kansas City A's baseball cap. The cap rarely left my head. Sometimes I slept with it on. I rarely missed an A's game on the radio and I harbored the eternal hope that one day they'd climb out of the cellar. I liked Norm Siebern but was totally puzzled why they needed him more than Roger Maris. It was strange for me to be missing so many A's games while away at camp.

I left my catcher's mask in the cabin. The Vacuum and his assistant, Milky, welcomed me with open arms. I arrived a little early and they put me at third base. The Vacuum hit several hard ground balls at me and showed no mercy. I caught every one of them and made decent throws to first base. They threw a few to me at the plate and I hit my usual grounders toward short. Dad never worked much with my hitting, and I don't remember him ever swinging a bat. He swung at golf balls twice a week, but seldom came home happy with his score. He usually came home happy, but not with his golf score.

About twenty guys of different ages showed up for baseball. The Vacuum and Milky worked with our infield play and outfield throws. I could tell that they knew the game, since they showed us proper positioning for relays and they had the outfielders throw one-hoppers to the infielders covering the bags. I loved fielding and felt in my element. I didn't care that some of the boys were older. I probably couldn't hit with them, but I could hang with them in the field.

The Vacuum divided us up and I noticed that he purposely picked the teams. It was a smart move to avoid anyone being picked last. I was put at second base and batted next to last. We played four innings; the game was close. I had several fielding chances at second with no errors, but I didn't hit the ball out of the infield in two tries. I didn't care; the baseball activity was a great time with no arguing, and The Vacuum and Milky had everything under control.

They both said to me, "Nice job! See you tomorrow."

It occurred to me that I'd just met nineteen new guys and we all got along pretty well. The age thing didn't seem to matter. The bell rang signifying lunch in fifteen minutes. The morning had rushed by! I needed some time to find my brother; the one-match fire was puzzling me.

Lunch was a decent time to catch up with the guys from the cabin and to just sit for a while. I noticed the hamburger on the pizza burgers. I was pretty sure that it was yesterday's meat, and I was thinking that it could stretch to tomorrow's sloppy joes. I didn't care; it all tasted pretty good to me and there was usually enough food for seconds.

Lunches continued to be pretty raucous. Dessert was followed by cabin cheers, goofy songs, and parading around the mess hall to screams of "Fire! Fire! Fire!" and "As the saints go marching in." Lou, the staff, and the older campers really got into that stuff while the younger campers just watched. I'm not sure we were in awe exactly; we just watched. I think this was a foreshadowing of things to come, since no one really expected the younger campers to be loud the first week.

I told The Bulk about handling the hatchet and making a fire, and he said that every year someone would gash a leg with an ax. He also said that he thought the slop fire was the most fun. He loved randomly tossing bark and wood into the fire pit and making it flame up with just one match. I told him I was going to see my brother about the match and The Bulk said he'd tag along. He acted as if he already knew the answer but was holding back. I asked if the camp doctor was in charge of gashed legs.

I was looking forward to rest period before afternoon activities. It had been an interesting morning and a fun lunch, but I wasn't so sure about the upcoming afternoon of swimming and canoeing. My thoughts of homesickness waned, since there wasn't much time to think about it. Swimming could change that—I wasn't sure about canoeing.

Soon I was off to swimming, less fearful than before, but still pretty queasy about the idea. I told The Bulk that I'd try to see my brother late in the afternoon. I didn't have any activities with The Bulk and I missed his knowledge about everything. It seemed as if I'd known him forever.

The concept of time at camp was becoming irrelevant. So much was happening in such a short period of time. I began losing track of the days of the week. Wednesday, Friday, Monday—it didn't seem to matter. I had only met The Bulk two and a half days earlier and I was already missing having him around.

Feeling a bit nervous, I arrived at the swim point, along with maybe twenty others. Most of the campers were young, but there were a couple older guys. The Pumpkins cornered me and told me to jump right in. Whatever nervousness I had brought to the swim point instantly went away, since the Pumpkin twins gave me little time to think.

We worked with my crawl and breaststroke and they showed me how to float on my back. They made me swim five or six laps, although it felt like a hundred. They had me stand at the end of the pier, bend my head forward, contort my body into a horseshoe shape, and hold the position as they picked me up and threw me into the water. It was my first dive! I didn't have time to think or worry about it, but it was my first dive ever!

Then they had me get out of the water and repeat the process. I never said a word through the whole ordeal. The third time, they had me position myself like a horseshoe on my own and then told me to dive in. I did it! It wasn't pretty—more of a belly flop than a dive, but by the third or fourth try, I had it. On the last dive, they instructed me to bring sand up from the bottom, and I did! The Pumpkins stared at me and laughed a bit. They told me that I wasn't supposed to sign up for canoeing until I had passed the camp's advanced swim test. Then they pointed to the canoe racks and told me to get going. I had passed.

As I left the swim point, I noticed an older boy who was barely able to swim away from the pier. He dog paddled in desperation and then grabbed the pier. He had been the right fielder on the other team that morning. He'd missed two pretty easy fly balls and had struck out twice. The Vacuum had acted as if he'd fouled-tipped several third strikes before reluctantly signaling him out. At that moment, I felt bad that the Pumpkins had worked with me. They should have worked with that older boy.

There were two staff members instructing the canoeing activity. They didn't know me and it appeared that my dubious start at camp hadn't affected them. The canoeing staff hadn't seen me catch the curveball or my embarrassment at the staff show. I worried about my performance all the time because I was convinced that everyone was noticing everything I did. However, the canoe activity was my awakening to the fact that I wasn't foremost in everyone's thoughts, and I wondered why I hadn't noticed that before.

Maybe it was natural for me to think that way; I really wasn't sure. Mom, Dad, my grandparents, Aunt Lucille, Aunt Estelle, Aunt Thelma, and virtually all my relatives had always put me on a pedestal. My brother was placed on a pedestal as well, and we seemingly could do no wrong in their eyes—at least that was always my perception. I wondered if my brother thought the same way.

There were fourteen of us at canoeing. The instructors fitted us with paddles according to height. The paddles had to reach our chins, which apparently constituted a perfect fit. They positioned all of us on the dock and had us dip our paddles into the lake. They demonstrated several strokes and we followed their examples, including the j-stroke, push-away, draw, sweep, and reverse sweep.

Over and over, they called out the strokes in no particular order. They stood over us and made sure we had the proper grips. They were no-nonsense guys and all of the campers followed their lead without goofing around. I just did what I was told, since I had little desire to be on the wrong side of the canoeing staff.

They showed us the proper way to pick up and set down the canoes, and then they told us we were going to take the canoes out the next day, so we should remember the strokes.

I headed back to the cabin to get out of my swim trunks and back into my jeans, t-shirt, and hat. The Bulk entered the cabin as I was changing and asked about my afternoon. I told him that I'd become a better swimmer in one day than in all my previous years of lessons. I also mentioned that I'd been too afraid to even speak at canoeing.

He just laughed and said, "Let's go see your brother."

As The Bulk and I climbed a path to see my brother, he said that he didn't like canoeing and was glad that he'd passed quickly last year.

I asked if anyone ever flunked, and he said, "A lot of guys have to take it two or three times before they qualify for the cabin canoe trip. Every now and then someone doesn't pass in time for the canoe trip and has to stay behind."

I asked, "Who does that boy have to stay with?"

"The cabin next door," said The Bulk. "It's not fun being a canoe flunky, which is what everyone labels you if you have to stay behind."

J-stroke, push-away, draw—I was already memorizing the strokes, since I didn't want to be a canoe flunky.

We arrived at my brother's cabin, one of five located on a steep ridge. The cabins were about forty yards apart, separated by pines, white birch trees, and a narrow path. There was a steep hill at the rear of the cabins, covered with woods so thick that one could barely see the lake. There were no paths leading to the lake from that point.

The Bulk opened the door and we walked in without knocking. A few boys were in the cabin, including my brother. He said hi to The Bulk and asked if I still wanted to go home. I kept quiet, wondering how my brother had gotten wind of my wanting to go home.

News traveled in strange directions at this camp. He finally said hi to me, but he seemed a little distant. I told him about my camp craft experience, and he said he got it.

Then he asked, "Do you get it?"

 Campingly Yours

The Bulk answered, "I got it."

My brother said, "Good!"

The main thing I got out of that was my brother's sense of humor.

I asked The Flash how he'd been able to make a one-match fire. When had he learned to light a match?

Some of the boys in the cabin overheard my question, and one of them said, "Flash, let's take your brother and The Bulk outside."

I learned that my brother's group was a bunch of cool guys from Milwaukee, Cleveland, and St. Louis. Most of them were good athletes and school leaders. It was obvious they were part of an "in" crowd. For some reason, they totally accepted my brother. I wasn't sure why, but they really liked him. The Milwaukee guys all knew the Bulk and also acted favorably toward him. Maybe his dad was their doctor and they were afraid of getting an unwanted shot—I didn't know. Regardless, because of my brother and The Bulk, I felt accepted, as well.

We went outside and maneuvered down the backside ridge toward the lake. I hung on to branches to avoid rolling down the hill, but my brother and the other boys managed the hill quite easily. The Bulk was a little smoother than I, but not much. We arrived at a secluded area where three boys from my brother's cabin were smoking cigarettes. A couple of Milwaukee boys joined in, as did the one from Cleveland. My brother abstained, but I couldn't tell if it was only because of my presence. I looked at the top of the trees to see if Mom was watching for smoke signals.

One of the boys showed me how to light a match and then had me try. I was too afraid not to try. It took me several strikes, and then a flame appeared. I tried a couple more matches with the same result. The Bulk lit a few, too. One of the leaders from Milwaukee put down his cigarette, glared at The Bulk and me, and said there was an unwritten rule that had been passed down through the ages. The Bulk interrupted and said that they didn't have to worry about Kid Flash and himself—and that was that.

Then The Bulk and I clawed our way back up the hill and headed back to our cabin.

I told The Bulk, "All I wanted to do was learn how my brother managed the one match fire."

The Bulk replied, "Now you know."

That evening we heard a Native American speaker from the area by the name of Dea Quay. He spoke about native lore and how his family had inhabited the area for hundreds of years. The older campers asked a lot of questions, as did the staff. They seemed pretty interested as Dea Quay detailed the plight of his ancestors. Toward the end, he put on a headdress and some bells and danced and sang a tribal chant. Then he had volunteers join in. That part was pretty neat, and the older campers became proficient at Quay's two-step.

The Bulk and I tried the two-step dance chant, too, and soon the whole camp had joined in, even Lou and Renee. I watched as the campers had great fun with that simple dance, and I was surprised to see tears running down Dea Quay's wrinkled face as he waved goodnight to us.

The Bulk and I chanted and two-stepped all the way back to our cabin. It made me think about General Custer and his troops. It was too bad they never attended summer camp.

I lay in bed, less awake than the previous two nights. It was my third night, and I was tired. A couple of the guys were goofing around, but I didn't pay any attention to them. I stared at the cobwebs. I had begun to love those cobwebs, and I wondered if those same cobwebs had been around for Dea Quay's ancestors. He was old, kind, and gentle. I would have been bitter if I had been Dea Quay.

I tried to concentrate on the canoe strokes. I bet those cobwebs had hovered over a few canoe flunkies through the years.

"I don't want to be a canoe flunky...zzzzz...I learned to light a match, but no one told me how to keep it going. I bet The Flash has never smoked...zzzzz...I should have helped that boy at the lake...I hated seeing him struggle with the dog paddle...Maybe I can help him catch a ball."

I wasn't really homesick anymore. I had too much to do the next day to think about home.

Campingly Yours

"I didn't see Snarl today…zzzzz…The Vacuum likes me…I can't wait to show Mom and Dad the camp…zzzzz…Tomorrow, swimming, j-stroke…Get it? Got it. Good…night…zzzzz…"

5

Sherman

The camp craft instructor gave each of us a box of stick matches. He said we could play with matches legally during the activity, but we couldn't light matches anywhere else around camp. He showed us how to strike and light a match and more importantly, how to shield the flame from the wind. He also said it was fine to ask a friend to help shield the flame.

He then handed us each an old piece of birch bark and showed us how to light it. After all of us had been successful in lighting the birch bark, he had us hover around his pre-assembled log campfire. He said the bark needed to be strategically placed at the lower level of the campfire, with smaller wood built up around it. He then demonstrated how to assemble the campfire in a log fashion, pointing out each layer. He told us that in order to pass the camp craft activity we'd have to gather our own wood and birch bark, assemble either a teepee or log fire, light one match, and watch the campfire glow. One match, one try—that was it. Then I headed to baseball, determined not to become a canoeing and camp craft flunky.

The Vacuum and Milky weren't there when I arrived at the ball diamond a little early. The

 Campingly Yours

older boy I'd seen struggling to swim was sitting on the bench by himself, wearing an old beat-up ball glove and just staring out at the field. I watched him for a minute or so, but he didn't look up; he just kept staring at the field, wearing a look of disbelief, as if his hometown Kansas City A's had just lost the World Series. In my case, I would have had the same stare if the A's had ever *made* it to the World Series.

I walked over to him and said, "Hi, my name is Kid Flash."

He looked up and said, "Hi, I'm Sherman."

He asked if I'd pitch a few balls to him. His language was broken and I had a little trouble understanding him. He looked to the side a bit as he grabbed a bat.

I threw him two pitches, and he whiffed at both of them, not even remotely close. I noticed that he was swinging his bat at exactly the same point each time, just below his armpits, so I threw him a low one on purpose—which he missed by two feet as he again swung at armpit level.

I said, "OK, Sherman, you're going to hit this one."

He said, "I've never hit one before."

Again I said, "You're going to hit this one."

I threw the next pitch just below his armpits, which was actually a bit high and out of the strike zone, but he swung and connected with the upper half of the ball, sending it rolling slowly toward third. I headed to my right to pick up the slow bouncer and saw Sherman running to first base. When he'd made it to first, he stood stoically on the bag, and as I trotted toward first, Sherman just stared at me.

"Are you OK?" I asked.

"I've never been on first base before," he said, displaying a slight smile.

Others started to arrive, including The Vacuum. I was pretty sure they hadn't seen what happened. I told Sherman to get his glove and I'd throw a few to him. He ran to the bench, picked up his tired-looking glove, and then stood still. I signaled him to third base, and when he'd made it to the bag, we began playing catch. Soon most everyone had arrived and they also began to play catch, mainly in pairs.

Sherman missed every ball I threw to him and I began to notice a pattern. He put his glove in the exact same spot every time, to the left of his body, about armpit level.

I said, "Use both hands and you'll catch the next few."

He said, "OK."

I threw the next ball close to where he always held his glove, but he put his right hand in front of the glove and the ball hit his bare hand.

As he massaged his hand, I mildly shouted, "This time try just one hand—your glove hand!"

I threw the ball to the same spot—and he caught it! I didn't know who was more excited, since I knew I couldn't throw that accurately every time. Sherman beamed at me and I knew he was happy, but he didn't say anything. A few moments later, The Vacuum called everyone in—he was going to pick teams for a game.

Sherman struck out three times and missed several balls in right field, but I didn't say anything. I played well, but kept pretty quiet. No one made fun of Sherman. The Vacuum wouldn't have let that happen. As I left the ball field, I said goodbye to Sherman. He asked me to help him with his swimming, and I started sinking at just the thought of it.

• • •

During rest period, I asked The Bulk what he knew about Sherman. He said it was Sherman's fourth summer at camp. He wasn't sure how old Sherman was—he guessed maybe fourteen or fifteen. He said Sherman mostly just sat at his cabin table and stared. The counselors tried to work with him, but the campers rarely said much to him. The Bulk thought maybe Sherman was a bit slow.

"My dad says that camp is good for Sherman," said The Bulk. "He also says that Sherman won't get any better. He says that Sherman's just one of many sad cases in life."

As I thought about what The Bulk was saying, he continued, "Lou and Renee accepted Sherman to camp and let it be known that no one could make fun of him. My dad told me that Lou and Renee had two sons. One of them died very young and the other one is in an institution."

The Bulk went on to tell me that the recreation hall at the camp was named after the son who died. The son in the institution was unable to care for himself, but Lou and Renee also had a daughter who was fine. Just as I was asking The Bulk if he thought Lou and Renee looked at all of us as their sons, the bell rang and it was time for third period. I headed off to swimming.

When I arrived, the Pumpkins didn't throw me in the water. Instead, they told me to swim six laps, float on my back for a minute, and practice a couple dives. They said they'd check on me, but they were going to be working with two other boys who needed more help. I finished my laps and again saw Sherman doing the dog paddle a yard from the pier. He wasn't being helped, but he didn't seem to be in danger, since he was in shallow water.

I swam over to Sherman and said, "Hi!"

He asked me to show him how to swim, but I told him, "I can play ball, but I'm not so good at swimming."

He lunged from the pier and dog paddled, getting only as deep as his armpits. It seemed that everything he did was at armpit level. Then he lunged back to the pier.

I said, "OK, Sherman, I'll give it a try."

I hoped that I could do for him what the Pumpkins had done for me.

Sherman bolted from the pier while I got under him, with the intent of leveling him off. He panicked and dragged me under, desperately holding on to my arms. He was strong—a lot stronger than I would have thought, and he outweighed me by at least sixty pounds. I was still, by any measure, not a strong swimmer.

Sherman flailed on top of me for what felt like minutes. I finally got my head above water to grab a quick breath, then down I went again. It didn't matter that we were only in three

Campingly Yours

feet of water—it felt as deep as Lloyd Bridges dove in *Sea Hunt*—and Lloyd was allowed to take oxygen down with him!

I became desperate and squirmed in every direction, trying to get loose, but Sherman was too strong and in panic mode. I couldn't get above water long enough to catch another breath. Finally, I heard an explosion in the water and a moment later, the Pumpkins were grabbing Sherman and me and pulling us apart.

They hauled the confused Sherman up onto the dock and when I joined them, my Pumpkin counselor said, "We'll let you know when you're qualified to give lessons!"

Sherman sat staring out at the water, and I did, too, trying to catch my breath. Then Sherman jumped back in and again began to dog paddle by the pier. I stood and left for canoeing, toweling myself off as I jogged along the shore.

My mind was filled with all sorts of "what ifs." I was sure the Pumpkins were angry with me, but I didn't think Sherman knew enough to care, especially after seeing him jump right back into his dog paddling routine. I knew that Sherman hadn't meant to hold me underwater, but what if the Pumpkins hadn't been alert? Had they witnessed the whole thing or just the tail end of it?

All I could think about was being underwater, not being able to grab a breath, and having a ton of weight holding me down. Gasping for air—what a horrifying feeling. It was the opposite of a fish gasping for water, dangling on the hook, squirming to get loose, drowning in air, with a big something holding him up and not letting him get back down to breathe water again. Sherman had been my hook, line, and sinker, but he hadn't perceived it that way. I didn't think Sherman perceived very much—and I knew that I needed to understand more about him.

There was no more time for me to think. It was time to obey the canoeing instructors. They had us pair up, grab a canoe, and carry it into the water. They told me to get into the stern—the backside—where the canoeist controlled the boat. I had a bowman, and together we directed the canoe in a pretty straight line. I figured it out pretty quickly; it wasn't

 Campingly Yours

complicated for me. I paddled on the right with the bowman on the left. If the canoe started going left, I did an easy j-stroke, a normal stroke ending in a slight rudder position, which eased the canoe to the right. If I changed sides, I told the bowman to also change to his right, and a j-stroke eased the canoe to the left.

All the strokes made sense to me and I quietly and quickly became somewhat proficient. The instructors told us to have the bowman back paddle and for the stern to do a sweep stroke. It was pretty cool to maneuver the canoe into a one-eighty. Then they showed us how to swamp the canoe, flip it over, hang on to the side, and swim with it back to shore. I was thrilled with that maneuver—it was sure a lot easier than having Sherman on top of me.

We emptied the canoes on the shore. Next, the instructors had us play leapfrog with our partner from stern to bow—without tipping over the canoe. After that, they had us balance on the gunnels for ten seconds without falling. Both leapfrog and gunneling were fun and pretty easy, and I left canoeing feeling confident. I could tell the instructors thought most everyone had done well. There were a couple of guys who looked like they might have to face being canoe flunkies, but I wasn't one of them, and I was glad. For being such strict, no-nonsense guys, the canoe instructors sure made the activity fun.

On my way back to the cabin, I bumped into Snarl. He told me to stay away from Sherman because he was too big for me in the water. News sure traveled fast at the camp!

Snarl said, "Come to basketball tonight after dinner. I'll put you on my team."

I said I'd see him there, although being on Snarl's team meant that twenty percent of the team would be pretty lousy.

• • •

Over the summer, there were all sorts of evening programs, including skits, campfires, special speakers, sing-a-longs, luaus, community cleanups, barbarian and toga festivities, sports nights, color war competitions, capture the flag contests, and organized free periods. My favorite was the organized free period, when most activities were open at night and staff was assigned accordingly. Those who enjoyed crafts headed to the crafts shop, like my brother. Those who enjoyed sailing headed to the waterfront, like my brother. Those who enjoyed photography headed to the darkroom, like my brother. Those who liked land sports headed to baseball, basketball, or football—like me, all the time, every time.

Basketball was a blast. I was teamed with two guys from my brother's cabin (the smokers) and Snarl had a really tall counselor join our team, so Snarl's presence didn't matter as he bumbled up and down the court, pushing for rebounds and occasionally getting a slop basket. He argued a lot and always claimed he'd been fouled. Most of the guys just ignored him. I was the smallest one there, so I mostly just dribbled and passed, and I only scored a couple baskets.

The guys in my brother's cabin really took to me. They were definitely cool kids and leaders. They seemed a little ornery and definitely a little cocky. I could tell they were destined to be good high school athletes. My brother had nothing in common with them, but they included him as one of the cool ones.

It was great fun to play without caring about who won or lost. When the bell rang, signifying that the evening period was over, all of us said "nice game" and that was it—well, everyone except Snarl. He just waddled his way back to his cabin. I felt no pressure during the game and I was playing with all older guys. Everyone played hard, but no one seemed to care about the final outcome. I couldn't wait for the next evening free period. Maybe I'd try football—or basketball again; it didn't matter. I wondered if my brother was one of the cool guys because he smoked with them—naw, not The Flash.

• • •

The counselors said we had to write a letter home and get it done before they turned off the lights. Mom had packed a bunch of self-addressed stamped envelopes. I wasn't sure if she knew that I actually was familiar with our home address. Maybe she just figured I'd write more letters if the envelopes were ready to go.

Dear Mom and Dad,

I was homesick, but not anymore. No offense. I taught Sherman how to catch and hit a ball. Sherman almost drowned me, but I was saved by a couple counselors.

Canoeing was fun. I had a blast at basketball. This guy named Snarl picked on me, but he's OK.

Guys in The Flash's cabin smoke, but don't tell anyone or I'll get in trouble. The food has been good. There's a neat guy named The Vacuum. He's a really good baseball player. I got to play with matches today, but don't worry.

My best friend is The Bulk. His dad is a doctor. I'll show you all around when you visit. Lou and Renee are really nice and Lou talked to me. Goodbye for now.

Love, your small camp son,

Kid Flash

• • •

Tired but wired, I decided not to talk about the swimming incident. It had been frightening and I'd experienced the feeling of drowning—but I never wanted to know that feeling again. The thought of not coming out of the water—I wondered if fish ever did any thinking. The thought of not getting back into the water—and a hook to deal with. Squirming for life; squirming to get away from Sherman.

I'd let Mom and Dad know that the incident was no big deal—and that would be it. I didn't want to talk about it to anyone.

"Do the fish that escape warn the others?...zzzzz...It felt good to be accepted by those cool kids...zzzzz...It seems like ages ago when I caught the curveball. The Bulk was right. It wouldn't have mattered…*zzzzz*…How does the Bulk know so much? I miss Mom and Dad. I should have told them that in the letter…*zzzzz*…I'll tell them in the next one."

I was actually looking forward to canoeing and camp craft, but not to swimming. I stared in the dark at the cobwebs. What a tangled mess they were.

"Maybe they're an organized mess…*zzzzz*…How do they last on the ceiling so long?… *zzzzz*…Maybe The Vacuum will teach me to hit better…*zzzzz*…'This land is your land, this land is my land, from California to the New York islands, this land is made for you and me'…*zzzzz*…but was it made for Sherman?…*zzzzz*."

6

Fun at River Rats

Three weeks of camp passed quickly and our two-day canoe trip was scheduled for the next day. I had been accepted by all the age groups and was well known around camp as Kid Flash. Camp was flying by and I was sure that the days had begun to get much shorter the moment my homesickness went away.

I qualified for the canoe trip, as did everyone in our cabin. Indeed, a few of the other boys became canoe and camp craft flunkies, but sooner or later they'd pass the requirements. I made it through camp craft with a blaze of luck, or I should say because there was no wind. My stick match held its flame as I managed to light several pieces of birch bark to ignite my log fire. Swimming was the toughest requirement; if a camper couldn't swim efficiently, they didn't qualify for water activities, including the canoe trip. That was the rule—no exceptions.

I continued to enjoy free periods the most. Hanging around any of the land sports was always my cup of tea. I attended the baseball activity almost every day and became closer and closer to The Vacuum. Milky was a good friend as well, and he always gave me extra attention.

I threw baseballs and footballs to Sherman—not every day, but a lot. I also showed him how to shoot a basketball, but at swimming, I stayed away from him at all costs. I still

Campingly Yours

couldn't tell if he thought about much and I was sure he didn't remember almost drowning me. I was glad that no one picked on him. It let me know the camp held magic for all of us, and someday I wanted to find out that magic formula. How could a camp director and his wife not allow anyone to pick on a boy like Sherman?

I also wondered why the directors had allowed me to take a bowl of pudding in the face at the first meal. Why did they allow that to happen to first-time campers every year? I was still trying to figure out why my brother, the lanyard maker/sailor/ photographer, was so well accepted by the cool kids from Milwaukee and St. Louis.

Snarl continued to agitate people, but he managed to show his vulnerable side, as well. I didn't really know why I liked him—maybe it was just because he liked me. The Bulk continued to sprinkle sand on my bed from above. It became a morning ritual.

News around camp spread that a junior counselor had suddenly been sent home. He was cocky, but without much substance. My brother never had anything nice to say about him. I found out that the junior counselor had gotten mad at one of his campers and hit him—not hard, but he did hit the kid, so Lou sent him home on the next bus. The Bulk later told me that the junior counselor's parents had complained to Lou, but it did no good.

I wasn't sure what I would have done if a counselor had hit me. I probably would have been afraid to tell anyone, although I would have told The Bulk, and he would have helped me figure out my next move.

Campfires were a little long, but by the end of the key log ceremony, it seemed like the whole camp came together as one unit. I threw in my first key log the third week, thanking the Pumpkins for teaching me to swim, The Vacuum for all of his help, The Bulk for being my best friend, and Sherman for being a neat person. I thought Sherman would like that, but I suppose it gave me a little self-gratification, as well.

Our cabin canoe trip was approaching and I was nervous. The next weekend was parents' visitation and I couldn't wait to show Mom and Dad everything and everyone. I was looking forward to seeing Dad throw his roundhouse curve to The Vacuum and I wanted to show

Mom the cobwebs in the cabin, although I suspected she'd notice them right away. I wanted to tell her about how the cobwebs presented a purpose for thought. After all, they'd witnessed so much and had withstood the trials of so many campers. On with the canoe trip—I wanted the weekend to arrive.

• • •

I packed some underwear, a pair of jeans, a couple shirts, a pair of shoes, a towel, toothpaste and toothbrush, a flashlight, a mess kit, and a deck of cards into my sleeping bag, and rolled the bag up as tightly as possible. Wearing swim trunks, a t-shirt, my A's cap, and beat-up tennis shoes, I headed to the trip vehicle. Everyone in the cabin packed similar items and all of us put our tied-up sleeping bags into the canoe trailer. The tents and other camping gear were also packed in the trailer and then the trip leader strung a tarp over the gear in case of rain. The trailer held six canoes, fastened tightly with bungee cords.

Our leader was Wolf, one of the camp's trip staff, and our three cabin counselors came along to assist. Wolf made it clear that if any of us got out of line he'd let our counselors take care of the matter.

Wolf told us, "I'm your guide, but you're going to be doing all of the work."

Wolf immediately commanded respect, even from the counselors, but he spoke in a nice manner (not bossy) and I could tell he knew what he was doing. I could also tell he was a very likable guy. We loaded into the van and Wolf sat in front with Crash. Crash asked how I liked camp. I told him it was just fine.

He said, "Good! Now hang on tight and I'll do my best to avoid any cows."

After an hour's ride, we arrived at the put-in point on the Namekagen River. All of us unloaded our gear as Wolf, Crash, and the counselors carried the canoes to the river landing. The Bulk and I paired together; he took the stern.

We put on our life vests and pushed off, catching the current of the river. Wolf was in the lead and one of our counselors brought up the rear. Wide-eyed, I could feel the strength of the current and I saw rocks everywhere. It was up to me, as the bowman, to let The Bulk know of any impending rocks.

We'd been taught in canoeing activity to announce rock locations by saying such things as "deadhead to the left at ten o'clock," or "deadhead to the right at one-thirty." I tried to stay ahead of the game and help The Bulk steer accordingly, but the rocks appeared quickly and it sounded like The Bulk was getting a little annoyed with me after we'd slammed into several boulders.

By adult standards, the Namekagen wasn't considered a tough canoeing river, but it was plenty challenging for a bunch of ten-year-olds. For two hours, although it seemed like two days, I jumped in and out of the boat to push us off rocks. I think The Bulk had the better end of the deal.

Wolf landed ahead of us and told everyone to pull ashore for lunch. Peanut butter took on a pretty good meaning as we made sandwiches and ate chips. Wolf pulled out a cooler of bug juice and said we'd be heading out in thirty minutes. He also told us we still had three more hours of paddling to do before we'd hit the campsite.

Lunch period was brief, the Peter Pan slid down quickly, and then Wolf had us get back into the canoes. He said there was a good chance of rain and he wanted us to make the campsite by mid-afternoon.

The Bulk and I sifted through a few one-rated rapids. They were pretty scary, but presented a carnival-like thrill. We heard thunder a couple times and saw some flashes of lightning. Wolf had us paddle near shore, telling us we only had a half hour to go, but we all paddled in a bit of a panic, since the lightning was getting pretty close.

Finally, Wolf pulled to shore and we all followed. Everyone was relieved when we heard Wolf say we'd made it to the campsite. The rain had just begun to come down hard as we hurried to pitch the tents. Our clothes were getting soaked and Wolf turned over the canoes and put all the bags and gear underneath them. I thought that was pretty smart on his part.

The counselors and Wolf helped with our tents, since there was no way we could have pitched them on our own. Four of us crammed into a three-man tent. We grabbed our bags before entering, but everything was pretty drenched. The canoes helped a little, but the rushing rainwater formed a stream that encompassed the bags.

Wolf shouted, "Everybody stay in your tents until the rain passes!"

He said he'd keep us informed. He carried a flare for emergencies, which he told us was the best way to call for help.

The four of us unrolled our sleeping bags and found most everything soaked. Early evening was upon us; we were wet and cold with no dry clothes to change into. I could hear complaining and even crying from the other tents, but I was too cold and wet to complain. The Bulk got his flashlight to work, so the four of us played a card game called Schmier. For me, the game was appropriately named, since I never won a single hand. Schmier was quirky but fun and it helped the time pass more quickly.

The rain subsided after an hour or so and Wolf called for everyone to come out of their tents. He already had a fire going and had crisscrossed rope around several trees close to the fire. He had us hang up our sleeping bags, jeans, and whatever else would fit on the line so the fire could dry them out. Since it was all new to me, I painted Wolf as a genius. How had he managed to get a fire going in the rain?

We all gathered around the fire to warm up. Wolf and the counselors brought out the food to be cooked and Wolf had us get our mess kits, which consisted of two aluminum pans, some silverware, and a tin cup. Wolf gave each of us a piece of foil and told us we only needed our silverware and one of the pans to use as a plate. Our cups were for the bug juice. What exactly was bug juice? I'd first heard the term at camp, so I assumed it was reserved for camp use only. It usually had a fruit juice-like flavor, pretty heavy on the sugar and pretty light on the juice. I couldn't recall Mom ever serving anything that resembled bug juice, but for some reason bug juice earned a lot of notoriety at camp.

Wolf announced that we'd be making tinfoil dinners. He demonstrated by chopping up hamburger meat, onions, mushrooms, carrots, tomatoes, and cheese and putting them onto the dull side of the foil. Then he neatly rolled and wrapped the foil, shiny side out, and placed it on the coals, not directly on the flames. All of us grabbed the ingredients of our choice, chopped away at them with the mess kit knife, wrapped and folded the foil, and put the tinfoil dinners onto the fire, keeping track of which one was ours.

I used all of the ingredients and loaded mine to the max. I wanted to make sure to pull out the right one, so I stared at it nonstop for fifteen minutes and then ootched it off the coals with my mess kit pan.

Mom's finest four-course gourmet meals had never tasted as good as that tinfoil special—sorry Mom; I was wet and starved. Everyone complimented Wolf as he gathered the ingredients to make us a chocolate cake.

Wolf said, "I'm giving you a break because of the rain, but tomorrow you're all going to gather wood, make the fire, and cook your own breakfast of bacon and eggs."

We finished the tinfoil dinners, cleaned our mess kits, and gathered our dry clothes. It was a relief to put on smoky jeans and a sweatshirt. After awhile, Wolf served his open fire cake and we devoured it in seconds. Then he let the fire burn and had us get into our tents by nine o'clock.

He said, "Tomorrow will be a four-hour paddle and I want everybody up for breakfast by eight."

Sleeping in the tent was pretty neat. We got our flashlights to work and played Schmier for an hour or so until Wolf shouted to tell everyone to turn off our flashlights and go to sleep. I rolled up my towel and used it for a pillow. The ground was a little rocky and on a downward slope, but I finally maneuvered myself into an adequately comfortable position. Wolf had made sure our tents all sloped downward just a bit to prevent rain from running into the front flap area. We all listened to and respected Wolf. His presence wasn't intimidating, but there was something about him that assured us he knew what he was talking about.

There were no cobwebs in the tent and I couldn't help thinking about the cobwebs back

in our empty cabin. I supposed they were used to an empty cabin most of the year. Summer must have been the bright point for those cobwebs. They probably came to life when all of the campers arrived. It was probably a long, slow winter for those cobwebs.

Maybe it was a long, slow winter for the camp directors, too. Lou and Renee seemed to come to life when the campers arrived, though I figured they probably had better winters than the cobwebs. I missed the free periods and wondered who was showing up for morning baseball—and I was sure that no one would be throwing a ball to Sherman. I actually missed Sherman, too.

Mom and Dad were coming in three days. Everyone's parents were coming to visit. The three other boys in my tent were all snoring, and The Bulk was the loudest, but I remained wide-eyed, wanting to fall asleep.

I could visualize Dad throwing his roundhouse curve to The Vacuum. I'd have to warn The Vacuum not to comment on the non-movement of Dad's curve. I wanted to show Mom that I could actually swim.

I forgot that my brother would have to show them around, as well. I thought about introducing them to Snarl. I doubted if anyone had ever done that before. I'd only received three letters from home. Nothing much was happening there, anyway. The rain started again. It had a soothing sound as it pelted the tent.

"I miss camp…zzzzz…I don't want to miss out on anything good…zzzzz…Who talked to Sherman? I'm glad to see my brother doing well with his group…zzzzz…I wonder why my brother doesn't come see me all the time?…I still owe him big time and want to pay him back…zzzzz…I need to find the right moment—maybe when he least suspects it."

The rain continued to pelt against the outside of the tent.

"A tent is a cool place to sleep…zzzzz…goodnight, Vacuum, Lou, Renee, and the kitchen staff…zzzzz…goodnight, Mom and Dad, see you soon…zzzzz…can't wait."

Wolf got everyone up early and gave us our job assignments. Some gathered wood for the fire, some took down and rolled up the tents, some cooked the bacon and eggs, and some were on cleanup duty. Wolf said that we had to leave the campsite cleaner than we found it. That was his firm rule and he told us to remember that commandment forever.

Everyone did paper pickup and a general once-over, and then we loaded the canoes and headed downriver for a four-hour paddle. The counselors started singing rowdy camp songs and we all joined in. We sang, splashed each other with our paddles, and got serious whenever rapids approached, so the time went by quickly. We stopped for lunch, paddled two more hours, and made campsite by mid-afternoon—and what a neat campsite it was!

It was called River Rats and had a large wooden pavilion in the middle, surrounded by all sorts of areas to pitch tents. There were several campfire pits and a place to swim. Wolf told us that the site was very old and full of interesting history. He said other groups would probably be camping there as well, so he found a nice area for our tents and a good campfire pit. We unloaded the gear, pitched our tents, and then jumped into the river to swim. We played in the current for a while and tried to swim upstream.

A short time later, a group of Girl Scouts set up camp and Wolf invited them to join us after dinner at the campfire. The counselors jumped back into the river and tried cleaning themselves up a bit, but The Bulk and I figured we didn't need to get clean for anyone, let alone a bunch of girls.

Most of the girls were teenagers, but we soon found out that their counselors were the reason our staff members were sprucing up. One of the girls had a guitar and we sang together by the fire. Both groups had s'mores, which almost made it worth the ordeal of having to sing with girls.

Even so, The Bulk and I ducked out to see the River Rats pavilion. The building looked like it had been around forever. There were all sorts of names and dates on the walls—many of which I recognized.

The Vacuum had signed: "Good luck to everyone."

Snarl had added his signature to River Rats lore on one of the upper rafters, though I wasn't sure how he'd gotten that high without bringing down the entire structure. There were loads of names from the 1940s and '50s, and I felt like I was at a camp-canoeing wall of fame. The Bulk and I found a pen and scribbled our names in a low corner, thus officially incorporating us into the lore of River Rats.

We returned to the campfire and found Wolf telling a story. The counselors from both camps had mysteriously disappeared. Only Wolf and an older Girl Scout leader remained with the campers, but no one seemed to miss the staff members. The Bulk and I figured maybe they'd gone to sign the pavilion.

Wolf completed his story and told us to head for the tents. He said we had a short paddle in the morning and then we'd be picked up by Crash. The girls said goodnight and thanked Wolf for his hospitality.

I was tired and looked forward to another night in the tent. I was excited to see Crash in the morning and was thinking of Mom and Dad's visit. Everyone fell asleep. I was briefly awakened in the middle of the night by laughter, and it sounded a little rowdy, and I heard Wolf milling about as he'd gotten up to see what the noise was all about. I heard him quietly tell some girls to go back to their campsite, then he mumbled the same to our counselors. The guys thanked Wolf for watching over everything and said they owed him one. Wolf agreed.

I whispered to The Bulk, "It sure took them a long time to sign the wall of fame."

The Bulk said, "Yeah. Goodnight."

• • •

We cleaned the campsite and made sure it was in better shape than we'd found it. The Bulk and I waved goodbye to our names, inked for posterity, as we paddled downriver. After an hour of easy paddling, we spotted Crash by the shore. He was a welcome sight; two and half days on the river had been enough for me and I was actually looking forward to a warm shower and getting some of the three-day dirt off my body. I would never have admitted that to my brother, but I suspected that there were times when he wanted to clean up, as well.

We packed all of the gear into the trailer and the counselors loaded the canoes. As we piled into the van, Crash handed us our mail. I was excited to receive a letter from home! Mom had signed Dad's name, since he seldom wrote. All of the guys were reading their mail, and I ripped into my envelope to see what was happening at home.

Mom's handwriting was quite distinct. It had a touch backhand and was set in perfect placement. When she ate corn on the cob, she always formed a perfect row across; she never missed a kernel—and her writing lined up exactly the way she ate corn. She was often asked to contribute her artistic penmanship for other people's anniversary, Bar and Bat Mitzvah, and party invitations. She wrote as beautifully and artistically as she prepared meals—and as perfectly as she treated other people.

Her news let me know that everything was fine at home, but boring. She told me that Dad golfed a couple times a week—and moaned two times a week about his score. She said that Dad told her he was going to change his swing each time he came home. She let me know the relatives were fine, the weather was hot and muggy, and that camp sounded like a lot better place than home. She was glad to hear that I'd made friends and was no longer homesick. However, in the last paragraph, she mentioned that she wouldn't be able to visit camp due to personal reasons and that Dad had decided to stay home, too, because he didn't want her to be alone.

 Campingly Yours

Mom emphasized that she was fine, not sick, and told me not to worry. She said she had notified Lou and Renee and they had told her that my brother and I could make a quick call home over the weekend if we wanted to—collect, of course.

She signed her letter, "Much love, Dad and Mom." (She taught me to always put the writer's name last.)

That was that. I sat motionless in the van, which was hard to do with Crash driving. I was crying inside, but I held it together outwardly. There would be no curveball to The Vacuum, no cobwebs for Mom, no Snarl, no Sherman, no showing off my swimming skills, no parents visiting camp.

The other guys were laughing and singing songs, but I just stared out the window, trying not to show my emotions. I wondered if my brother knew about it. Our parents hadn't visited my brother last summer, either, but I'd never really thought about it. I just assumed it was because I was home and they didn't want to leave me. I'd never given any real thought to it—until that moment.

7

Visitation, But No Mom and Dad

The weekend arrived and it was time for the parents to pile in. Several counselors lined the camp road to direct traffic and help park cars. I sat near the entrance, hoping that something had changed and that Mom and Dad decided to surprise my brother and me.

A lot of license plates crept by, with Illinois, Wisconsin, Nebraska, Minnesota, and Ohio leading the way—but no push button Plymouth station wagon with Missouri plates. Mom thought it was the ugliest car ever made, but Dad was proud of it, and at that moment I would have thought it was the prettiest automobile on Earth if I had seen it coming down the old camp road. I finally resigned myself to the fact that Mom and Dad weren't going to show up and I headed off to find my brother.

What a sight, watching all of the parents filtering out of the cars and seeing all the boys hugging their moms. Some were even hugging their dads, and I even saw dads kissing their sons. My grandfather and dad always shook my hand; I never saw dads hugging or kissing their boys. I thought that was strictly a daughter thing.

I finally found my brother and we watched more cars enter, more hugging and kissing, and lots of gifts being handed out. My brother looked at me and I looked back at him. I wanted to cry, but it was hard for me to tell about my brother.

 Campingly Yours

He said, "I knew they weren't visiting, but I didn't want to let you know too early. It was a lonely time for me during last year's visiting weekend, too, but I'm glad to have you here with me this time."

That made me feel a little better, knowing my brother actually was glad to have me around. It was hard to tell how many campers didn't have their parents visit, but I knew there weren't many.

A short time later, my brother and I went to find Lou and ask if we could make our call home. Unfortunately, both Lou and Renee were inundated with parents. It looked like they were giving a party for 300 guests and they had to make small talk with each one, so there'd be no phone call for us for awhile.

There were the normal activities in the morning, allowing parents to see their sons in action. A lot of parents participated with their sons. They shot arrows and rifles, hit tennis balls, sailed, and pretty much got in the way of their sons wherever possible. My brother headed to crafts and said he'd be making lanyards all morning. I told him I was going to go to baseball and try to get into a game. We agreed to meet at lunch and make our call then.

I strutted to the baseball field with my A's cap firmly planted on my head. Several fathers were already on the field and The Vacuum was hitting grounders and fly balls. Some of the fathers were showing off, but I could tell The Vacuum wasn't very impressed. I noticed a lot of the fathers wore gold chains around their necks, silver and gold bracelets, and shiny rings on their fingers. That all seemed foreign to me; Dad never owned any of that stuff. He said he never wore his wedding ring because it made him fidgety. It never bothered Mom, since she knew she wasn't in danger of ever losing Dad (especially when he drove his push button wagon around town).

The whole scene was a bit amusing to me; the dads showing off their shiny chains and lousy baseball ability. I was missing Dad and knowing that he didn't need all those material dangles to prove he was the best dad ever. His push button Plymouth wagon would have fit perfectly between the Lincolns and Cadillacs—and The Vacuum would have given his seal of approval to Dad's roundhouse curve. I must have been feeling sorry for myself. The Vacuum put fathers and sons together accordingly and got the game started. He put me in right field, which was absolutely fine with me.

Several of the shiny fathers came up to me and applauded my two catches down the right field line. They were actually quite nice and they made me feel pretty comfortable. They said they were sorry my parents were unable to attend and that they'd like to meet them one day. I had initially judged them to be loud and showy, and maybe they were, but they also demonstrated a caring side. I could tell that they were the best fathers ever to their own sons.

I headed to crafts to find my brother. One of the guys said my brother had been summoned to the sailing area, so I jogged to the bay where the sailboats were moored. One of the fathers, who apparently claimed he was a great sailor, had capsized an X-boat with his son and wife aboard. No one was hurt, but Lou was pretty upset and had asked my brother and two sailing counselors to take another X-boat out to pick up the family.

I could see across the bay to where my brother and the counselors were climbing into the boat. My brother was handling the main sail and he guided the family back to shore. The two sailing staff members jumped in to retrieve the capsized boat and put my brother at the helm to bring in the others. I was standing by Lou at the shore.

I asked Lou, "Why aren't the sailing counselors bringing in the family?"

Lou looked at me and firmly stated, "The Flash can handle it."

Lou grinned as my brother smoothly attached the boat to the moor, and as he did, I looked through Lou and saw my dad. Lou congratulated my brother as he came ashore. Then he reminded us that we needed to call home—collect—after lunch.

Lunch was an outdoor barbecue and my brother and I sat by the canoe racks, away from the masses. I told him that it was pretty neat watching him sail in the bumbling father and his family. My brother said he brought in beginning sailors all the time, and it was no big deal.

He said, "The father told his family the sails were bad and blamed the boat for the capsize."

 Campingly Yours

I asked my brother how he was able to sail in a bad boat, but my brother just grinned and reminded me that Dad worked on Saturday until noon. It was time to call home.

The camp secretary took down our phone number and dialed zero for the operator.

She said, "Collect from The Flash."

I laughed at the "collect from The Flash" part; my brother laughed at the collect part.

My brother took the line first as Mom answered and accepted the call. Mom and Dad only had one phone. My brother was smiling while telling Mom about the sailing incident and several of his camp adventures. Then Dad took the line and my brother repeated his stories, word for word. My brother's eyes watered a bit as he said goodbye and then he handed me the phone.

Dad stayed on the line, and I said, "Hi."

He told me how slow things were at home and that it was hot and nothing much was worth mentioning. He asked if anyone knew how to throw a roundhouse curve and if my hitting had gotten any better. I said no to both, although I suspected he knew I was fudging on the curveball part.

He said he'd received a letter from my counselor stating that I was participating in all sorts of activities and being a good kid. He told me to keep it up and that he'd hear all about it when I got home. That was it from Dad, so he put Mom on the phone.

Mom was as happy to hear my voice, as I was to hear hers. She asked all about camp and my new adventures. I interrupted her and asked how she was feeling. She paused and assured me that she was feeling fine and for me not to worry. She said she'd had setbacks now and then, so it was best for her to stay home. She quickly moved the conversation back to camp and I spewed as much information as I could before the secretary said our time was up. Mom didn't cry as she said goodbye. She said she knew I was enjoying camp and she was proud of both my brother and me. I said I'd see her in a few weeks and we hung up.

My brother and I then headed back to the canoe racks and sat for a while. I asked if he was sad. He asked if I was sad.

A short time later, we saw Lou talking to a tall, refined-looking woman and directing her my way. My brother told me he'd see me later in the day and quickly scurried off.

When she got closer, the woman asked if I was The Flash.

I said, "No, The Flash is my brother, but he just left."

She asked, "Oh, are you Kid Flash? If so, you're really the one I wanted to see."

I stood up and nervously shook her hand. She grabbed me and gave me a breath-stopping hug, locking me in a hold I couldn't break. When she finally released me, I grabbed a quick breath as she put an arm around me and guided me to meet her husband.

After walking some distance, we found her husband—standing next to Sherman. Smiling, the husband shook my hand without a word and then walked away, holding Sherman's hand while his wife remained with me. I got ready to grab another breath in case she decided to hug me again.

She told me that they were Sherman's parents and they'd brought me a gift. I tried to speak, but she stopped me and thanked me for helping Sherman, not just with sports, but also with showing him that he could make friends.

She said, "Sherman isn't able to comprehend much, but he knows that you've been trying to help him."

She took my hand and led me to the second ball field, farther away from the mainstream activity, where we found Sherman's dad throwing him pitches. Sherman swung each time and missed. As Sherman's mother and I reached the diamond, his father handed me his glove and asked me to pitch to Sherman. Then they sat on the first base bench while I lined up Sherman at the plate.

I took a few steps in front of the mound and threw my first pitch—too low. Sherman swung and missed. I threw the next pitch directly at armpit level, and Sherman connected with a ground ball up the middle. Sherman ran toward first base while his parents stood and cheered. Sherman's mother gave her husband a hug, and I felt sorry for Sherman's dad.

The mother cried openly and the father took off his glasses and wiped his eyes. Then they both approached me on the mound and said it was the first time they'd ever seen Sherman hit a ball.

Meanwhile, Sherman was standing stoically at first base as his parents handed me their gift. Then they walked over to first base and hugged Sherman while I opened my gift. It was a banner for the Kansas City A's. I held it up and waved it toward the three of them. As I watched them hug, I could see Lou in the distance with his arm around my brother.

After dinner, everyone was called to the council fire area for an evening campfire—a traditional campfire held for the parents. Lou and Renee opened the ceremony with a short story about how they had founded the camp and then emphasized the beautiful surroundings. Lou said it was a golden opportunity for the parents to forget about the hustle of the city and enjoy the tranquility of the north woods.

Some of the parents were talking during his speech and Lou promptly asked them to either be quiet or leave. He said the campers knew not to talk during solemn moments, and he expected the same from the parents. My brother and I were sitting together and we opened our eyes as wide as they could go, staring at each other. We didn't dare say a word, but I thought it was really cool how Lou had gotten the parents to be quiet. I could tell my brother felt the same. Even the fathers with shiny chains quieted down. Nobody left, and the audience remained silent and attentive.

Lou ended the campfire by asking us to repeat after him, and the parents all complied: "And now, may the Master of All Campers be with us until we meet again, and may the trails that we follow, though they be of different paths, lead straight unto him. Night, you all."

I stayed by my brother's side as the parents said goodbye to their sons, kissing and hugging them again. It was a huge crying scene, until Lou finally grabbed a megaphone and shouted that it was time for the parents to go. A few minutes later, they were all gone, and camp was about to become normal again.

Lou stepped in our direction, put his arms around us, and said, "Goodnight, Flashes."

We said, "Goodnight, Lou."

Then we heard another, "Goodnight, Flashes."

It was from Renee, who also gave each of us a hug. Her hug was gentle; I could breathe. However, both hugs I'd received that day had meant a lot to me. Both hugs were from mothers who had sons with serious challenges.

The guys in the cabin were pretty wound up when I got back. They were full of all kinds of food that parents weren't supposed to bring to camp. The Bulk offered me some popcorn. I asked him why parents had taken the chance of bringing food to camp. Lou would have scowled at them if he'd found out.

The Bulk said, "I think Lou knew. There's an unwritten law that all the food that parents bring has to be consumed or thrown out by morning."

Knowing that, I indulged in popcorn and brownies with the rest of the group, and the counselors made sure everything had been devoured before we went to sleep. The Bulk said there would be no trace of illegal food in camp by morning.

When I finally went to bed, I looked up at the ceiling, again intrigued by the cobwebs. I was sad that Mom hadn't gotten a glimpse at them. That was probably just as well. She would have wanted them gone—but maybe not after she'd heard my side of it. Dad would have loved meeting The Vacuum. He wouldn't have been one of the fathers talking during the campfire. His push button Plymouth wagon would have been a hit with the counselors. They would have thought it was Broderick Crawford pulling into camp with a patrol wagon.

Finally, the counselors hit the lights and told us all to go to sleep.

"Mom would have let the cobwebs be if she knew they had meaning…zzzzz…Lou cared more about the campers than he did the parents…he couldn't wait for the day to be over…I could tell…zzzzz…Renee seemed OK with everyone, but Lou wanted to get back to normal camp…How did Sherman's parents know I liked the A's?….Who told them about me?... zzzzz…Did Lou have a plan for all the campers…or just for my brother and me…no, all of the campers…zzzzz….Was Lou the Master of All Campers?…not the parents…zzzzz…Was

 Campingly Yours

it an accident that my brother was called to help the bumbling sailing father?...What if Sherman hadn't hit the ball?...I owe my brother another one...*zzzzz*...that makes two...I hope I can pay him back one day...*zzzzz*...Something's not right with Mom...but I can't tell what it is...*zzzzz*...I'm looking forward to normal camp again...Lou is, too...*zzzzz*...He's the father to all of us during the summer...Dad would approve...*zzzzz*...Mom would, too... *zzzzz*...'This camp is your camp, this camp is my camp...*zzzzz*...this camp was made for you and me'...and Sherman...*zzzzz*..."

8

I Want to Stay Just a Few More Days

Camp life quickly reverted to its normal laid-back state, except for lunch and dinnertime. Those meals were generally over the top with noise, while breakfast remained somber. The Bulk reminded me that a lot of the staff stayed out late and didn't want to hear loud noises in the morning. I wasn't sure what he was getting at, but he reminded me that our counselors at River Rats had been out till the wee hours of the morning—and not just signing their names on the rafters.

The next three and a half weeks flew by so fast that my nighttime dreams muddled into one beautiful fog-like experience. I played ball daily, made more friends in a few weeks than I'd made in a lifetime at home, became very close to The Bulk and The Vacuum, learned to like beanie weenie and all the other leftover hamburger meals that followed, endured a morning and part of an afternoon at an all-camp photo session, was never homesick anymore (even if a counselor yelled at me), missed playing catch with Dad but knew I'd be doing that soon, stared at the cobwebs every night, threw balls to Sherman several times a week, memorized the camp song ("Forest Green") and Lou's Master of All Campers closing at campfires, learned all sorts of fun and crazy camp songs, never sniffed another pudding with whipped cream, remained amazed at how everyone congratulated one another after winning

 Campingly Yours

or losing, and chuckled as Snarl found some sort of trouble almost daily.

I watched ten-year-olds and fourteen-year-olds hang out together, something I never saw at home. I never could tell counselor ages. The sixteen-year-olds could have been twenty, the twenty-year-olds could have been thirty—I had no idea. Lou and Renee must have been my parents' age.

No one messed with Lou. I once saw him get angry with a junior counselor who was goofing around during a solemn moment. After that, the counselor and anyone else, for that matter (especially me), made sure not to get on Lou's bad side. Later that week, I saw Lou with his arm around that same counselor.

Renee remained like a mother to all the campers, and to the counselors, as well. She was more than the camp mother; she was our confidant. She performed daily the most difficult part of conversation—listening. My brother continued to be somewhat of a cult hero. My counselors did a nice job of molding our cabin into a cohesive group. I could tell they liked us a lot.

The older guys came back from a weeklong Canadian canoe trip, and Wolf was overheard saying that the boys griped with each stroke into the wind and with each mosquito bite during the portages. Yet when Lou asked the group to give the camp a narrative on their trip, they said it was the most rewarding adventure they'd ever attempted and they couldn't wait to do it again. I could see Wolf mumbling to himself.

There were only two days left and Lou kept professing that there was still a lot of camping to do. We kept busy with our activities, but going home was in the air. I was excited to see Mom and Dad, but I wanted to stay at camp a few more days.

The first night of camp, I remembered hearing one of the counselors talking about how camp could get into a person's blood. At that time, I only wanted camp to bleed out of my system and into a North Woods septic tank, but I thought about that comment a lot during the summer. How could camp get into my blood? I didn't understand it at the time, but as the end of camp drew near, I found myself wondering just *when* camp had managed to get into my blood.

The staff performed an end-of-the-summer variety show. It was an annual next-to-last night evening event. Most of the show consisted of making fun of campers, counselors, cabins, trips, bugs, bug juice, food, rainy days, lousy athletes, good athletes, lanyard makers, and Lou and Renee. There was no mention of a catcher's mask. Most of the skits were in good taste and most of the campers could handle the good-natured teasing. The staff all gathered on stage at the end and sang camp songs—mellow ones, sad ones, lonely ones, and goodbye ones. Lou ended the evening by telling us there was still a lot of camping to do and to make the most out of our remaining time.

Lou never mentioned going home until breakfast on the last full day. All of us knew that the end of camp was near, but Lou tried his best to keep it a well-guarded secret. The head counselor made the transportation announcements. Most campers were assigned to buses headed for Milwaukee and Chicago. Those flying to Omaha and Kansas City were assigned to ride with Crash to Minneapolis. We were told to pack our trunks and duffels and leave them in front of the cabin.

We needed to save our sleeping bags and decent clothing for the trip home. Our packing was to be completed by lunch. The counselors made sure the clotheslines were empty and a huge lost-and-found area was formed in front of the lodge, where I was amazed to find some of my socks, underwear, and a pair of jeans. I wondered who'd been using those all summer.

I stuffed my clothes in no particular fashion into my bags, yet there was a lot of empty space. I was hoping Mom wouldn't notice my lost-and-not-found items. The Bulk said his parents had been surprised the previous year when he brought half of his clothes home. He said they weren't angry and actually applauded him for his fifty percent retention rate!

At lunch we were handed the back page of our camp photo album, which was designated for autographs. In the afternoon, everyone ran around camp gathering signatures and good luck sayings. Our photo album would be mailed in the fall and the autograph page would clip to the back of the album. Picture day had taken place in the middle of the fifth week, and we'd each had an individual portrait taken and then we took an all-camp picture. It took forever, since the counselors were goofing around and it was the muggiest day of the summer. I'd been handed a rifle for my portrait, even though I'd never shot one before.

I wanted to make sure to get as many autographs as possible. I found my brother and his group, Snarl, The Vacuum, the Pumpkins, Wolf, Milky, Sherman, Crash, the canoe instructors, and of course, my cabin mates and counselors. As I ran around camp, I had guys sign my book who didn't even know me very well—and I did the same for them. I wasn't sure if I was supposed to, but I also sought out Lou and Renee. I decided not to look at the signatures until camp was over.

That evening, our last night, there was a traditional final banquet. The lodge was decorated, the lights were turned down, there were candles on the tables, and we were served steak and a great dessert. Various awards were given out for archery, Red Cross swimming, most improved tennis, and most spirited team member, just to name a few. My brother won fastest lanyard maker and top sailor, but the best award of all went to Sherman—for most improved baseball player.

After the banquet we all headed to the rec hall for the annual request night. Lou was the master of ceremonies and we could request any songs or skits from that summer or any summer in the past. It was fun hearing songs from the camp musical again, rehashing some of the staff show funnies, hearing guys mimic Abbot and Costello's "Who's On First" routine, seeing guys fitting their fists into their mouths, and watching guys distort their bodies in strange ways. That went on for an hour, until Lou and Renee sang a song poking fun at all the counselors. It was really funny stuff, and it must have been rewarding for Lou and Renee to watch the staff members duck down in embarrassment.

Next, Lou had all of us stand and we chanted what years we had attended camp to the tune of "Mary Had A Little Lamb."

"We were here in '61, '61, '61; we were here in '61; where is 1960?"

Each person remained standing through his or her years before sitting down. The last ones

Campingly Yours 🌲

standing were Lou and Renee, singing, "We were here in '45; where is '44?"

Then they finally sat down.

The mood toned down as Lou called on a camper from the oldest cabin to give the Camper Farewell speech. Lou told us that it was an honor to be chosen to give the speech.

I listened as a fifteen-year-old reminisced about his first days at camp. He talked about homesickness, griping on canoe trips, losing big games, and not winning many awards. He said that he'd been put in a cabin with boys from other areas and he'd often felt left out. He said that he was in his fourth summer before he realized what camp really meant to him. He talked about friendships, trust, seeing the campers and staff go the second mile to help others, the thanks extended at the key log ceremonies, realizing that the staff's ridicule of Lou and Renee in shows was only in jest, and figuring out that Lou and Renee laughed at the ridicule.

At age fifteen, he paid notice to the beautiful sunsets and the dense forest surrounding camp. He said he'd begun to feel the serenity of the lake and was happy when his counselors woke him at midnight one night to see the northern lights. He'd begun to understand the meaning of the solemn moments at campfires. He expressed his wish that each new camper would someday have the same enlightenment and grasp the uniqueness of camp and all it had to offer. He concluded, on behalf of all the campers, by bidding everyone a fond farewell.

Everyone applauded respectfully while Renee gave the camper a hug and Lou called on a staff member to give the traditional Counselor Farewell. That counselor, who was finishing his ninth summer as a camper and staff member, took center stage and began tearing up before he'd even said a word. The room was totally quiet as Lou encouraged the counselor to do his best.

The nine-year counselor began by emphasizing that he'd been a lousy camper. He'd moaned his way through meals, ducked out of activities, been unable to sit still during campfires, picked on younger campers, hated losing, annoyed his counselors at bedtime, and had failed to learn half the activities offered at camp. He said he'd made a few friends but wasn't well liked by his cabin. The only reason he'd returned each year was because his parents had forced him. He later found out that he'd been non-requested by most campers every year and that Lou had always had trouble placing him with a group.

When he was sixteen, the age of being invited to return to camp as a CIT, he said that he hadn't received an initial invitation, even though all the other boys had already been invited. Ironically, he had wanted to return to camp that year, but his parents couldn't control the outcome.

He told us that he'd finally gotten up his nerve and called Lou to discuss why he hadn't been invited back. He said Lou had cleared his throat and hesitated—it was apparent that Lou was stalling. Then Lou told him that he and Renee would need to make a personal visit to discuss the matter. Later that week, he told us that Lou and Renee came to his house and were greeted by his parents. After making small talk, Lou had then asked to speak to him, alone.

The nine-year counselor teared up again as he continued, "Lou spent ten minutes going over all my positive traits, including a hidden, but kind heart. He said that beneath all that complaining, bullying, and lack of ambition was a boy waiting to show something special. Then he told me that at age sixteen, it was time to step up."

The staff hopeful had then asked why Lou had only mentioned his good traits. What about all the bad stuff that had caused him not to be invited back?

Lou had again cleared his throat and said, "Camp is a melting pot of characters. Not every staff member is an all-American jock."

Lou had then chuckled when he talked about a staff member who had developed a following because he was able to make fishing a fun activity. He'd come back from two hours on the lake with happy campers telling tall tales of catching a northsky (half musky, half northern).

The counselor went on, saying, "Lou also mentioned a staff member who was overweight but was popular because he could do a duck waddle that made everyone laugh. He reminisced about a rifle instructor with two first names who could hit a bull's eye from a hundred yards, but couldn't hit a baseball if his rifle depended on it. He was a pied piper for the non-athletic campers.

"I could see that Lou looked proud as he talked about one of his all-time popular staff members who always played the lead in the camp musical as a camper and later directed the play as a counselor. Then he shook his head, thinking about a counselor who had stayed out late way too many times, bragged about risqué adventures to campers, and was overly competitive when coaching campers in basketball. But Lou said he kept inviting that counselor back because he was a devoted counselor and his campers loved him and came back every year to be with him."

That bedroom discussion with Lou was a turning point in the young counselor's life. Lou asked him to write an essay on how he could fit into the camp melting pot in a positive way and how he could make a difference in a camper's life. Lou told him to put some serious thought into it and then mail it back to him.

The nine-year staff member concluded his farewell speech by thanking Lou and Renee for allowing him to return that year as a CIT and each year thereafter. Tears rolled down his face as he said that he knew he'd been a camp character—and not always a positive one—but a character that was accepted. He said he hoped he'd made a positive difference in at least one camper's life, and then, on behalf of all the counselors, he bid everyone a fond farewell.

Renee went to the stage and gave the counselor a hug as Lou shook his hand and said, "Well done, Snarl."

I clapped quietly along with the others as I thought about my catcher's mask. It wasn't the mask that had made a difference that day; it was Snarl. In his own ornery melting pot way, Snarl had made a difference in at least one camper's life—I knew that for sure.

It was very quiet as we left the building in an orderly fashion and headed to the tennis courts overlooking the athletic field. At the far end of the field was a flame, burning the camp's initials in effigy. Lou spoke about the great summer and how we had become men.

Renee cried as she said she looked forward to seeing all of us during the "off season." Lou asked us to remain silent, to stare at the effigy, and to visualize our fondest moments of the summer. We all stood in no particular order; everyone had arms around each other.

The Vacuum came to my side, put his arm around me, and said, "Be good, Kid Flash."

Lou's voice cracked as he joined Renee in singing "Forest Green" and we all joined in. It was a most serene version, mixed with coughing, sniffles, and outright crying. I'd never seen so many boys cry before.

As the effigy faded away, we repeated after Lou: "And now, may the Master of All Campers be with us until we meet again, and may the trails that we follow, though they be of different paths, lead straight unto him."

Everyone mumbled, "Night, you all," and then we headed back to our cabins as the older boys and several counselors lingered on the courts.

I lay in bed that night with many thoughts racing through my head. I said goodbye to the cobwebs and told them I'd visit them next year. Would there be cobwebs in my new cabin? Would Mom and Dad take us to the hamburger place again or would we have to go to a nice a restaurant? I wondered if there would be dessert with whipped cream. I could ask Dad to smell it—or maybe Mom. No, bad idea. I couldn't wait to see them and to tell them about everything that had taken place.

"And I'll tell my friends about camp…zzzzz…Why did Lou honor Snarl with that speech? It was sad to see Snarl cry…The Vacuum put his arm around me…I hope he comes back next summer…zzzzz."

I whispered goodnight to The Bulk.

"Thanks, Bulk, for filling me in on everything…zzzzz…I couldn't have made it without you…Thanks for kicking sand on my bed all summer…I wonder if my brother's friends smoked the last night…not my brother…I forgot to pack my catcher's mask…I'll get it in the morning…zzzzz…I can carry it on the plane…Maybe the stewardess will make fun of me…zzzzz…Who's saying goodnight to Sherman?…I can't wait to see Mom and Dad…get the curveball ready, Dad…zzzzz…Crash is driving us…hold on tight…I wanted to stay a few more days…zzzzz…was Lou the Master of All Campers?…did every camper lead to him?…The Bulk is a good friend…have a good year, Bulk…zzzzz…be good, Vacuum…zzzzz…'This camp is my camp, this camp is your camp, this camp is made for you and me'…and Snarl."

• • •

The buses arrived bright and early; the head counselor was screaming for everyone to take their assigned bus. Crash made an announcement that he'd be loading the flight people as soon as the buses pulled out. Boys were shaking hands and hugging, and some were crying, but mostly it was a time of smiles and laughter. I stared at the scene. I thought it was kind of a happy sad—a happy sad, that's what it was. Boys didn't want to leave camp, but they were ready to see their parents and friends back home.

Lots of guys said goodbye to my brother and me. The head counselor finally pulled campers apart and gave the last shout to get on the buses. The Bulk and I shook hands and he boarded the bus. So long, Bulk—thanks for being my best friend.

Roll was taken and then two buses crept out onto the camp road as some staff members waved goodbye and some ran alongside the buses for a while. No one seemed to want to let go, but it was time; campers had spent eight weeks, staff members nine, and it was time to return home.

Moments later, we loaded our van as counselors came our way to say their goodbyes. So long, Vacuum, Pumpkins, Milky, Wolf, and all the counselors. Snarl gave me a shove—his form of affection. I laughed and got into the van. Counselors disappeared pretty quickly. Crash leaned on the horn as we headed out onto the camp road.

At the end of the road were loads of staff members, all mooning our van. Indeed, it was quite an "end" to a magical camping season, my first.

9
First Night Home

Crash somehow missed all cows and managed to get us to the Minneapolis airport on time. Then we waved goodbye to Crash and boarded a Braniff jet prop. My brother and I sat together and were both exhausted but fully awake. Anxiety had taken over, but we were excited to see Mom and Dad.

My brother told me that I needed to view going home as the "off-season" and camp as the "on-season." He said it would be hard for me to explain camp to my friends. After all, he was The Flash only at camp, and my Kid Flash status would have to wait until the next summer.

Midway through the flight, I opened up my autograph page. It was filled with scribbling and I read each one slowly. The Vacuum wrote that he'd thrown his best curve at me and considered me a great friend. He said I'd make a few errors now and then, but to remember the ones I caught. He concluded with: "See you on the ball field next summer."

Snarl said I was a smart-alecky kid and that he'd push me around again if I returned the next summer. He also said thanks for being his friend.

Renee said I'd be a camp lifer and that she expected my mom to have her kugel ready at the reunion.

Campingly Yours

Lou wrote: "Kid Flash, great first summer, see you at the reunion, and see you next summer."

The Bulk said that I was his best friend.

My brother wrote, "See you at home."

Wolf said that he'd take me on a harder trip the next summer and to be ready.

It took me most of the flight to read everything. I was sad to leave all of these people, but also was anxious to see Mom and Dad. It was truly a happy sad.

As I put the page away, I noticed on the bottom was a small picture. It was a very precise, artistic rendering of a bat and ball. Inside the ball was crudely written: "Thanks, love Sherman."

We landed safely and my brother and I headed down the steps, trying to eye Mom and Dad. They were standing at our gate, Mom waving and laughing and Dad wearing his grin. Mom hugged us and Dad shook our hands. We gathered our baggage, loaded the car, and off we went. I noticed that Dad didn't have a conference with Mom, so we must have been reasonably clean.

They gave each of us a new shirt and told us we were going to have a nice meal. That sounded fine with us; we were hungry. I actually liked the camp food, but the thought of restaurant food was equivalent to a camp pizza and pop party.

We all ordered Kansas City strips and it seemed like the whole cow was served. My brother told a few stories about his cabin, his canoe trip, and the sailing program. I interrupted and bragged about how he'd rescued a goofy family on visiting day and how Lou seemed proud that he could handle the situation better than the parents in distress.

Mom and Dad were quite interested in our stories. They let us do most of the talking and only chimed in with further questions.

Mom asked me, "What did you think of Lou and Renee? Were they around when you needed them? Did they get to know you very well? Was Renee a big part of camp? Did they make you feel at home? Were they fair or too strict?"

I thought about Mom's questions and said I'd get back to her, maybe that night. We thanked Mom and Dad for the great meal and then we all headed back to the car for the half-hour ride home. We talked about camp happenings and Mom had to give Dad several nudges to keep him awake. Our camp stories didn't bore him; he often dozed at the wheel. Maybe he felt secure in his push button wagon. Maybe they had sent us to camp for fear that the alternative would be unsafe, long family outings. No, my mind was again wandering, not wondering.

I experienced a strange feeling as we pulled into our driveway. It was only as I entered the house that I really knew camp was over. I didn't want to let go of camp, but it was over. It was great being with Mom and Dad again, but camp was over.

Mom tucked me in that night. The first few nights of camp, I had wondered how she could have abandoned me and left me to fend for myself, but as she tucked me in, I thought that maybe I had abandoned her. I'd had fun at camp and had not needed her to show me the way.

She asked me about Lou and Renee again. I paused and then said they were like second parents to all the guys. Lou commanded our respect and most of the guys were somewhat intimidated by him. I told Mom that Lou knew everyone's name within a week, and so did Renee. I always wanted Lou's approval and hoped he'd notice me in a positive way. I'd look Lou's way when something funny happened at a campfire because I wanted to see if he laughed or not. When something not so good happened, I'd look his way for his reaction.

There was a lousy feeling in the air when Lou was upset with something, but then, I felt the same way about Dad. I always glanced at Dad to see if he approved of my homework, hitting, fielding, or most of my everyday stuff.

I told Mom, "I didn't want to say anything about this at the restaurant, since I thought it might hurt Dad's feelings. I thought he might think I liked Lou as much as him."

I told Mom that Renee was a very sweet lady who was always willing to listen. She was everyone's summer mom and I didn't think anyone needed her approval, although we all had it. I said that Lou ran the camp his way while Renee was the voice of reason and kindness.

Mom reassured me that my view of Lou and Renee was right on target. My brother had voiced similar comments the year before. She said that they wouldn't have sent us to that camp if Lou and Renee hadn't been viewed as second parents. Mom said that Dad had known from the first time he met Lou and Renee that their camp would be the right place for us.

After a few minutes, Dad peeked into the room, grinned, made a funny face, and then gave me a thumbs-up. He told me to look out the window the next morning for something special.

I laughed with Mom and said, "Dad doesn't intimidate me. He's too goofy for that to happen."

She laughed and said goodnight.

In the darkness, I lay in bed with my eyes wide open. It was very quiet, almost eerily quiet. I turned on the light and looked for cobwebs on the ceiling—but there were none, not with Mom heading up the household. I turned off the light and could have sworn I felt sand raining on my bed from overhead.

I whispered to The Bulk—no response. I saw flashlights streaking across the bedroom and heard our counselors telling us to knock it off and go to bed. I remembered Mom saying that when my brother was a baby she and Dad had stayed in a hotel in Kansas City, leaving my brother with my grandparents. Mom said it was the first time they'd ever left him. She said that both she and Dad swore they heard him crying.

I thought for sure that everything I was sensing that night was actually happening, but not so. I thought about all the great things that happened to me at camp and I laughed while thinking about my first two days. I never would have guessed that I could laugh about being teased and being so homesick.

"I already miss The Vacuum. It was great having a college-age friend. I know he really liked me. It was great…he'd better return next summer…zzzzz…Dad has a surprise for us in the morning. He probably picked up something for my brother and me for making it through camp. I hope the new shirt doesn't count for anything…*zzzzz*…the shirt was for dinner… *zzzzz*…Mom and Renee would be great friends…they think alike…*zzzzz*…Lou isn't goofy like Dad…Dad never intimidated me…*zzzzz*…I have to tell Dad that he's my only dad, not Lou…*zzzzz*…I miss organized free nights, the ball field, and even canoeing down the river to River Rats…*zzzzz*…Welcome home, Mom and Dad…*zzzzz*…Welcome back to Missouri, Flash and Kid Flash…my brother and I won't have those names here…*zzzzz*…Thanks, Snarl, for picking on me…*zzzzz*…'This camp was made for you and me'…and my catcher's mask…Thanks, Dad."

10

The Arrival of Charley

I t was nearing 8:30 a.m. as I peeked out the window. Mom had said Dad was only playing nine holes. Hmmm! There had to be something special happening if Dad was only playing nine holes. I was glued to the window, looking for the beautiful push button wagon—and then I saw it. It was Dad! I yelled to my brother to look out the window. Dad was pulling in!

Dad got out of the car grinning as he opened up the passenger door. He knew we were looking out the window. Out of the car squirted a puppy, white with varied black spots. He seemed to be mostly beagle and part terrier. My brother and I bolted out the door like the true Flash and Kid Flash while Mom trotted behind us.

Dad grinned and said, "This is Charley."

Charley fanned his tail and licked us all over. Dad had saved the dog from the pound, since someone had thrown him away. Someone hadn't wanted to take care of Charley, but my brother and I did. What a surprise!

Mom brought out a small bowl of milk and Charley lapped it up. My brother and I ran into the yard and Charley darted after us. I looked back and saw Dad's grin, and I remembered the last time I'd looked out the window to watch Dad and his bulldog. I was happy to see Dad's grin again. What a great feeling.

At the dinner table that night, Dad gave us his views on dog ownership. He said a dog wasn't for everyone, yet he felt sorry for children that didn't have one. He said a dog could create a wide variety of emotions, ranging from extreme aggravation to total joy. A dog could be a psychologist and a great conversationalist; after all, a dog could only listen. Dog ownership involved a lot of work and loyalty. The owner had to be just as loyal as the dog. Owning a dog could also be very expensive, with all the food, shots, de-worming, and potential illnesses. Dad said that Charley would be our best friend, especially when the world around us was difficult.

"Count on Charley to stick with you, and you with him," said Dad. "A lot of parents don't allow a dog in the house because they don't want the hassle, but I think those parents are depriving their children of something special. The biggest problem with owning a dog is that they don't live very long, and watching your dog die can be extremely gut-wrenching."

I knew exactly what Dad was talking about.

Dad continued. "It becomes a sad end to years of joy. I treasured all the happy memories with Bulky, but now we'll do the same with Charley."

It occurred to me that having a new dog was another form of happy sad.

• • •

Over the next few days, I made the strange but fast transition from camp life back to hometown living. My brother proved to be correct; none of my friends were interested in my camp stories. No one laughed when I described the pudding in my face or the antics of Snarl. They didn't seem to care much about The Vacuum's curveball and my brother's sailing rescue. Mom and Dad listened and cared, but no one else seemed to. It didn't take me long to stop telling camp stories, except at home. I had my brother to reminisce with about the summer, and he had me—and that was good enough.

My attitude about daily life away from the house changed, as well. I compared school happenings, after school pickup games, every nonsense argument that led to a fight, older boys who were too cool to hang out with the grades below—basically everything—to how things happened at camp. I missed hanging out with eighteen-year-olds. I missed knowing 200 guys who thought I was okay. I missed the daily guidance of counselors, and I missed Lou and Renee. I also missed all the attention. It was hard, and maybe unfair, to compare everything to how it would have happened at camp, but that was how my mind worked. My main solace was my brother, Mom and Dad, and Charley. It was great having such a close family.

My other relief was the newsletter that arrived from camp—like clockwork—at the beginning of each month. I knew my brother enjoyed reading the newsletter, but after spending a summer at camp, I also realized how exciting it was to have a monthly newsletter arrive in the mailbox. I assumed that Lou and Renee wrote them, but I never really knew.

The first two paragraphs were designed to teach us something about being moral or going the extra mile. Abe Lincoln's failures before he became president were mentioned, as was being extra thankful on Thanksgiving. There was a quote from the president of Harvard, saying that one summer of camp was more valuable than four years at his institution. I liked that comment. Spending a summer at camp and skipping four years of college; that sounded like the best way to get a degree.

I read quickly through those paragraphs to get to the good stuff—the list of who would be returning. Was The Bulk going back? The Vacuum? What about Sherman? I was excited to see the names of those I really wanted to return—and I was apprehensive and worried when I didn't see someone on my wish list of names, which meant I had to wait until the next newsletter. What about my name and my brother's name? Maybe Mom and Dad wouldn't be able to afford to send us back. I hadn't asked them about it. I assumed I'd return, but what if it wasn't in the cards?

I kept quiet and looked forward to Lou and Renee's visit. We hosted the annual camp reunion and Mom made her famous kugel for Renee. It was so much fun for me to see the camp movie, and I actually popped up on screen a few times. My brother spliced the film for Lou before it decorated our living room carpet.

Lou had a private chat with my brother and me. It made us feel important and I could tell that Lou was sincere in hearing our thoughts about camp. He asked if we were going to return. We both said we wanted to go back to camp, but we weren't sure if Mom and Dad would be able to send us again.

Lou and Dad talked quite a bit, and even though they'd met only a few times, it seemed as if they were good friends. As we said goodbye, Lou shook our hands and Renee gave us hugs. It was great seeing Lou and Renee, and the reunion reinforced my focus—I was anxious to get back to camp.

Two weeks later, the camp newsletter arrived. I tore into the envelope and skipped the opening life lecture. I skimmed the list of returning campers as fast as I could—and my name was listed along with my brother's! I was going to return to camp!

The Bulk's name was also listed, and under the Staff News, The Vacuum's name was listed. I couldn't wait to get back to camp. I called Dad at work and Donna, the secretary, said he was busy. I told her it was an emergency. She said he'd call back in a few minutes, since he was checking #2 steel on top of a gondola.

A short time later, Dad called and asked what was wrong.

"Is Charley OK?" he asked.

I told Dad that Charley was fine and thanked him for sending me back to camp. Dad told me to get out the football, loosen up my legs, and be prepared to do a few post patterns toward the weeping willow when he got home. I could see Dad's grin through the phone.

11

My Brother
Hoisted
on Shoulders

was in the middle of my fourth summer and camp life had fallen into place for me. Every year I looked forward to returning more than the last. Mom never visited, and Dad stayed home with her. Dad said that he and Mom didn't want to interfere with our camp life, and though I understood the interference line with Little League, I didn't when it came to camp. My brother and I figured that something larger was wrong with Mom, but we let the matter lie. Parent visitation was a bit lonely for us, but we always enjoyed the call home.

I had accumulated loads of camp friends and my brother had kept his status of cult hero. The Bulk returned each year and we remained best friends. He always knew what was happening next and I was smart enough to ask him pertinent questions. Other campers trickled into my summer life. Few kept their real name for long, since staff members assigned nicknames quickly. I had a core group of friends in my cabin and I looked forward to being with them each summer—including Moose, Farb, Brillo, and The Bulk.

Brillo was my biggest sports competitor. He was six feet tall at age thirteen and very coordinated. He could punt a football fifty yards, hit a baseball a mile, and play tournament tennis. He was destined to be a star high school athlete and he was always picked first, no matter the sport. The Bulk was just as big, and a decent athlete. Moose was a combination of decent athlete and intellect. Farb wasn't a great athlete, but he was a good team member. He was also very knowledgeable about sports and world affairs. I had to use quickness and smarts athletically, since I was the shortest and weighed the least, but I was always picked on the higher end and somehow my camp teams did well over the years.

The Vacuum returned for several summers, as did many of my favorite staff members. Lou and Renee had a way of maintaining old-time staff; counselors wanted to return as much as my friends and I did. Camp was in our blood. I had figured that out my first year. I just didn't know how much of my blood was being engulfed.

The last night of camp remained magical and I was left with that same empty feeling each time camp ended. I knew that some of the boys and my favorite counselors would be saying goodbye to camp for the final time—not for any bad reason; they just knew it was time to move on. Wolf and Crash moved on, as did the canoe instructors. The Pumpkins returned through my third summer and I hung out with them a lot. Then they both went off to attend Ivy League schools, and that was it. I never heard about or from them again.

That part of camp was puzzling to me and made me wonder if camp was in everyone's blood as much as it was in mine. It was hard knowing I might not see someone again. There were so many boys and staff each summer, and probably eighty percent of them returned the following summer. It was the other twenty percent that worried me. With each summer that passed, I lost a few close friends. I could only hope that the Pumpkins remembered me as much as I did them.

I figured that one day the time would come for me to head in a different direction. Fortunately, that time seemed an unimaginably long distance away. The goodbye bus scene was always loaded with crying eyes, hugs, handshakes, and the uncertainty of who'd be returning. Dad let me know early on that I could return to camp as long as I desired. He never brought up the cost. Dad never complained about money—well, maybe about the cost of an ice cream cone. He often bragged about all his losers in the stock market and how his roulette number would hit as soon as he walked away from the table. I don't remember Dad ever boasting about himself, except for his roundhouse curve.

. . .

United Nations Day always felt a bit mystical to me. The campers and staff were divided into four teams with each team representing a country in the U.N. I compared it to the Yankees vs. Dodgers, UCLA or the Packers vs. anyone, Wilt vs. Russell, or the U.S. vs. Russia in the Olympics. Spirit was always extremely high and the noise level remained off the charts all day. I was amazed at how important and intense that day was.

Each team had three camper leaders and one counselor serving as the advisor. The four advisors were close friends, but they distanced themselves on United Nations Day. Lou touted camp as being a low key, noncompetitive program—but not on U.N. Day.

Teams were announced several days before U.N. Day, and we practiced our events with staff coaches. There were four full series of events, and every camper competed each period. Events were held in baseball, basketball, flag football, volleyball, sailing, water skiing, archery, riflery, lanyard making, ping pong, obstacle courses, relay races, three-legged races, crab walks, all-team tug of war, tether ball, canoe gunnelling, row boat races, and a huge swim meet the last period of the day.

At the end of the swim meet there was an all-team watermelon polo competition. Two teams entered the swim area at one time, and then Lou dropped a greased watermelon in the middle of the swim area, blew his whistle, and the first team to place the watermelon on the opposing team's pier was declared the winner. I lived for that day, thought about it during the winter, constantly kicked myself for a bad play I'd made the previous summer, and smiled just thinking about my team winning the day.

That fourth summer I played shortstop for our baseball team. We had a strong team,

including two guys from my brother's cabin and Brillo. We won our opening game easily and were waiting to play the finals against the other winning team on the main diamond. We were staying loose, since the other game had gone into extra innings. We heard loud cheers of excitement and saw boys jumping for joy. The underdogs had won and were headed our way for the championship game. It was my brother's team. They had a lousy team, but they had managed to win their first game.

We were the visiting team and coasted to an early 6-1 lead. They scored two runs on walks and an overthrow to first base—by me. I was feeling pretty lousy heading into the top of the last inning, having made that error and knowing that our team only led by three.

I led off with a drag bunt single and Brillo drove me home with a two-out double. But that was all we could muster—a 7-3 lead with the last half inning to go. They drew two walks after the first batter flew out. My team was a bit cocky, especially the guys from my brother's cabin. I think they figured there was no way our team was going to lose to an inferior opponent. I kind of thought the same thing, but I tried not to show my feelings.

One of the cocky guys, our captain and a smoker from my brother's cabin, decided to pitch, since he knew he could throw strikes. His first pitch was down the middle, but one of their two known hitters lined a single to left, scoring a run. It was 7-4, with their strongest hitter coming to the plate and my brother on deck.

Our pitcher called time out. He conferred with our coach and a couple of guys and said he wanted to walk the next hitter to get to my brother, The Flash. Most of the guys knew The Flash could out sail them, out lanyard them, and shoot a clear midnight picture, but they also knew that my brother didn't often get involved with camp sports.

For some reason, the advisor of his team had put him in the baseball lineup and for an even stranger reason, the advisor had set up the lineup for him to bat fifth, right behind their best hitter. I understood why our pitcher wanted the intentional walk to get to my brother. I went to the mound to hear what was being said. Everyone agreed that my brother would be an easy out; everyone but me. They said it was better-than-even money that he'd hit into a double play and the game would be over. I started to chime in, but opted to stay silent. I wanted to win that game in the worst way, since it was U.N. Day.

My brother strutted to the plate with the bases loaded. I wanted to win the game, and if he hit a grounder my way, I was resolved to go for the double play. I wanted to tell our cocky, smoking pitcher to keep the ball outside, since my brother was a good pull hitter, but again I kept quiet.

My brother fouled the first pitch off to left for strike one. I noticed our left fielder was playing too shallow, but I kept quiet. I wanted to win the game. Thoughts of that Little League game flashed across my scoreboard brain.

Strike two came as my brother watched a perfect pitch go by. I wanted to win that game. I wanted to tell the left fielder that my brother could hit.

I wanted to say, "Move back, be ready, a single is OK."

The next pitch was delivered high and inside. The Flash whacked a rope just out of the reach of our leaping left fielder. There was no fence, and the ball kept rolling. I darted way out for the relay, but by the time I got the ball and turned, my brother was already crossing the plate. No tripping, no accidental slide—just the same picture of my brother being hoisted on the shoulders of the whole team.

I had wanted to win that game—but I had also promised myself that I'd pay my brother back someday. I was never going to tell him. He'd hit the ball, and I just kept quiet. I had paid him back.

After the commotion settled down, our team chanted a cheer for the winners. The winners chanted a cheer for us. Our cocky pitcher shoved my brother in a Snarl-like way of congratulations. The opposing advisors shook hands and laughed. I stood on the bench and played Dad. The Flash looked my way and saw my grin— he knew.

12

Mom, Dad and the Merry Fairy House

I **was sixteen and had just finished my sophomore year. My brother had left for** camp a week early to attend the required counselor orientation. It should have been my CIT summer, but I opted to stay home, play ball, teach tennis for the city recreation department, and work with Dad.

Lou and Renee were upset at the winter reunion when I told them I wasn't returning to camp. At the time, I thought they were angry with me, and they were disappointed. Lou took me aside to explain the value of the CIT summer. He said I'd make a fine staff member one day and that he was very sorry to lose me. His sincerity was genuine—at least I knew he hadn't made the same comments to Snarl—but my mind was made up. Lou said I was welcome back any time. Renee hugged me and said that she would miss hitting tennis balls with me—and that was it. For me, there would be no being at camp for the bus arrival, no magical time of seeing friends from other cities, no Bulk, no Vacuum, no hearing Lou call out cabin assignments, and no opening staff show.

On the first day of camp, there was no me. I just sat in Dad's office, lost in the ozone of camp. My trance probably lasted five minutes, but so many things raced through my mind. My face was longing for the sweetness of pudding and whipped cream. The Flash was at camp, and I was jealous. I wanted to know every happening every second, minute, hour, and day. I could have assisted The Vacuum with the baseball program. What had I been thinking? Lou was right. Renee tried so hard at tennis—and I never told her that I purposely hit every ball to her forehand. Did the new campers notice the cobwebs? Probably not.

Dad waved his hat in front of me to get my attention.

He said, "Since you're getting paid, you might consider going to the metal room to learn how to separate red and yellow brass."

When I let him know that I was feeling blue about missing the first day of camp, Dad began telling me a story.

He said that he and Mom were an old-fashioned couple, and for them, it had been love at first sight. He said they just knew that they were going to get married at some point. Then Dad told me how he had walked away from the relationship for a while, thinking maybe he wasn't ready to move so fast. He didn't go out with anyone else, but he didn't call Mom during that period.

Dad said he daydreamed about all the great times they'd had together. He reminisced about the first day they met, the dances, the ice cream, meeting each other's families, and the time he told her he loved her for the first time. To my surprise, Dad told me that walking out on Mom turned out to be the best thing that ever happened to him, but I got his drift and asked how long he stayed away.

Dad grinned and said, "Five whole days. Now go sort the brass."

Keeping busy during the days proved to be my salvation. I taught tennis to grade school children in the morning, worked at Dad's junkyard in the afternoon, and played Ban Johnson ball two or three nights a week. It was the first time I'd ever been around Dad during the day to see him at work.

Dad had majored in journalism at Missouri University at about the same time Walter Cronkite attended the journalism school at the University of Texas. Dad and Walter were born months apart in St. Joe, probably at the same hospital. After graduation, Dad wrote for a Corpus Christi newspaper and planned to be a columnist and work his way up the ladder of success. Then he received a call telling him that his father had been struck in the leg by a piece of iron that had darted out from the shears. My grandfather developed an infection and eventually lost his leg.

Dad felt compelled to help out for a while, so he left his newspaper job. "For a while" ended up being twenty years, since my grandfather was unable to work every day after that. The business had been in the family since the early 1900s, and Dad said he eventually learned to enjoy the everyday action of the junkyard. Dad said it was probably a good thing for the Columbia Broadcasting System that Walter wasn't called to help my grandfather.

The junkyard employees and customers made an interesting cast of characters. Willie the crane driver couldn't afford a house, so Dad let him live in an old bus at the back of the yard. Willie was a dead ringer for Charlie Allnut, Humphrey Bogart's character in *The African Queen*. I wasn't sure where Willie showered—or if he ever bothered with any form of ablution. I also wondered how he kept warm in the winter.

Willie took to me and made sure no one gave me grief for being the boss' kid. He showed me how to run the crane, swing the magnet to pick up iron, and drop the load into a Southern Pacific gondola. Willie swung the Bantam with ease and precision, an art not many could or should have considered, including me.

My first solo attempt was almost a disaster. I accidentally let the magnet drop, and it came within a deck plate-width of crushing Wilbur, but he just laughed, since he was still drunk from the night before (probably from all the nights before). After that, though, Willie suggested that I stick to the metal room and have Paul teach me the art of sorting. Red brass was worth more than yellow brass, since the red had more copper content.

Paul weighed 350 pounds, spit tobacco everywhere (including on me), had black hands from never washing, and was cranky all day, every day. Paul, like Willie, had been at the junkyard when my grandfather was in charge. Neither of them had made it through grade school, and most of the employees were similarly uneducated.

It was my first experience hearing the f-word in almost every sentence, as well as constantly hearing about people's mothers. The place came to a standstill when a woman walked into the yard. It didn't matter what she looked like; the guys all spewed what they'd like to do to her—except for Willie. I never heard him say too much about anything, except his crane.

Elmer handled the new and used steel on the north side of the lot. He took me under his wing and showed me the ins and outs of the grades of steel and how to handle the customers. He said used steel was simplified to fifteen cents per pound, and that made it easy for me to help customers who needed odds and ends.

Elmer was made from a slightly different mold. He had lots of children and was devoted to his wife. I don't think he ever made it through school, but he was instinctively smart and he could be trusted. Dad made him the foreman of the yard and Elmer took his job seriously. Elmer confided to me that when he started he had no money, a wife, several kids, and no place to live. He said that Dad gave him building materials and brought in outside help to put up a home.

Elmer worked hard, saved a little, and several months later met Dad after work to pay back some of his debt, but Dad wouldn't take the money. In fact, Elmer said that his next paycheck even included a bonus for his devotion to the yard.

Late one afternoon, just before closing, I noticed a man crying at Dad's desk. It was Doug, one of the guys who helped with new and used steel. He'd been there for years and I could hear him pleading with Dad for $20. He said he was being evicted from his apartment and needed to pay rent that night. Dad asked Doug about the previous week's $20 and the $20 the week before. Doug said that he'd pay it all back as soon as he could. I watched Dad hand over the $20 and overheard Wilbur say he'd see Doug at the gin mill.

Dad appeared oblivious to his surroundings. It seemed almost as if he purposely didn't know what was going on around him. Then it occurred to me that maybe he knew every single thing that was going on. He was at the epicenter of all the swearing, lying, stealing, spitting, and mother talk.

He knew that seedy customers would sneak into the yard at night, take a few pounds of stainless steel or aluminum, and sell it back days later. He knew that some would load extra dirt or snow into their trucks before weighing on the scales and then dump it all off before reweighing their empty truck. He knew that some of his frequent customers would come in and shoot the breeze with him while having their accomplices try to gain an extra pound of worth out back.

Many of the junk dealers, battery peddlers, and number one steel distributors would come from small towns to bring their goods to Dad's yard. Most were decent people, not crooks. They came in one or two times a month from a radius of fifty miles or so and each one would sit with my dad and talk about life and junk. Dad was king of the area's junk world and all his customers admired him, as did his workers and the gonifs.

Driving home, I asked Dad why he let people borrow from him without paying him back. I also asked if he knew about the petty thieving going on out back. I told him that it had been an awakening for me to see him in action and it was really cool that all the people considered him to be a higher being. I told Dad that he was king of his world, the benevolent dictator of junk.

Dad didn't say anything until I stopped rambling, but as we pulled into the driveway after our nine-minute ride, Dad gave me one answer. He said that he liked the fact that he was recycling goods and that he could sleep easy at night. He also told me that he hoped I'd always be able to sleep easy at night.

• • •

One night that summer, I was sitting in bed with Charley curled up by my side. My brother was at camp and would be heading to college shortly after his return. Charley was a nightly regular in my bed, and at middle age, he was the ultimate family dog. He never messed in the house, always asked to be let out and in, was a hit with all my friends and relatives, roamed the neighborhood at will, and listened to whatever I had on my mind.

That night, my mind was filled with reflections and I spewed my camp thoughts to Charley. I told him about my third summer, when Lou had placed me in a different cabin, away from my core group of friends. The new group was absolutely non-athletic. They read comic books all day and had nicknames like Spaz, Wiener Dog, The Laugher, Oatmeal, and Dr. Square. The rest of the camp looked at that cabin as a bunch of misfits, and we'd been dubbed the Merry Fairy House.

The third night of that summer, my former group kidnapped me and petitioned to put me back in their cabin for the rest of the summer. Lou got wind of the incident, scolded the boys (and their counselors) the next morning, and then had me sit in his office until he was ready to see me.

After a ten-minute eternity, Lou stepped in, cleared his throat, put down his pipe, cleared his throat again, and began speaking. (Charley even looked worried at that point in my story; at least he seemed concerned as he nestled his head on my leg.)

Lou said, "Kid Flash, do you remember how happy Sherman's parents were with you?"

Lou told me that Sherman's parents had confided to him that no one had ever given Sherman the time of day, let alone found a way to help him hit a ball. Lou said the boys in my new cabin could handle each other okay, but they would be teased mercilessly mixed with other groups.

"I notified your parents of your upcoming cabin placement just before summer, and your dad told me it would be a valuable learning experience for you," said Lou. "You can still have a great summer, but it's up to you. Now go get 'em, Kid Flash."

Apparently Lou must have looked at that whole cabin as one big Sherman.

The Sunday after my kidnapping was a camp challenge day and the Merry Fairy House had been challenged to a basketball game by my former cabin. We were about to be further embarrassed by Brillo and The Bulk, both six-footers, the surly Moose, the scrappy Farb, and a few other above-average players. My new counselors were clueless about sports, so I had just two free periods to teach the cabin how to play basketball.

Charley gave me his full dog attention as I told him that there had been no time to work on offense, so I devised a two-three zone defense.

Since Spaz, Oatmeal, and Dr. Square were all pretty tall, I had them spread out under the basket while The Laugher and I defended out front. It turned out that The Laugher was pretty quick. I showed our counselors how to pass the ball in different directions and demonstrated how to move with the ball in our zone defense. The cabin began having fun. They weren't dummies; they'd just never played competitive sports. They shuffled back and forth and kept their hands high. I told them not to hit anyone or commit fouls and to keep their hands high.

I then had the counselors take some shots, knowing they'd miss, so our guys could fight over the rebounds. Dr. Square and Oatmeal were surprisingly strong, though they didn't know it. I told them to hang on to the ball after a rebound; not to throw it away—just to hang on to it.

After an hour of defense, we shot around a little. The Laugher could actually make a lay-up consistently. Everyone else collaborated for zero baskets. I thought that if we could grab a rebound, I'd have the ball thrown to me and I'd try to get a few points by getting the ball to a streaking Laugher before the other cabin caught on.

Charley was at the edge of the bed at that point in my story. I figured he either had to do a number one or he was really curious about my story.

Our group had practiced the next day for almost two hours and our defense was beginning to make some semblance of sense. We were pitiful at offense, but at least the guys seemed to be having fun.

I took Charley outside to lift his leg and then both of us scurried back to bed. Charley could tell I was excited to get to game time.

I had assumed that most of the camp would be disinterested in the upcoming massacre, since there were other games to be played. Surely there had to be more to camp life than the upcoming slaughter of the Merry Fairy House.

The referees were two staff members from the other cabin. I was happy with that, since they were good guys and knew basketball. The opening tip-off went to them and I screamed for everyone to get back into our zone position. The Laugher and I hustled back and forth in the front court, trying to harass their guards. They slipped in a pass to Brillo, and though our guys kept their hands up, he banked in a three-footer. I brought the ball up, made one pass, we lost the ball, and they scored an easy lay-up.

I brought the ball up, made another pass, we lost the ball again, and they again scored easily. Six to nothing, and I called time out. The Laugher said he could dribble the ball up and throw it to me. I had emphasized to everyone that we could stop stop the other team with our zone defense if we ever got a chance to set it up.

I tossed the ball in to The Laugher, and he wasn't bad at bringing the ball up. He flipped a pass to me and I lofted a twenty-footer—swish.

I was feeling it; if we could only stop them. I yelled for everyone to get into place. The other team, for some reason, took an outside shot, missed, and Dr. Square grabbed the rebound. He threw the ball to me; I took one dribble, and then hit a streaking Laugher. He made the lay-up and our team jumped up and down while I screamed for them to get back into position.

Our counselors were jumping for joy, although I wasn't sure if they knew what they were cheering about. Brillo got the ball and was immediately surrounded by the Merry Fairy House. Since Brillo didn't like passing, he threw up a shot—no good. I grabbed the rebound and again hit the streaking Laugher for two more points. Tie game!

They called time out and started arguing as a crowd began to gather. Word always traveled fast at camp. Meanwhile, we were jumping up and down and congratulating The Laugher.

The rest of the half, we held it close. I threw in five more baskets from various angles—I was feeling it, and our zone defense frustrated them. As the end of the half drew closer, a large crowd was cheering our every move. The other team finally stopped The Laugher and slopped in a couple baskets before the half, and they led 20–16—but we were still in the game.

The Vacuum came over to our huddle at halftime and offered a few tips. He suggested that The Spaz, who hadn't been in the game yet, could make a surprise lay-up, since no one would bother guarding him.

They got the second half tip and scored before we could set up our defense. The Laugher brought the ball up and handed it off to me. I dribbled to the right side, faked a pass out front, and then noticed The Spaz standing all alone under the basket. I lobbed a pass his way. He caught it, sent an awkward one-handed shot into the air—and it went in! No bank—all net!

The crowd went wild as our zone continued to frustrate our opponents and Dr. Square pulled down another rebound. He threw to The Laugher, who in turn hit me for a streaking lay-up. We were only down by two, and it seemed that the whole camp was watching, including Lou.

They missed on their next two trips, and then I banked one in from the side. Game tied—I was feeling it. There were days when I couldn't make a shot, but that day wasn't one of them.

To my amazement, the crowd began chanting, "Merry Fairy House, Merry Fairy House" as I hit a streaking Laugher for two more points—and the lead!

"Merry Fairy House, Merry Fairy House" rang through the air and our guys were eating it up. They weren't familiar with Bill Mazeroski, Jesse Owens, Wilma Rudolph, Don Larsen,

Campingly Yours

Joe Bellino, Bobby Thompson, or Lenny Moore, but during those magical moments, we all had a little of each of those heroes in our blood.

The other cabin eventually regained the lead, since we couldn't seem to stop Brillo. I hit a few more shots before fizzling out, and we lost the game by nine points.

At the buzzer, the crowd, led by Snarl, hoisted our team onto their shoulders, chanting, "Merry Fairy House, Merry Fairy House!" For that brief moment, the Merry Fairy House had reached the top of our camp world—maybe the whole camp world. From my heightened position, I noticed Lou in the background, wearing my dad's grin.

Goodnight, Charley.

• • •

Some things around our house were considered taboo. We knew that Dad skipped golf a lot on Wednesdays to take Mom to Kansas City, but we didn't ask questions about why. One day, I decided that the time had come for me to find out what was going on with Mom. My brother was soon heading to college and I was going to be a junior in high school.

Mom always took Dad's hand when walking or climbing steps, and she never took an escalator—never. She said she had a slipped disk from an attempt at bowling and needed help getting around. We'd heard about her slipped disk problem for years and never thought twice about it, but the story was starting to sound a bit suspicious.

I was ready to sit down with Mom, have an open talk about her situation, and clear the air about whatever was troubling her. I thought about the conversation for weeks, and several times I was close to initiating it, but I always held back. Later, I would blame myself for not pushing the issue sooner.

I had just finished teaching tennis and didn't have to work at the junkyard that afternoon. A couple of my friends and I headed to the mall to grab a burger and hang around. Across the mall, in front of Montgomery Wards, there was some sort of commotion going on.

everal people had gathered and my curiosity got the best of me. My friends weren't as concerned, but I headed toward Wards to see what was happening. I arrived at the scene to find a woman crying, looking straight down at her feet, frozen in her shoes. She was sobbing. It was Mom!

Two men were trying to console her, but it did no good. She was panicking and just staring down at her shoes. For some reason, I thought about Sherman sitting on the bench staring at nothingness and how he had panicked to stay afloat at my expense. At that moment, Mom was panicking—but unlike Sherman, Mom knew it.

I rushed between the men and took Mom's hand. Suddenly, I was a Pumpkin, saving my mother from drowning in her tears. What was wrong? What was happening?

Mom grabbed my hand with no intention of letting go. Maybe she thought I was Dad. We quickly headed outside and hailed a cab. When we got home, I paid the two- buck fare and gave the cabbie a dollar tip. I was worried that Dad would have been mad at me for leaving a fifty percent tip. Mom said Dad had never been mad at me.

Seeing Mom crying, frozen, staring at her feet, feeling utterly alone while surrounded by people was the saddest thing I'd ever seen. What if I hadn't gone to the mall for a burger? What if the Pumpkins had been looking the other way that day? Dad, Bulky the bulldog, Sherman, Mom—all of them frozen in time—sadness happened randomly, and I was lucky to have such a caring family.

• • •

The Flash was coming home in a week and I was anxious to hear all about his summer. While my angst over missing camp had dissipated after a couple of weeks, I still thought a lot about my time at camp, the friends I'd made, and all the stories that only a camp person could understand. I planned to go back someday, and I hoped it would be sooner than later.

Mom sat down with me, before my brother came home, and began to explain her problem in depth. On Wednesdays, Dad had been taking her to a psychiatrist in Kansas City because she had a pretty bad case of agoraphobia. She became disabled with a fear of open places and the unknown. Agoraphobia had been a medical mystery for years and people affected by the illness often were mistaken for being eccentric or even drunk.

Dad knew about the shopping mall incident. She said it had happened one time before. She and Dad mainly vacationed in Las Vegas and stayed at Bally's each time, where she became familiar with the hotel, the same slot machine, the same restroom, and the same coffee shop.

Mom said she often was afraid to go out of the house, and she had an unusually severe fear of snakes. She couldn't even look at pictures of snakes in magazines. Dad had to pre-read all her periodicals and remove any snake pictures. She would scream if the image of a snake flashed on the television. (I knew about the snake thing, but hid the fact that I had the same fear.)

She told me that Dad had always wanted to travel to Europe, Yosemite, and the Grand Canyon, but she was afraid of new adventures and he opted never to travel without her. Mom said Dad had given up a huge part of his life for her, and she'd always been sorry about that. She also said that she was very sorry that I'd seen her in the mall in that condition. That day, she had tried to beat her fear—but she had lost, and she'd been embarrassed that I had been the one to find her.

I tried to lighten the mood by reminding her that she still owed me three dollars for the cab ride.

• • •

My brother would have loads of stories to tell me when he returned from camp, but I decided that I'd keep quiet with mine. Once again, I was tired but wide-eyed. I was thinking about the summer my senior counselor had given all of us a kiss on the forehead each night before lights out. Snarl and his few buddies had made fun of that counselor, and there seemed to be a general undercurrent toward him around camp, but I had no idea why, and The Bulk couldn't help.

I had no idea at the time that the counselor was gay. No one had ever brought up anything about being gay, so I never knew anything about it. How had Snarl known about it? I only found out about him after six summers at camp, and at sixteen, I still knew very little about it. I wasn't against it; I just didn't think it actually existed anywhere, except maybe in Hollywood. I'd always heard the word "queer," but it was usually directed toward others in jest. Kids used the word queer all the time in banter. My senior counselor must have been living in turmoil, not being able to openly express himself and his beliefs.

My thoughts drifted to when my brother and I were young and Mom and Dad took us to a new restaurant in Kansas City. A black family walked in but was refused a table.

Dad stood up and said, "We're leaving right now. Let's go."

I was confused at the time, but I remembered the father of that family giving my parents a twinkle-like wink as we walked out of the restaurant.

I turned out the light, but kept thinking of my gay counselor. I wished that I had known at the time, since I would have asked him all sorts of questions. Maybe he would have cleared up the queer/gay issue for me so I could have relayed it to Snarl and his few friends.

"My brother will have stories....zzzzz...I always understood why my friends sometimes didn't get camp—my camp...I've learned so much this summer...zzzzz...I just wanted one more summer at home...zzzzz...then I'll consider going back to camp...if Lou and Renee will have me...Now I know why Mom never visited camp...zzzzz...fear...Maybe she thought there were snakes at camp...zzzzz...I should have told her she would have been fine...Dad works with black people...I play ball with black kids...I've never known any reason not to...zzzzz...Mom and Dad were ahead of their time...so was Larry Doby...so was Lee Elder...and Buck O'Neil...so was President Kennedy...and his brother...those two would have been great lead-off hitters...zzzzz...Mom thought there'd be snakes at camp…that's why she never visited…*zzzzz*…When President Kennedy was shot…it was like everyone's bulldog died…everyone's…*zzzzz*…Goodnight, Charley…'This land is your land, this land is my land, this land was made for you and me'…and for gays, black people, and even snakes…*zzzzz*…Mom will visit one day…*zzzzz*…"

. . .

Moving angle iron by hand, wearing jeans, a t-shirt, and an A's ball cap in 98-degree heat with the same humidity, I decided it was time to reevaluate my situation. Had Dad done all of that physical labor before he moved into his disheveled office? Was he trying to teach me something? Did he want me to take over the junkyard one day so he could travel? How much money could a married couple lose in Las Vegas? I never heard much about them winning anything.

I hopped onto the back of a two-ton truck to unload dirty motors by hand. Wilbur and I rolled them off, which was no easy task. From my periphery, I noticed Willie climbing down from his crane. He grabbed a piece of iron and attempted to trot toward the office, and I'd never seen him in a hurry. Then Doug picked up another piece of iron and ran toward the office.

Wilbur said, "Something ain't right."

We jumped off the truck and heard Elmer shout, "They've got your dad!"

I sprinted to the office quicker than any of my first-to-third runs. I beat everyone to the entrance and found Dad surrounded by two seedy-looking guys, each holding a knife. I recognized one of them, so Dad must have known who he was.

Dad spotted me in the doorway and grinned. Why the heck would he do that? Did he think I shouldn't see him being afraid? Didn't Dad think I should see his vulnerable side? Didn't he know that I'd seen him with his bulldog?

The thugs wanted money and inched closer to Dad—until the far door crashed open and in walked Paul, Willie, Doug, Wilber, and Elmer, all holding steel shafts. They quickly surrounded the intruders and Paul, carrying 350 pounds of muscle and fat, spit tobacco on the men as he warned them that if they laid a hand on my dad, it would be the last mother-f-ing thing they'd ever do on Earth. Willie, with his hat slightly tilted and sporting his half-shaved beard, stared at the men to confirm Paul's threat.

Elmer, not the biggest, but probably the strongest of the bunch, walked directly between the two and growled, "You touch him and you're going to the shredder."

Doug reached inside his trousers, pulled out an empty vodka bottle, and then rapped one of the intruders on the head. The other guy tried to take off, but Paul quickly blocked his path. Then Doug took out another bottle and conked the second guy equally as hard.

I had just witnessed an amazing act of loyalty. Dad had done so much for all of those guys over the years, expecting nothing in return—and they'd finally found a way to pay him back.

During the ride home, I asked Dad how he could possibly consider grinning at me in such a moment of crisis.

He didn't answer my question, but he did say, "Well, I'll tell you one thing. My money has been well spent over the years. Doug sure turned out to be a good investment." Then he added, "And don't tell your mother about any of this."

13

A Torch
Has Been Passed

In the middle of my senior year of high school, after two summers away, I called Lou and told him I was thinking about returning to camp. Lou was pleased and said that he'd hold a place for me, but warned me not to wait too long. He planned to complete the staff roster by the end of January, so I should notify him no later than that.

Dad said, "Going back to camp will be a good experience for you."

I told him with a smile, "I've been away from camp a lot longer than the five days you left Mom."

"That's OK, as long as you didn't date any other camps," Dad said with a grin.

He never did explain to me how he'd managed to grin while two guys were threatening him with knives. Someday I'd find out.

I'd made my decision—I was heading back to camp. Lou congratulated me and said I'd be receiving my contract and general staff information in the spring. I wrote The Bulk and asked him all sorts of what-to-expect questions. He clued me in with one-liners filled with his usual knowledge and said he was glad I was returning. He also said that I'd do well as a counselor.

During my time away from camp, I still enjoyed reading the monthly newsletters. Of course, it was hard reading about upcoming events, knowing that I wouldn't be involved. There was just something about those newsletters that grabbed me, and when I saw my name listed under Returning Staff, I reverted back to age ten when my brother and I were listed as returning campers. It was the same feeling, and it made no difference that I was going to be eighteen that summer. The Bulk, from Milwaukee, was returning for his tenth summer, and Kid Flash, from St. Joe, would be returning for his seventh.

A lot of guys my age were going back, but many others weren't. The Vacuum had moved on after his twelfth summer. The Snarl was long gone, as were most of my boyhood staff idols. No Pumpkins, no Wolf, no Crash, no Milky, no canoe instructors, and No Flash. No Flash!

My brother had spent his ninth and last summer at camp. All my boyhood idols were gone. I'd be starting over. Campers returning for their third summer, as well as first-year campers, wouldn't even know my name.

Lou mailed me a contract and offered me $90. Wow, $90! Dad jokingly quipped that Lou's offer made what Dad had been paying me at the junkyard look bad—but I really didn't care about the money. I just wanted to go back to camp. A little more would have been nice, but I never questioned Lou. I checked with The Bulk and he said that was the going rate. We both concluded that Lou probably had a nice savings account.

Dad slipped $50 in my pocket and Mom handed me $30 on the day I left. I wasn't sure if they had collaborated, but I earned almost a whole camp salary while saying goodbye to them. Somehow, saying goodbye to them seemed to take on more meaning. Was I saying goodbye permanently? I was heading to college in late August and I'd only be stopping home after camp long enough to gather up my belongings.

They waved and stood at the top step as I drove off with a friend named The Binder. My grandfather had always waved from his doorstep until we could no longer see him. Every time we visited, we'd look back as we drove away to see my grandfather waving from his door. At that moment, I looked back at my parents as they waved until I was out of sight.

Dad was wearing a slight grin that seemed to fade as I got farther away. It was a sort of sad grin. I knew Dad had liked having me around for the two previous summers.

The Binder drove a '68 Mercury Cougar and was glad to have me along. He knew all the back roads and shortened the eleven-hour drive to nine hours. The Cougar's 427 engine also had a lot to do with the two-hour savings. The Binder's family had discovered camp from one of their customers from Omaha and had then shared their discovery with Mom and Dad. Word-of-mouth had led my brother to camp, as it did for most other campers.

The camp road was a welcome sight. It had been two years since I'd pulled onto that dirt road with its not-so-fancy hand-carved wooden sign. Entering camp brought back memories of Crash honking the horn, of people gathering, and of my brother being mobbed by his friends. Our entrance was quiet that day, however, since there were no campers yet; it was staff orientation week.

We drove to the camp office and were greeted by no one. The Binder didn't honk, and we entered pretty anonymously. It was dinnertime, so we headed to the lodge, which was where we found everyone. The feeling was strange. I didn't recognize half of the staff, since several had started during my absence and there were a dozen new counselors. Lou stood up and gave me a nice handshake while Renee gave me a warm hug.

The Bulk said, "Hi, Flash. Sit here by me."

Moose found me, as well, and the three of us sat together. The head counselor, named Supplecheck, patted me on the back and said it was good to have me back. I looked around for some of my boyhood idols—The Vacuum, Wolf, or even Snarl—but saw none of them. I was used to being coddled and favored by the staff as one of their favorite sons, but I'd become just another staff member. I had lived for U.N. Day, but it seemed strange to think that I could no longer play—I was a staff member.

A feeling of emptiness surged through me. The staff members hadn't rushed to see me when I got out of the car or entered the lodge. What I would have given to be a camper again, just one more time.

 Campingly Yours

After dinner, Lou took me into his office and told me that I'd be heading the summer baseball program. I was under the assumption that I'd be an assistant, since I was only a junior staff member, but Lou said I was *it*.

"I checked with your dad, and he said you can handle it," said Lou. "He said the experience would be good for you."

I told Lou that it would be difficult to follow in The Vacuum's shoes, since he was a camp legend, leader, and positive role model. I told Lou I thought it might be too much for me and that he might want to get someone else.

Lou cleared his throat, set his pipe aside, and sternly proclaimed, "You're no longer Kid Flash. From now on, you're The Flash! The Vacuum's shoes were always tied." Then he added, "The first staff meeting will begin after breakfast. Get some sleep and come to the meeting with both shoes tied."

The Bulk and I stayed up reminiscing into the wee hours of the morning. He told me that I was going to enjoy seeing the other side of camp and again told me that I was going to do well as a counselor. He talked about his own CIT summer and how it had taken him several weeks to adjust.

"I missed our camper summers of no pressure, no responsibility, of just being kids," he said.

I reminded him that the pressure was always on to win U.N. Day and that I felt all sorts of pressure the first day I wore the catcher's mask. The Bulk disagreed, saying that my catcher's mask had actually relieved me of any further pressure.

"If you ask me, everyone should wear a mask to camp," he said with a chuckle.

The Bulk had made a valid point. I'd only had two or three scary days at camp, but after that, I had led a pretty charmed life. What about the boys who hadn't been so favored?

"Well," he said, "I suppose the boys who don't fit in probably aren't aware of it, at least during their first few summers."

He also figured that those boys didn't later want to become staff members, and Lou was probably happy when they bowed out. The Bulk said that I was going to see a few staff members who had slipped through the cracks. They'd been so-so campers but had somehow managed to be asked back by Lou.

I asked, "Do you think Snarl fit that mold?"

The Bulk said, "Snarl created a unique mold reserved only for Snarl, so he couldn't slip through any crack."

We finally fell asleep, ready to face a challenge in the morning.

There were more than fifty staff members plus CITs at breakfast. The CITs sat together, the first-year junior counselors sat together, and I sat with my group of friends. The old-time senior staff members bunched together, as well, and the twelve or so new counselors also ate breakfast together. Supplecheck welcomed everyone and told us to report back in thirty minutes for our first meeting.

Pre-camp orientation was foreign to me and I had no idea what to expect. The Bulk hadn't filled me in about the meetings; I figured he wanted me to make my own judgment.

Lou chaired the first meeting. We started with introductions, each of us telling a little bit about ourselves—where we were from, what school we attended, how many years at camp, our cabin placement, and what activity we were teaching. What seemed like a pretty simple assignment turned into a full-fledged comedy routine.

Moose started with, "Hi, I'm Moose. I used to be so fat that everyone called me Moose."

The Farb told us his counselor had misspelled his name. It was supposed to be b-a-r-f spelled backward.

Simple sang his introduction to the tune of "Take Me Out to the Ball Game" and melodiously let us know that he was still mad about being left out of the all-star baseball game when he was an older camper.

Supplecheck and his wife, Ruth, sang a rendition of "When We Goin' to Get Married, You Little Ol' Buffalo Gal" and then told us who they were.

The new staff must have wondered what they had walked into and I was feeling like a new staff member. It was all pretty silly—and when it got around to me—oh, brother.

I deadpanned, "Hi, I'm The Flash. I used to be Kid Flash, but Lou yelled at me last night and told me to grow up and tie my shoes. I don't know about the growing up part, but I did tie my shoes. I'm a friend with all the guys with funny names. I was responsible for Simple not getting in that all-star game—because he stunk—and Farb is right, it should be Frab. I'm heading the baseball activity this summer. If you have any questions, ask The Bulk."

It didn't seem too funny to me, but everyone laughed at my deadpan approach. The new guys came up with some pretty good stuff, as well. Pre-camp staff orientation had officially begun.

After introductions, Lou and Renee calmed the group and then talked about how they had started camp from scratch. They borrowed money from Renee's family, found and cleared the 100-acre site, recruited a few boys and staff, and began their first season in 1945. I thought it was pretty interesting that they had envisioned the camp before it was a camp. Lou explained the goals of staff orientation and what we should expect to derive from the weeklong meetings. Then Supplecheck announced work period and everyone headed to their stations.

I was put on sickle crew with The Bulk and a few new counselors. Chopping down a grassy area was a lot easier than rolling motors off a two-ton truck. I was glad to be with some of the new guys; I didn't like how all the old-timers sat together. It seemed segregated to me and I vowed to make a point of sitting with different people. The Bulk had taken me in on my first day of camp when I'd just turned ten. I suspected that twenty-year-olds could be just as frightened and maybe even more embarrassed to show any signs of concern. I looked forward to branching out while keeping my longtime camp friends.

Lou invited one of his lifelong friends, a fellow camp director, to lead the afternoon meetings. His name was Jack and he had started an agency camp in the early 1950s. Jack was short, left-handed, a bit rotund, overly tanned, smoked a pipe, wore a goofy short-brimmed cap, and was an avid tennis player.

The meeting was titled "Understanding the Camper." We were divided into groups of

Campingly Yours

eight and each group was a mix of old staff, new staff, and CITs. I should have known that Lou would make sure there was a mix. Each group received a list of subjects and we were to openly discuss our feelings. We learned how to handle the homesick camper, what to do with the loner, how to handle the cabin bully, how to avoid cabin cliques, what to do if a boy didn't get along with the group, and how to handle swearing. Those were some of the more difficult issues brought to our attention.

It was also a nice way to learn about seven other staff members, since everyone had something to say. I mentioned that I'd been homesick for two or three nights during my first summer, but I hadn't let anyone know. I said that it would have been nice if one of my counselors had understood what I was going through and encouraged me. I told our group that maybe I'd make a special effort to detect any form of loneliness in my cabin and to check for tears at night. I was assigned nine-year-olds, so I assumed I had a good chance for homesick campers.

One of the new staff members made an astute comment, saying that it would be harder for him and other new counselors to understand the habits of campers. He explained his point by noting how the old-time staff had lived through so many of those issues and had first-hand experience. He wasn't complaining; just stating a valid point. I knew I had an advantage, having grown up at camp.

After an hour of discussion in our small group, we took a short break and then reconvened as a whole. Jack took center stage and opened the floor to the staff. He didn't lecture us, but accepted our questions and redirected them to anyone with their hand up. Opinions were bounced back and forth. It was a bit school-like, but most interesting, and I noticed there was something unique about Jack. I couldn't quite place it, but something about Jack attracted my attention.

Understanding the campers wasn't so simple; actually, it was quite complex. I felt like I was attending a combination sociology-psychology class, but with no pressure of a grade. I learned why one boy might feel left out or why another camper might constantly feel the

 Campingly Yours

need to pick on an easy target, and it was all quite interesting.

I also learned that some of the so-called toughest boys were the most insecure and that an outwardly happy camper might be crying at night. Hmm…that sort of rang a camp bell for me. Jack surprised me, and others, as well, when he told us that in all of his years in camping, he'd never met a bad camper.

He emphasized it again—he'd never met a bad camper! He claimed that it was easy to be a good counselor to the popular camper, but the great counselor took the time to develop a relationship with the boy who was being left out. The great counselor learned to gain acceptance with the cabin bully. The great counselor worked with the boy who was the biggest nerd and helped that boy develop a niche at camp. The great counselor listened and learned. The great counselor cared about all his boys, from the most popular to the least likable. The great counselor became a truly caring person and was willing to go the extra mile for his campers—*all* his campers.

Jack restated that the great counselor was a caring counselor and then finished by emphatically reminding us that he'd never met a bad camper. There was something different about Jack. Someday I'd pinpoint it.

That night there was an organized campfire and songfest. All of us acted a little crazy, going overboard with basic songs. John Jacob and his Jingleheimer Schmidt family were still part of the camp tradition. There were several talented guitar players and it was fun watching them fingerpick. A couple new counselors added songs to the repertoire and the staff began blending together—through the magic of music. Senior counselors taught the new guys some of the camp traditions, and all of it reminded me of why I had decided to return to summer camp.

We were assigned to sleep in our new cabins with our co-counselors. It was a good move for me, since I got to know my senior counselor and CIT rather quickly. My senior counselor was new and he quizzed the heck out of me until he finally pooped out. I answered what I could, and for one fine evening, I felt like I was walking in The Bulk's shoes.

The lights were out, my co-counselors were snoring, but of course my eyes were still open. There were no cobwebs in the upper rafters, but that was okay. I had checked my very first cabin earlier in the day, and those ancient cobwebs were still intact. I'd go see them once in a while and have a chat. They didn't talk back; they only listened.

"Jack would have liked those cobwebs…zzzzz…One day of staff orientation and I already know everyone's name…nice organization Lou, Renee, and Supplecheck…zzzzz…I don't miss home…I was always part of home…zzzzz…Dad's grin looked a little sad when I left…I had to go, Dad, and you even said it would be good for me…zzzzz…I'm also afraid of snakes, Mom…don't worry…I had no idea how much was involved in learning about the campers…zzzzz…Did the staff worry about The Flash and Kid Flash?…Did they talk about the smokers?…zzzzz…I had no idea they discussed things about us…Did they make fun of my mask?…zzzzz…Was Snarl paying attention at the meetings?…Have they discussed the same topics all these years…since 1945?…zzzzz…Did Lou bring those topics from another camp?…zzzzz…How could Dad grin with those knives pointed at him?…Mom, someday you'll see camp…zzzzz…Don't worry, Charley, Dad will give you special attention…The Vacuum and all those guys aren't here anymore…but camp is still going on without them… zzzzz…Someday I'll find out more about Jack…zzzzz…never a bad camper…'This camp was made for you and me'…and the new staff…zzzzz…goodnight, Charley…"

• • •

Staff orientation week breezed by quickly and the campers were due to arrive the next morning. We had to tie up all loose ends, and Supplecheck inspected all of our areas carefully. We needed his seal of approval before our time off would begin.

I let The Bulk know that I was surprised at how much the staff could accomplish in a week. We had painted four cabins, sickled and mowed fifteen acres of grass, wiped down and scrubbed twenty-five buildings, sanitized the lodge, washed hundreds of dishes, polished

 Campingly Yours

sailboats, hosed down rowboats, set up waterfront docks and rafts, swept pine needles off roofs, and had all of our teaching activities ready for the campers' arrival. We'd learned about potential camper problems and had discussed how to handle a wide variety of situations. We'd also discussed staff problems, such as not getting along, one person carrying all of the load while another sloughed his duties, and one staff member playing the nice guy to the cabin while the other tried to adhere to the camp rules.

Sing-a-longs were an integral part of camp, and we kept the traditional favorites while adding new songs from Crosby, Stills, and Nash, Bob Dylan, and the Lovin' Spoonful. A lot of the guys hammed it up and added comedy to the meetings. That seemed fine with Lou, but we could tell where to draw the line. Safety at all costs was emphasized, and not taking a chance was a constant theme.

Jack stayed just one day, but his impact was significant, especially on me. He attempted to impress upon us that devoting time and effort to our campers would pay off for all concerned. The theme of the week was that the campers always came first.

Supplecheck had divided us up throughout the week during work periods and meetings, but some of the guys still hadn't made the effort to get to know the new counselors. I was glad I wasn't that type of person. I wanted the new guys to feel welcome at my summer home.

As a camper, I'd never given any thought to what was involved in getting the camp ready. I just figured when Crash let us out the door, camp was supposed to be in place. I had no idea that the staff had spent a week talking about what makes the campers tick. I had never considered that Lou and Renee had a "philosophy on camping" that they taught to all the staff. I never knew that Lou and Renee had made the effort to have someone as knowledgeable and experienced as Jack come to share his expertise in understanding campers. Lou's staff had become close long before my first summer as a camper, long before Crash had let me out the door, and Lou and Renee had come up with the idea long before my brother had repaired the camp reel-to-reel.

Campingly Yours

14

The Cubs
Kid

Two buses and several vans honked their way into camp. It wasn't Crash pounding
on the horn, but the noise was the same, and so was the excitement as boys of all
ages and locations merged together, shaking hands and reuniting with their ten-month-lost
friends. I also saw new campers stumbling out of the vehicles, looking lost and overwhelmed.
No one greeted them; boy, I could relate to how they were feeling—and it occurred to
me that my life had instantly changed. The campers had arrived, and I was a full-fledged
counselor. My shoes were tied, and I was ready.

Everyone circled around the flagpole as Lou announced the cabins. Nostalgia washed
over me as I thought back to my first time hearing Lou shout cabin placements: "Kid Flash:
Cabin Junior Four. Bulk: Cabin Junior Four."

I came out of my trance to hear cheering as Lou called out, "Flash: Counselor of Cabin
Junior Two."

The cheers weren't just for me, however, since the circle of staff and campers cheered after
everyone's name. My co-counselors and I whisked our group of nine-year-olds, all new
campers, to Junior Two (J-2).

 Campingly Yours

It was fun watching the little guys unpack and try to organize their belongings. Ironically, my own mom still closed my bedroom door when company arrived, but at that moment I was in charge of helping nine-year-olds with tidiness. My co-counselor was new and had three years of college behind him. Maybe he'd be the one in charge of tidiness.

We took our cabin group around the campgrounds and highlighted the various areas of interest. They asked a zillion questions and I gave them my best Bulk imitation.

Again, I zoned back to my first day of camp. Who would be the camp Vacuum and was there a new Snarl lurking somewhere to pounce on one of my new campers? Where was my brother, in case I needed him, and would Lou be standing in the distance, watching me?

I snapped out of my trance and noticed that none of my boys had a catcher's mask! Thank goodness. I was determined that no one would get picked on the first day.

The bell rang, signaling dinnertime. I knew my new campers would soon be wide-eyed, watching and hearing their chaotic first meal. I also was curious to watch the new counselors react to the first meal craziness. New is new, no matter what your age. I had learned that in staff orientation.

When we'd all sat down at our tables, Lou raised his hand for quiet, but of course, that only lifted the noise level even higher.

I had our cabin shout, "We are cabin J-2, J-2, Ja-aye-2. We are cabin J-2, where is J-3?"

The domino effect went on until the oldest cabin concluded their chant with, "Where are Lou and Renee?"

Then Lou and Renee took the microphone, staff members and campers pounded on tables in euphoria, and finally the room settled down. Lou said a nice grace of thanks for everyone's safe arrival and the first meal began—my first counselor meal. The tasty pasta with garlic bread and vegetables that lined our table reminded me that parts of camp life hadn't changed and probably never would change, but maybe I could change something. What was wrong with something new?

I whispered to my CIT in a nonchalant manner as the dessert was being served to our table. The CIT complained to the cabin that the pudding and whipped cream had an awful odor. I proclaimed that the dessert was fine and brought it close to my face for a sniff. Wham, the CIT pushed my face into my bowl—a direct hit. I was a mess and started to cry (fake, of course). All the boys in the cabin fell over with laughter; no one felt sorry for me—and no one felt sorry for any of the new campers in my cabin.

. . .

That night, my co-counselor lit a candle and talked about what he wanted to accomplish during the summer, beginning the same bedtime ceremony ritual I remembered from my first night of camp. Some of the guys were showing watery eyes through the fire's reflection. When the candle came to me, I offered my wish that all of them would someday look at camp as their second home, as I did, and that someday camp would be in their veins.

One little boy was crying while he explained that his grandparents had made him go to camp. He didn't want to be there and he knew he wouldn't like camp. He asked if I could send him home.

The last boy to speak claimed that camp was going to be fun and that he'd help the crying boy. He said that he was sorry my dessert had been wasted, but I told him that it was nice that he was willing to help the crying camper. I also let him know that the dessert was far from wasted and then said goodnight to everyone.

The campers sniffled their way to sleep, but, of course, I was awake, thinking about the first day of camp—their first day of camp.

The day had seemed to be uneventful—no one catching a curveball, no Snarl pushing a new camper around, no staff poking fun at new campers in the show, and no cobwebs on the ceiling of J-2—but I kept thinking about my camper who wanted to go home. His first day must have been horrible. Why had he asked me to help him? Maybe he'd taken my dessert crying seriously.

 Campingly Yours

I jumped out of bed, made my way to his bunk, and found him awake, crying. I whispered to him that he should sign up for my baseball activity the next day. He told me that he loved the Cubs and attended games with his grandfather.

I said, "How about that Lou Brock trade they made a few years ago?"

He said, "That was a few World Series ago and a lot of stolen bases ago."

I put his Cubs hat on his head, put his glove under the covers with him, told him to get some sleep, and grumbled that at least his Cubs hadn't moved to Oakland.

Goodbye, my Kansas City A's, and goodnight, Cubs Kid.

The next day, I waited for campers to arrive, as my baseball activity was about to begin—my first from a counselor's perspective. I was the student, about to become the teacher, even though I didn't even have a camping degree, let alone a master's. I hadn't even taken a college course yet!

The field was ready and I tried to look the part with my blue Kansas City ball cap (not the A's—the *Royals*). It wasn't an easy cap to wear, but I was the only one suffering, since no one else at camp seemed to care. Even so, I knew that The Cubs Kid would have suffered if the team behind his embroidered "C" cap no longer existed—and I knew that his grandfather would have been devastated, too.

The Cubs Kid and all the others from my group made it through physicals and signed up for canoeing, camp craft, and swimming. I told the guys I'd help them with canoeing—there'd be no flunkies allowed in our cabin. However, they'd be on their own with swimming and lighting a match.

Most of the tears had dissipated, but The Cubs Kid was another story. If anyone looked at him cross-eyed, he cried. If I raised my voice, even in jest, to him, he cried. He was a cute, blond haired, cuddly little boy that my Aunt Lucille would have squeezed to death. Aunt Lucille was still squeezing my brother and me, so I was certain that she would have suffocated The Cubs Kid.

"Help me, Jack," I thought. "You didn't mention anything about this. How do I stop the crying?"

Then I remembered that Jack had mentioned attacking the problem at the source. Why was The Cubs Kid crying, and what was the cause of his problem? I was his counselor, and I was determined to do my best to reach the root of his problem.

Twenty campers of all ages strolled onto the baseball diamond, including The Cubs Kid. I had an assistant and we treated each other as equals. There was no reason to have a sergeant-midshipman atmosphere at camp, especially on the ball field. Even in the cabin, co-counselors shared responsibility. There was no need for one counselor to act more in charge than the other. Sure, the senior counselor was older and took on a few more duties, but not enough to boss the others around. The camp atmosphere didn't call for that kind of hierarchy, and most of the eighteen-year-olds had been at camp several years before heading to college. They were pretty well on top of things when it came to camp know-how.

Once in a while, a staff member would try to take charge, act like he knew more, and try pushing his way to the top, but it was only a form of power surge and the type of attitude that spread negatively with the rest of the staff. The staff would grumble that so-and-so was trying to be Lou's right-hand man without Lou's consent and the power-seeking staff member would soon have most of the counselors, including his friends, turn against him.

However, the interesting thing about camp was that a staff member, or a camper for that matter, could undergo a positive attitude adjustment, after which all would be forgiven almost immediately. There had been several guys over the years that no one wanted to be around who returned the next summer with a changed personality—and they were instantly accepted as a result.

I wasn't sure that Snarl had ever been totally accepted, but I remembered that on my first day I totally feared him, but by the end of that evening, I thought he was a pretty decent guy. Camp could bring out the worst in a person, but that person could also turn it around almost instantly.

The twenty boys tossed balls around for a while, and then I had them sit on the bench.

They were used to The Vacuum and his crew, but my assistant, Rooster, decided to break the ice by giving a mock lecture about how their baseball glove was their best friend. That humorous lecture did the trick, and when Rooster had finished, I was able to chime in, as well. Even The Cubs Kid laughed as Rooster quizzed them to see if they'd been listening.

We divided the guys and staff members into two teams. Rooster placed The Cubs Kid at second base and the Kid's cousin at third, and then Rooster pitched, to keep the game moving along.

The cousin's name was Little Tom. He, too, was blond and wore a Cubs hat, but he wasn't a crier. Little Tom was nine years old and he looked like he could play. He was pretty small for third base, but that's where Rooster placed him.

The first batter lined a single to left. The second batter hit a slow bouncer to short, and I held my breath as The Cubs Kid caught the throw for the force out at second.

The runner was out by three steps, but I decided to fake an argument with Rooster, saying that the second baseman missed the base. I jumped up and down, screaming that the Cubs guy at second was way off the base. Rooster shouted for a vote, and both teams raised their hands saying the runner was out. I ran to The Cubs Kid and pointed to him, kicked dirt on second base, and faked anger as I walked back to the bench. Rooster accused me of being a bad sport, and everyone booed me, including The Cubs Kid.

When I got back to the bench, I looked at The Cubs Kid and he smiled back at me. I told him to quit laughing or I was going to smash a line drive right at his belly—but he just smiled back at me.

There were two outs and a runner on first, and I was at bat. I pointed my bat, Babe Ruth-like, at The Cubs Kid, but he just lowered his stance to indicate that he was ready. I swung and missed the first pitch, showing even more anger. (I wasn't sure if they could tell I was faking that part.)

I stared at The Cubs Kid and then, without using my brain, lined a screamer toward third, right at Little Tom's head. That split second seemed to take as long as my first two days as a camper. What had I done? How could I have hit one that hard at a nine-year-old? They were going to carry him off in a stretcher and Lou was going to use my $90 to help pay his medical bill. The Cubs Kid would start crying, knowing he'd lost his cousin. Way to go, Flash—excuse me—way to go, Kid Flash.

All those negative thoughts were streaking through my brain as I started out of the batter's box toward first base. I squinted my left eye toward third base, and then I heard a POP! Little Tom had managed to stick his glove in front of his face and had caught the ball for the third out. Everyone rushed toward him while I breathed a huge sigh of relief. The team was hoisting Little Tom on their shoulders. As I watched, I saw The Cubs Kid's arms outstretched as he joined in the shoulder-lifting celebration. Way to go, Flash!

I walked over to Little Tom and pointed my finger, warning him that he'd better not catch my line drive again. Little Tom just threw a smirky smile my way.

The period ended, but it didn't matter which team had won. As The Cubs Kid was leaving, he told me he had a great time and that I was goofy. Then he locked elbows with Little Tom and they trotted away. Little Tom turned around and smirked at me again, and I pointed at him with mock menace. The Cubs Kid laughed and twirled his glove. I was happy—I had saved $90.

15

Moose Without a Mother

Weekly staff meetings were held on Wednesday nights. **No time off was** allowed, and everyone was required to attend. The only ones allowed to miss were counselors who were away on overnight trips. The staff officers of the day (ODs) roamed the villages to check on campers and ducked in and out of the meetings. Lou chaired the meetings and called on the village directors to talk about the happenings within their age group.

One night there was a complaint from the CIT director that several senior counselors were never around at night, so the CIT of that cabin had to put the campers to bed. That was a no-no, since CITs weren't allowed to cover a cabin by themselves. Supplecheck sternly looked at all of us and said that no CIT should be left alone again during the summer.

Supplecheck was a great person who managed to instill fear in all of us. He was 6' 6" and a former college track and football star who would later become a high school track and football coach in Colorado. He had his job to do and he expected us to do our jobs—no ifs, ands, or buts. If a staff member sloughed off his duties, Supplecheck would soon find out and assign that person extra work. We knew if a person had been caught, just by the number

Campingly Yours

of extra details that staff member was being assigned.

Supplecheck walked the camp daily to check activities. He was everywhere. We all liked him. He was intimidating, but we liked him. What a great right hand man he was for Lou. Supplecheck had a funny side now and then, too, and it was great when that side appeared.

Next, Lou asked if there were any problem campers we should discuss. One counselor said that there was a very homesick boy in his cabin and asked us all to be aware of him. Lou told us all to learn his name and to keep a special eye on him during our activities. We were encouraged to go out of our way to make him feel useful. The boy really liked crafts, so Lou suggested that the art counselor give him a special project to complete. Lou said that it was necessary for the homesick boy to feel important—and needed.

Another counselor said that he thought some of the older boys were sneaking out into the woods to smoke. My mind drifted a bit, thinking about the guys in my brother's cabin that first summer. I wondered if anyone had brought their names up during a meeting. They were pretty sneaky and probably never got caught, and I knew The Bulk and I never told on them.

Lou said that smoking was a fire hazard and he wanted their names right away. Great, I thought. My brother's friends could have burned the camp down, and it ultimately would have been my and The Bulk's fault.

Then I wondered if my name or my brother's name had ever been brought up at a meeting. Maybe at the first meeting during my first summer they had all laughed at my catcher's mask. I bet they had also talked about Sherman. Staff meetings were an awakening for me—I'd had no idea until that first weekly meeting that the counselors talked about particular campers.

The Cubs Kid still cried often, but I didn't want to spread his name in front of everyone. I was convinced that he was no longer homesick; he just cried. The root of his problem confused me, but I was glad I was able to make him laugh and I was happy that he seemed to like camp and no longer asked to go home.

The weekly staff meetings were a bit tedious, but they were pretty insightful. Staff orientation had lasted a week, but it soon became a distant memory. The weekly meetings brought back the unity of the staff and reminded all of us that we had a job to do—to take care of the campers.

By the third week, most everyone knew each other and I made sure to know each camper's first name. Last names at camp didn't matter much, and many were just known by their nickname. I doubt that most even knew if The Bulk had a last name—and Moose was just Moose. I'd never really thought about Snarl. One day my English teacher asked me to define onomatopoeia.

I just said, "Snarl."

My first-day stunt at the baseball field had just happened and wasn't planned, but I used that form of humor a lot in the cabin that summer. The nine-year-olds liked wrestling, so I got beat up almost daily. I delivered some mild flying mares and sleeper holds, and even performed the figure-four leg lock once in awhile.

One night after the evening activity, I set up a cabin wrestling match and placed fake blood in my pocket. Two of the boys attempted to flip me on my head, and I aided their effort. When I turned over, I had fake blood all over my face. The boys froze when I grimaced and announced that each one of them was going down. I put a headlock on two boys, one in each arm, and whack, I got nailed in the back of the head with a folding chair. One of the boys must not have realized my blood and anger were theatrics. I fell to the ground, all the boys pinned me for the down-and-out count, and I developed an immediate migraine. Sprawled on my back, fake blood on my face and clothes, and in actual pain, I looked skyward—only to see The Cubs Kid staring me down. He laughed and told me I was goofy. I had made The Cubs Kid laugh—so it had all been worthwhile.

Jack had emphasized that there were no bad campers, and I could pretty much get a read on most of the kids after three weeks. Jack was right; no camper was bad. Some whined a lot, some were a bit spoiled, and some were sneaking a smoke now and then, but they all had likable qualities.

The Cubs Kid still cried often, but he wasn't homesick. He hung around me; maybe because he thought I was goofy. Actually, it was because he was smart and knew that I was giving him a lot of attention. My antics made him laugh and I think he figured out that my goal was to make him laugh and to forget about crying. I could tell that The Cubs Kid was seeking a friend—an adult friend. His grandfather was his friend, but maybe The Cubs Kid was too young to look at it that way—but why his grandfather? What about his mom and dad?

• • •

My desire to understand more about The Cubs Kid caused me to reflect on Moose. One winter afternoon, Mom received a call from Moose's dad, saying that he was in St. Joe with two of his sons—Moose and his older brother. I was twelve years old, and by that time I'd become close friends with Moose.

Mom suggested that Moose's family stay at the Pony Express Motel and invited them to dinner. She immediately threw the ingredients together for the meal before Moose's family arrived. They lived in Tucson but were relocating to Milwaukee, and their trip had directed them through Missouri.

It was my first time seeing an out-of-town camp friend away from the camp setting, and it was odd to see Moose dressed in decent pants and an ironed shirt. I probably looked strange to him, as well, without my A's cap.

Dad and Mr. Moose talked clothing (Mr. Moose sold coats) and junk and had an easy time getting along. Mom joined them in a serious conversation while we kids were told to hang out in our bedrooms for a while. Moose's brother went with my brother. They were both into science and math, so that worked out rather well.

Moose walked into my bedroom and made fun of my combination of baseball posters and Johnson/Humphrey buttons. There was also a Goldwater poster, saying: "In your heart, you know I'm WRONG." I'd taken the liberty of rubbing out and changing the last word of his quote. I was under the impression that Goldwater wanted to blow us all up, and I remembered Dad mumbling something about not wanting to get annihilated, so I sided with Dad.

Moose said we'd been sent to our rooms for a reason. His mother had died, and his dad didn't want to talk about it in front of the kids. Moose told me that she'd been sick for a long time, and they had been living in Arizona to benefit her health.

He said, "It was pretty neat to have a swimming pool, and the winters were warm."

I could tell that Moose was trying to be cool about the whole thing, since he then quickly changed the subject to my Goldwater poster. He was surprised that I was interested in politics.

I said, "I don't really know much about it, but if I could vote, it would be for Johnson and Humphrey. Mom and Dad are going to vote for them, and that's good enough for me."

Moose said, "Goldwater's from Arizona, so I've heard a lot about him, but I'm pretty sure my dad will be voting for Johnson."

I froze, turned pale, and wanted to stuff my A's cap in my mouth. Why had I announced how Mom and Dad were going to vote? Why hadn't I just told Moose how Dad was voting? Moose didn't have a mom! I felt like a complete idiot!

Moose apparently saw my pain and told me not to worry.

"My mom is still alive to me," he said, "and she thought Goldwater was a lunatic."

As Moose's family was saying goodnight, I pulled Moose aside and asked him not to tell our camp friends that I had political stuff in my room.

He said, "Don't worry, Kid Flash. Your image will remain untarnished. I'll see you next summer." Then he added, "By the way, I think your mom and dad are cool."

I'd never thought about any of my friends not having a mother. What if Mom—I couldn't even think about it. Losing Bulky had been too much for me—and too much for Dad. How had Moose been able to talk about politics? Who cared about politics? His mother was dead!

I had trouble even thinking the words "his mother was dead." Moose had been left with an emptiness that no kid should ever have. I was the lucky one—Moose the unlucky one. He'd been dealt a bad break, and I vowed then and there that I'd always remain his friend, even during arguments.

16

Visitation Weekend and Still No Mom and Dad

The parents were due the next day, so Lou called a special staff meeting to go over details. Four weeks had flown by (actually five, including staff orientation), and I was receiving my master's degree in counseling through on-the-job training. Orientation and subsequent meetings were helpful, but living the experience was worth more than any form of pre-camp schooling. Lou handed the meeting over to Supplecheck, who in turn handed out our parent visitation assignments. He assigned five staff members, including The Binder, to park cars, which meant that parents' night would start a few minutes early. Supplecheck had Rooster and me handle baseball—that was all, so we got off pretty easy.

Lou reminded us that we needed to meet all of our campers' parents and should introduce as many campers as possible to the parents, as well. Supplecheck warned us to be punctual and not to mess around—enough said. Then Lou asked if any of the campers had parents not visiting. No one raised a hand. It appeared that everyone's parents were coming—apparently there wasn't a single agoraphobic parent in the entire group.

Memories of my first parent visitation day raced through my mind. How lousy that must

Campingly Yours

have been for Mom, and it was probably even worse for Dad. I knew he was anxious to see the camp, to throw a curveball to The Vacuum, and to watch my brother and me in action. In a way, my parents had suffered worse than my brother and I. I just hadn't realized it at the time. On my first parents' weekend, my brother rescued a boat—while Dad was rescuing Mom.

Cars were pulling in at a record pace, with The Binder leading the way. License plates from all over the Midwest were displayed, with Illinois taking the lead from Wisconsin as the most common.

Dad no longer had his push button wagon; he'd replaced it with a 1967 Mercury Marquis Coupe. It was the first model, black-on-black, with a red leather interior. What had gotten into him? Maybe it was a mid-life thing. The 410 engine moved out pretty well and my brother and I looked forward to our occasional chances to take it out. Unfortunately, I knew that car wouldn't be pulling onto the camp road—and Dad never would have considered letting The Binder behind the wheel.

The campers were going to put on a Broadway show for the parents. It was a big production and those involved had been rehearsing for three weeks. The show director was usually a former camper—the same concept as having me head up baseball. Campers played both the boys' and girls' parts as they danced and sang to the raucous applause of the parents. In the past, the staff would go crazy after each scene so parents could get a first-hand feel for the overall camp spirit. Lou loved it when the staff showed their spirit in front of the parents, and the staff liked receiving Lou's approval.

That night, Supplecheck asked Moose to gather up some guys to help move chairs to Mike Hall, the recreation center named after Lou and Renee's son who had passed away at age one. A bunch of us carried out the detail and finally there was one chair left on the lawn. Moose picked up the chair, but I told him it looked heavy.

Suddenly, Moose fell over in pain, so I told him I'd help with the chair. We both grabbed a leg and feigned the weight of the chair, barely getting the chair off the ground as we moaned about the heaviness. Moving the five-pound chair normally would have taken thirty seconds, but we turned it into a twenty-minute ordeal, screaming in pain each step of the way and crying for more help to move the chair. Several counselors gave us a hand and played along, and soon a growing crowd of parents and their boys was gathering to witness our impromptu opening act for the upcoming performance.

Everyone cheered each time we inched the chair closer to Mike Hall, and when we finally arrived at the doorstep, a voice screamed, "Move away! The Bulk-o is here."

With the chair sitting next to the entrance, the huge crowd was chanting, "Bulk-o, Bulk-o, Bulk-o" as The Bulk proceeded to lift the chair over his head in a weightlifter's stance and waddle his way into Mike Hall.

He carried the chair and set in down in the front row to a hero's welcome from the crowd. Watching Lou laugh with approval meant a lot to me. Lou's approval was always great; almost as satisfying as Dad's.

Moose had started that crazy stunt, I had joined him, and soon most everyone had been sucked into the non-rehearsed madness. Carrying a five-pound chair was a simple act in most places, but at camp, we had turned it into folklore. Faking an argument at baseball, getting hit on the head with a folding chair, and struggling to carry a five-pound chair for twenty-one minutes was all part of camp *shtick*. My brother, Lou, and all the other capsized sailors were hoisted on shoulders to reward their futility. A nerdy little camper with a catcher's mask had been the brunt of a staff show skit. What kind of place accepted such out-of-the-norm behavior? My boys camp!

Lou introduced the show *Oliver* and then made a special announcement about a former camper, The Chipmunk, who'd recently been chosen for a lead role in a well-known Broadway play.

When The Chipmunk was a staff member, he'd always directed the camp show. I remembered my first two summers, when The Chipmunk played the lead in *Fiorello* and *The Music Man*. He was fun to watch and had a great camp voice. A great camp voice was anyone who could sing better than the rest of us and could hit all of the notes. A great camp voice was anyone who was several notches above Bob Dylan, but nowhere near Nat King Cole. A great camp voice would have been Sheriff Andy Taylor.

Lou then announced, gleaming with fatherly pride, that he and Renee had been personally invited by The Chipmunk to attend a Broadway performance in the fall. The Chipmunk had become a legend to all camp theater hopefuls.

Rooster and I had prepared the ball field for a large turnout. The Vacuum had randomly mixed teams with parents and sons together, and Rooster and I had no reason to change that tradition. Rooster pitched for one team, I threw for the other, and everyone had a fun, noncompetitive morning of baseball.

The Cubs Kid and his grandfather attended the second period game. The grandfather pulled me aside for a private conversation. He asked me to make a ballplayer out of his grandson and expressed the desire for his grandson to play for the Cubs someday. I told him that wouldn't be a problem, since he'd picked the easiest team to make, and the grandfather chuckled at my comment.

With thoughts of Jack in my mind, I changed the conversation and asked the grandfather to give me some insights on The Cubs Kid. Why did he cry so easily? Did he have poor self-esteem? Did his parents sit in folding chairs cheering his every move on the ball field? Did he have a dog? I could have asked The Cubs Kid those questions directly, but at $90 a summer, I wasn't ready to classify myself as a professional child psychologist.

The grandfather was very nice and had a sense of humor. He avoided most of my questions, but he did confirm what I already knew. His grandson was a good kid in need of guidance. He emphasized that he wanted that guidance to come away from home during the summer, and he thought camp was the best place for his grandson. He also let me know that his grandson idolized him, but as hard as he tried, he couldn't always be there for him. I thanked the grandfather for his insights and headed for the mound.

• • •

S ome of the parents were pretty good athletes and it was fun watching them interact with their sons on the field. It was the same mix of parents I remembered from my first summer; the faces had changed, but nothing else. I wasn't sure how Dad would have performed on visitation day. I couldn't remember ever seeing him hit; he only pitched. I was curious if that had anything to do with pitchers being notoriously bad hitters. Probably not, since most of the pitchers in Little League and high school were top athletes, as well as good hitters. It made me wonder at what point those great pitchers became such lousy hitters. I supposed that Bob Gibson was probably just as puzzled about that.

Thinking about how Dad would have enjoyed visitation day brought back mixed emotions. Would he have fit in with those flashy parents wearing jewelry and putting on airs? All that glittery stuff bothered me when I was ten, maybe because my parents hadn't visited and I was lonely. Would Dad have enjoyed all that stuff? He wore a thirty-year-old watch and no rings. What about his push button Plymouth wagon parked next to all of those other fancy machines? What if one of the counselors had mentioned that Dad's slow curve dropped due to nothing more than gravity. I would've been upset if anyone had made fun of his curveball.

I brought my thoughts back to the present and decided to call home after lunch. Since I had counselor status, I no longer needed Lou's permission to make a phone call. As parents sat with their boys gorging on the barbecue lunch, I took that time to duck out and make my collect call.

Dad answered the phone and accepted the charges. I asked how golf was going and he said he'd actually reached the par five sixteenth in two. The only problem was that he'd gotten so excited that he four-putted. The next hole, a short par three, he'd hit his first one out of bounds, but Dad proudly boasted that he'd then teed up again and stroked his next shot into the cup for a par.

Campingly Yours

With his characteristic laugh, he said, "It was a great way to achieve the hole-in-one experience without having to buy all the drinks at the Nineteenth!"

Hearing Dad brag about his lack of success on the golf course (when he'd actually had a couple great shots) made me realize that he wouldn't have noticed the shiny cars next to his push button wagon.

He said that Mom was fine and was in the backyard with Charley, but when I asked how Charley was doing, Dad shifted back to his par three excitement.

I got a little serious and let Dad know that I was having some throwback feelings about visitation weekend. He said he wished he could have visited my first summer. I asked if he would have been embarrassed hanging around all those big city parents with their flashy cars and jewelry.

"What if your curveball hadn't moved that day? What if Snarl or one of the other guys had made fun of it?" I asked.

Dad interrupted my questions by letting me know that he wouldn't have had time to throw his curveball. He said he would have been too busy watching my brother rescue the family on the sailboat.

Then he added, "It sounds like you're worrying about all the wrong things. Would you have been worried for me or for yourself?"

He said he'd say hello to Mom for me and that his new Mercury Coupe was fine, but everyone kept asking him what happened to his push button beauty.

Finally, he said, "Talk to you later. Oh, and don't worry about me. People have been chuckling at me for years. I think your mother likes it that way."

Evening refreshments consisted of cookies, coffee, and lemonade. Parents were saying their goodbyes, and finally Lou gave a firm announcement that it was time for the visitors to call it a night.

The Cub Kid's grandfather came my way, shook my hand, and said, "Flash, keep up the good work. The Cubs Kid looks up to you."

The staff finally rounded up the campers and everyone headed back to their cabins. My guys were pretty tired and many of them were a bit weepy, but it didn't take long for them to fall asleep, even the Cubs Kid.

I was also tired, but it was nice to lie in bed and reflect upon the day. The cobwebs had made it through another parents' weekend. I missed my time with those cobwebs. No doubt some of the mothers would have complained about them if they had bothered to look up. Those cobwebs had helped me make it through my first summer.

"Maybe the new campers in that cabin have other ways of making it through…zzzzz…I owe something to those cobwebs…Maybe someday I'll figure out how to pay them back… zzzzz…Mom has never played with Charley in the backyard…In fact, I don't remember Mom ever playing in the yard at all…zzzzz…What did Dad mean, was I worried about me or him?…zzzzz…Dad said he was used to people laughing at him…I bet he meant with him…zzzzz…Moose's mom is still alive, at least to Moose…what else matters?…was Bill Miller's heart forced to agree with Goldwater?…zzzzz…Camp's had a lot of legends over the years…even if those legends aren't legendary to everyone…zzzzz…Will I become a legend to The Cubs Kid?…zzzzz…or to any of the campers?…Charley and Mom in the backyard… Dad probably just tipped his cap on the seventeenth…not much emotion…well, maybe a grin…zzzzz…My first visitation day as a staff member…no Flash…no Mom or Dad…I think I handled it okay…zzzzz…but it brought back that lonely feeling…zzzzz…Time to fall asleep, too much thinking…zzzzz…Thinking, that's all I ever do…zzzzz…Hope you're OK, Charley…zzzzz…Dad's lucky to be oblivious to things that don't matter…He waltzes to his own tune…zzzzz…'This camp is your camp, this camp is my camp'…zzzzz…'This camp is made for you and me'…and The Cubs Kid…zzzzz…Thanks Woody, for the tune."

· · ·

Lou judged parent visitation day as an evil necessity. He never admitted that out loud, but a lot of us could tell. The parents paid the bills and ultimately were the financial force that kept the camp running. Some of the parents also didn't seem too thrilled with the weekend, since they could detect the disruption of the camp flow, but I found the dynamics rather interesting. A few of the parents talked during quiet ceremonies, butted in line at meals, snuck in bags of food and candy, and tried to give off a bigger-than-thou aura. How coincidental it was that their sons acted the same way.

Some of the boys cried wildly during the goodbyes, hugged their parents, and neither side would let go. Those parents drove off with a lasting impression that their son was an unhappy mess. However, those crying boys were usually fine again in ten minutes, and once camp had returned to its normal flow, parents' weekend quickly became a distant memory.

Lou used to grumble that after every visitation day he fielded several calls from distraught parents who thought their sons were in holy hell. I often thought it was too bad that parents couldn't transform themselves into cobwebs, hang around camp for a couple days, and see for themselves what a carefree, safe, fun, independent, crazy, and caring life their sons were actually leading. Those cobweb parents might have learned some goofy songs and realized that no one really cared what people looked or acted like at camp. They'd also view an exciting bunch of diverse staff members leading the way for their sons. They would have seen the guidance of Lou and Renee and how camp was a remedy for the turbulence of the city.

Those cobweb parents could have watched a disabled camper hit a baseball or a crying nine-year-old finally begin to laugh. Those parents could have watched a cool "in-crowd" son apologize for his rudeness to the whole camp at a campfire key log ceremony. It would have been great for those parents to experience how a typical camp day worked. They would have learned that Jack was right—there was no such thing as a bad camper. Parents' weekend was necessary, but it didn't display camp life in its true form.

I wondered if Jack thought there were any bad adults. No, probably not. They were all kids at one time.

17

Forgive Me, Charley

The second four weeks raced by and as always, camp life had a way of going too
fast. Most of us wished we could slow the pace. United Nations Day remained a big
event and I enjoyed coaching various events for my team. The faces on the field had changed,
but the intense atmosphere and competitive spirit remained. In fact, most of camp remained
pretty much as I remembered it from my first summer.

Lou didn't want to change the face of camp, so the cabins, grounds, lodge, and food stayed
relatively the same. The newsletter always offered the normal pattern of information. Lou was
a profile in camping courage—he stuck to his beliefs, and it was his camp. The rules were his
and the overall philosophy was his. We all knew it and parents knew it. If parents complained
too much, Lou recommended that they try another camp. Lou was fair to the staff. I
respected him, somewhat feared him, wanted his approval, looked to him for guidance, and
viewed him as a great mentor. No one purposely crossed Lou, and most every staff member
respected and trusted him. Renee was the calming force behind it all. Lou needed Renee and
she was there for him, just as she was there for all of us. To many of us, Lou was the Master
of All Campers.

．．．

During the last week of the session, Lou called me into his office. Of course, I was a little leery about why. He went through his ritual throat clearing, put his pipe down, and cleared his throat once again before speaking. Then he said he had three matters to go over with me. The Vacuum had called and said that the word on the camp street was that the boys really liked the baseball activity. He had also said that he was happy that Rooster and I were continuing his baseball traditions.

Next, Lou mentioned that he'd received a call from The Cubs Kid's grandfather, saying that he was pleased with my relationship with his grandson. Lou said it reminded him a little bit of the past and how a little camper wearing a catcher's mask had made friends with the baseball instructor.

At that moment I was feeling pretty good, especially since the last time I was in Lou's office he'd yelled at me and told me to grow up and tie my shoes. It was nice to get a compliment now and then. But then he again cleared his throat and reminded me that he had one more matter to discuss. Oh well, a couple compliments were probably more than I should have expected.

Lou said, "Flash, you're lost in life right now. Your hair is a mess, your clothes are scraggly, and you're not excited about school. Baseball as a career must not be going well for you or you wouldn't be back at camp. Figure out what you want in life. My perspective, Flash, is that someday you'd make a great camp director. You're too young now, but get your life in order, keep your shoes tied, and someday we'll talk about it again."

Lou finished by saying that he'd also spoken to my dad earlier that day, and that my dad was a pretty smart guy.

Campingly Yours

As usual, the last night of camp consisted of a banquet and a request night. The traditional end-of-the-year song was fun for me.

"I was here in '69, '69, '69, I was here in '69, where is '68?"

I sat down and then stood up again for '66 and lasted until '61. Of course, Lou and Renee remained standing till 1945. The camper and counselor farewell speeches brought tears to most, but I drifted off, thinking about the night Snarl had given the counselor farewell. The faces had changed, but the meaningful words stayed pretty constant.

Afterward, we headed to the tennis courts to watch the burning of the camp effigy. Lou and Renee quietly said a few words about the summer, words that were similar to what they'd said during my first summer. I stepped quietly to my left and found The Cubs Kid.

I put my arm around him and said, "See you next summer."

All of us sang the camp song, and then Lou had us repeat after him: "And now, may the Master of All Campers be with us until we meet again, and may the trails that we follow, though they be of different paths, lead straight unto him. Goodnight, you all."

Some of the staff members remained behind and sang Lou and Renee's favorite song, "With Someone Like you, a Pal So Dear and True."

"Goodnight Renee, goodnight Lou, Master of All Campers. See you next year, Cubs Kid."

. . .

The bus scene continued to be a paradoxical happy sad experience for me. Campers cried and hugged, and I shook a lot of hands while saying my goodbyes. I bumped The Cubs Kid, Snarl-like. He laughed—he didn't cry—and told me I was goofy. The buses slowly crept away as some of the counselors rushed to the end of the road to give their traditional moon show. I stayed behind, since mooning wasn't my thing. I liked staring at the buses as they

Campingly Yours

slowly pulled away.

And so ended another camping season.

Those last few days of camp were a real hustle for the staff. There was a time limit and everything was final. By the time the buses pulled out, all the parent letters had to be completed, no camper clothes were to be left behind, all camper awards had to have been given out, cabins and activity areas had to be cleaned to a spotless condition, and the final summer newsletter and birthday lists were to be handed out on the bus. Immediately after the buses rolled away, counselors had a few hours to finish cleaning the entire camp, since families were due to arrive for post-camp later that afternoon.

Family camp was a tradition that Lou and Renee had started at the very beginning, and Lou didn't want any of the big city mothers complaining about unclean accommodations, so staff members weren't released to say their goodbyes until Supplecheck had given his OK.

I didn't stay for family camp. I was a purist and didn't want to see camp out of its true form. Visitation weekend was enough of a change for me, although I did wonder if any parents ever had the nerve to complain to Lou about anything. That would have been fun to watch.

When all our work was completed, we were given the summer-is-over signal from Supplecheck. I loaded all my stuff in The Binder's Cougar, said my goodbyes, and vroom, The Binder raced his Cougar down the camp road. No bus-like creeping for The Binder. We sang camp songs, reminisced about the summer happenings, and made it home in record time—with no speeding tickets. The luck of The Binder had prevailed.

• • •

I rang the doorbell sometime after nine, and out popped Mom and Dad. Mom tried hugging me while Dad shook my hand. Of course, they wanted to hear all about the summer.

Campingly Yours

"A hole-in-one, Dad," I said. "Well, a par, anyway. That must have felt pretty cool. Hey, where's Charley? Charley, where are you? It's me! I'm home. I told you I wouldn't desert you. I'm going to keep you up all night with all my stories. Here, Charley, here, Charley!"

No Charley.

Dad left the room as Mom quietly told me that Charley had died in July. She said that he'd been unable to move his back legs and was suffering—and an operation wouldn't have helped.

She added, "Your dad took him to the vet and stayed with him while the vet put him to sleep."

Mom said that she and Dad hadn't wanted to ruin my summer, so they hadn't told me about it.

"We knew you'd understand," she said, "and if Charley could have talked, he would have confirmed our decision."

With a heavy and empty heart, I told Mom that I was going to sleep and would tell them all about camp in the morning.

No Charley.

I stretched flat on my back, staring at the ceiling with my nightlight on.

No Charley.

I hadn't been there for him. I had deserted him during his time of need. Charley and I had been so close during the two years since my brother left for college—and I hadn't been there for him.

I was glad that Dad *had* been there for him. He'd had to sit there while the vet put Charley to sleep. How could Dad have gone through something like that again? He'd had to do what I should have done. I would have used my entire summer salary to fly home and be with Charley. They should have told me. Charley had spent his whole life with my brother and me around, and with me exclusively for two years.

"I should have stayed home…Didn't Dad know I saw him with Bulky?…zzzzz…Dad knew everything…*zzzzz*…Dad told Lou I'd make a good camp director…*zzzzz*…Mom never was in the backyard playing with Charley…*zzzzz*…I wonder if Charley could think. Did he look around the room for me before the vet took him away?…*zzzzz*…I should have been there… *zzzzz*…he was suffering…*zzzzz*…I should have been there for him…*zzzzz*…So long, Charley. Please forgive me…*zzzzz*…I know that Dad put Charley in the front seat…*zzzzz*…Forgive me, Charley…forgive me…*zzzzz*…"

18
Winning the Lottery

I spent nine summers as a staff member; that was a long camp life for most. The Bulk,
Rooster, Farb, and Moose hung around, as well. Supplecheck remained head counselor
through all those years and we became close friends. All of us watched a lot of interesting
characters filter in and out of camp.

Finding a direction in life was no easy task for me and the Vietnam War era presented
heavy-duty alternative thoughts. Lou and Renee's role became increasingly challenging, as
well. Most counselors had long hair and asked tough questions—"why" questions.

Mom and Dad's role as parents also became harder as my brother and I aged. We were
asking questions but receiving no logical answers. Archie Bunker wasn't logical, but his
scriptwriters were. Bob Dylan didn't have a great camp voice, but he put an enormous
number of logical questions in tune. Muhammad Ali voiced his beliefs and lost his job. I was
placed in a draft lottery, and so was my brother. I never would have imagined The Flash and
Kid Flash being thrown into a lottery; winner gets to attend a war—or maybe the loser was
considered the lucky one. We were led to believe the lower-half lottery numbers would lead
us to the draft. It was indeed a confusing time.

The lottery was announced my second staff summer. I was teaching

on the ball field at the time. College wasn't really my thing and I was already three credits behind, which made me eligible to be drafted. I liked living in our country. Where else could I have experienced Snarl, Sherman, The Bulk, and The Vacuum in my first summer camp adventure? Dad always grinned after I'd gone to my knees to throw someone out. In a lot of suppressed countries, I might have been on my knees for totally different reasons.

The USA was it for me, but Vietnam wasn't. Not only did I not believe in the war, but my phobia of snakes also became extreme. It must have been hereditary (thanks, Mom). *CBS News* had Walter Cronkite giving us the daily death toll: five Americans, and 351 Viet Cong. I never really knew who tallied those figures, but Walter showed us pictures of soldiers mucking their way through swamps full of wildlife, including big-time snakes. The war, snakes, my lack of enthusiasm for college, and then the lottery announcement—what would be next?

A close friend from home called and left a message for me. The camp secretary handed me her scribbled note that said my lottery number was twenty—TWENTY! I moped back to the ball field and sat on the bench, staring at nothing, Sherman-like. Move to Canada? Lose an unhealthy amount of weight? Shoot my middle toe out? Swallow tin foil? Drive a crane without earplugs? Find Alice and litter outside her restaurant? Go to Vietnam and wade with snakes? What was it going to be?

I sat with no clear answers, feeling sorry for myself. Pudding and whipped cream, boys laughing at me—at that age, I could justify feeling sorry for myself—but I was in the middle of college, with great parents, healthy, playing ball, and still attending camp with my close friends. What about all the people with no money, in wheelchairs, on respirators, with no legs? What about all the Shermans out there? Yet there I was, feeling sorry for myself.

What about one of Lou's graces during my first summer: "I once felt sorry because I had no shoes, then I met a man who had no feet."

I had feet and needed to do something with my life. Maybe it was time for me to re-tie my shoes.

Just before lunch, Renee told me that Mom had called. Renee said they'd had a nice conversation and that I should give Mom a call after lunch. Renee and Mom probably talked about kugel. Maybe not—it could have been they had a nice conversation about not wanting to lose anyone to a confusing conflict. Either way, it wasn't going to be an easy call.

Collect from The Flash, Mom took my call.

"Hi, Mom. Have you been to any malls without Dad lately? How's Dad's golf game?"

"Congratulations," Mom shouted with joy. "You beat your brother's 244 drawing."

"What do you mean, Mom?" I mumbled. "I'm number twenty, with no place to go."

She joyously exclaimed that I was 355—355! I didn't understand. I'd been given a message that I was number twenty.

Mom told me she distinctly remembered the date she'd given birth to me—and the lottery had been picked by birthdays, 366 drawings. I thanked Mom and said I'd call her back later in the day. I told her I was in the middle of an emotional roller coaster and needed a few hours to digest it all. Then I asked the camp secretary to review the message she'd written down for me. She looked at the note and said that a friend had called and said he was number twenty in the lottery. HE was number twenty!

By way of apology, the secretary said, "Maybe I scribbled it down wrong."

I was overjoyed and immediately headed out to the first base bench to contemplate what had just happened. I wasn't worried about my number twenty friend, since he had more medical problems than any Army unit would want to endure, but I felt sorry for anyone with a lousy number. I sat there thinking about how a person's entire life's possibilities could be picked out of a hat. Maybe fate was just a hat drawing.

What if Grandpa Sig, Mom's father, hadn't decided to duck out of the Romanian army, sail to America, head up the Mississippi, cut over on the Missouri, and end up in my hometown—his hometown? No Mom, no Dad, no catcher's mask, no me.

So many confusing thoughts were processing through my mind. My whole life was feeling like one big lottery pick. I needed a night off, and I knew that Supplecheck would OK it.

Dad meeting Mom, Mom meeting Dad—was it fate that both of them had won that lottery?

· · ·

Taking occasional time away from camp was healthy for the counselors. All day and night with campers without a break would have driven some counselors to insanity. Even Lou and Renee ducked out to the Tally *ho* restaurant on Wednesday evenings. That was the only scheduled time they left camp. They owned the camp and bore all the liability, so they probably didn't feel comfortable leaving very often—and the restaurant was only five miles away.

The staff didn't own the camp, so we needed to take a breather every now and then. We were allowed one day and two nights off per week, one beginning after dinner and the other after the evening program. That was plenty of time off, and no one complained. Supplecheck regulated our time away and made sure that we never left an activity or cabin uncovered. That was an understood rule for the staff. If a counselor skipped out at night without permission and got caught, he faced Supplecheck's wrath the next morning.

I wanted to celebrate my lucky lottery fortune, so I announced to the staff that the beer and pizza were on me for those who could take the night off. I even asked Supplecheck to come along if he could get away. The legal drinking age was eighteen, so that included everyone except for some of the first-year junior counselors and CITs. For many of the younger staff, camp was the most freedom they'd ever experienced, and the same had been true for me during my junior counselor summer.

No mom or dad calling to check in every hour or two, asking, "Where are you? When are you going to this person's house? Who's driving? Are you wearing a seatbelt, and what time should we expect you home?"

Lou wasn't one to stay up late—and counselors knew that they'd better come back quiet, because he was a light sleeper.

Balsam Lodge was located on the camp's chain of lakes. Counselors could get there by boat, a five-minute car ride, or even by foot, walking the camp ridge (the same one where my brother's friends had smoked) and keep going about a half-mile or so. Then we'd have to wade knee-deep across a channel, which would then take us to the shore of Balsam.

I took an advance of $21 from my salary. Pitchers of Leinies (Lienenkugel beer, a local brand) were $1.50 and tap beer was twenty cents. Large homemade pizzas were three dollars and the owners usually gave us a few freebies for being good customers.

I rode with The Binder, which cut the normal travel time down to a three-minute ride. Seventeen counselors were able to take the night off and they were more than happy to take me up on my offer of free beer and pizza. There were normally a few girls hanging around the place as well, and I told them they were included in the party until my money ran out. There was also a bowling machine that cost a quarter. If anyone rolled a 233, they'd win a free six-pack of Leinies.

I was feeling it that night, and so was Farb. We both needed one pin in the ninth frame, and we both nailed it. We were feeling it. I reminded Farb to role a gutter ball on his last roll, or maybe he reminded me, I don't remember. So we won two more six-packs for the group. Then Supplecheck walked in and everything got very quiet for a few moments. None of us had ever been out with Supplecheck. Was he going to report our overindulgence? Was the party over?

"Flash, I heard you were buying," rumbled the 6' 6" intimidator.

He grinned, somewhat Dad-like, and said he'd take a whiskey with a Leinie chaser. Oops, that order dented my tab limit, but the relief of having Supplecheck with us was worth more than I ever could have imagined.

Several of us sat with Supplecheck for an hour as he told us past camp and home stories. He was actually human, normal, and not really a bigger-than-life intimidating untouchable.

He told us that he'd attempted to play pro football and had actually played in the Canadian league for a couple years. Then he settled into coaching and never looked back. He had his summers free and planned to remain head counselor for a long time. Supplecheck was happy and for him, his life was set—school in the off-season and camp every summer. He told us he had a job to perform, both at school and at camp, and he expected everyone around him to do their jobs.

Then Supplecheck stood up and headed out, warning us not to stay out too late, since our jobs started in the morning with the wake-up bell. To our surprise, he winked as he made that comment.

Almost eleven percent of my summer salary was spent on that night of celebration, but getting to know and understand Supplecheck was worth every penny. Maybe I should have felt guilty for celebrating my high lottery number. Then again, maybe it was OK to have a little celebration now and then.

Supplecheck—what a great right hand man, he was worth every one of Lou's dollars. We no doubt drank and ate too much in a typical boys-being-boys fashion that night. At two a.m., the owners of Balsam Lodge turned out the lights and The Binder drove me home. I had no idea how the others were getting home. Binder missed the S-curve on the curvy camp road and accidentally parked the Cougar in a swamp.

Mom and Dad had warned me not to drink and drive, and Lou had warned us of the implications, but we didn't listen much. We lived in a catastrophe-oriented society, and our near miss ended in a swamp. How ironic it was for me—the guy celebrating a great lottery number so I wouldn't have to wade with snakes in a swamp.

Early the following morning, a tow truck rescued the drenched but unharmed Cougar. It was wise for us to let Supplecheck know what had happened, since he was going to find out sooner or later. Supplecheck's wrath wasn't something The Binder or I were happy about, but we hoped that telling the truth would ease the verbal lashing and the upcoming extra assignments we were sure to receive.

We sat with Supplecheck in his 7 x 9 office and in a firm voice, he muttered, "Dhuder, Flash, the three of us have something in common."

Supplecheck then told us he wasn't going to let it happen to him again, and neither should we.

Then he added, "Now get out of here and go do your jobs."

Drinking and driving was common in those days and not wearing seatbelts was the norm. Dad used to pile ten kids in his push button wagon with no seatbelts. Mom and Dad sometimes would have a drink at a restaurant and then drive us home.

Alcohol and cigarette advertisements were on television and in all the major periodicals. Dizzy, Pee Wee and Elwood promoted Falstaff every Saturday, and the Mick and his buddies took that to heart.

The drinking age in Kansas was eighteen for 3.2 beers. Lots of girls hung out at the 3.2 drinking taverns, just a few miles across the Missouri *Paper Moon* bridge. Wednesday nights were huge at those Kansas taverns. Sixteen-year-olds had no problem getting in. The first time I had the nerve to sneak in, I ran into my Uncle Louie—oops. Uncle Louie had never been married, liked a cold beer on a hot day, and played cards with his cronies for a few bucks. He was Grandpa Sig's brother, somewhat the roustabout of the family, and was jokingly accused of looking like the head of the Mafia. Uncle Louie let me know that he wouldn't tell if I didn't tell—he was a great guy. I didn't remember seeing any cabs. Everyone drove their own cars home, including Uncle Louie.

19

Ramona

The camp program, including rituals and traditions, didn't change much over the years. Once in a while a new cabin was built, a staff member would conjure up a different evening activity, and modern folk songs were added to the musical repertoire. Mealtime noise continued at peak level, U.N. Day stayed competitive, cabins challenged one another on Sundays, new campers needed to pass swimming, canoeing, and camp craft, and the cobwebs still hovered nicely in my first cabin. Campfires remained constant on Friday nights, and Snarl-like apologies were offered at almost every key log ceremony.

Lou continued to clear his throat and Renee's guidance remained strong. Staff shows were always upbeat and Lou and Renee were the brunt of similar jokes every summer. Lou guided the sailboat, named *The Frantic*, into wires yearly and boys were hoisted onto shoulders for all sorts of non-winning reasons. The off-season was always considered synonymous with winter. Spring was the coming of camp, and fall was reflection time on the past summer's memories.

What brought me back every summer? Why did so many come back year after year? The program didn't change much, so why weren't we bored? First period activities, second period activities, lunch, rest period, third and fourth period activities, dinner, evening activity, and then bed. There was nothing too original about a typical day at camp. There were plenty of other things to do at home—ball teams, family trips, and summer school (oops, that would have been a mistake).

Why did so many boys keep coming back to camp, and why to that camp? That boys camp was the only camp I knew, so nowhere else mattered. What had Lou meant when he said that I'd make a good camp director? I was too young and couldn't do what Lou did! Besides, Lou was the director at the boys camp, and I could never leave it.

By my fourth staff summer, it felt strange to know that I was actually older than most of my boyhood idols when they were staff members. Some had only been nineteen and twenty, but they seemed so old to me then, and without thinking about it too much, I probably was considered an equivalent idol to some of the current campers.

The Cubs Kid was enjoying a great camper career, and maybe I did have a positive influence on his life. Did he look at me the same way I had looked at The Vacuum? I looked up to loads of counselors over my camper years. Not that I considered them all idols, but they displayed character traits that made camp a better place for the campers.

Wolf was a good example of someone I admired. His attitude about taking care of the environment left a lasting impression on me. Wolf was my first encounter with someone who really cared about our surroundings and the first person who taught me that I should try to make a positive difference. Indeed, Wolf did make a difference, and his influence carried over to Moose, who became the camp trip director. Moose informed both campers and staff that all campsites had to be left cleaner than when we arrived. I learned that from Wolf, Moose learned that from Wolf, and Wolf probably learned that from someone else who had a big impact on his life. Faces changed over the summers, but certain character traits consistently reappeared.

The head of the nature program during my fourth summer, and for several summers to follow, was totally immersed in our environment. He had a great following of campers, and together they built a nature trail that encompassed the whole camp. That was a huge project, and Wolf would have been thrilled to know his ideals were continuing in full force at camp.

 Campingly Yours

I grew up at camp with Greenman, and he became the swimming director. Greenman ran a tight ship on the waterfront and boys improved their swimming and lifeguard skills. The Pumpkins had performed that role for me when it came to learning to swim, and Greenman did the same for a lot of boys just like me. I hoped that I was passing on some of The Vacuum's ideals to campers on the ball field. Moose, Wolf, Greenman, The Vacuum, and the nature counselor all had a following of campers. Were we idols to some of our boys, maybe? The Vacuum must have also had idols when he was a boy.

What about Lou? He attended an old-line boys camp and was its waterfront director before he became a camp owner. Did Lou have staff idols? Was Lou an idol to some of the campers? Who was the Master of All Campers before Lou started the boys camp? Maybe it was all part of camp evolution. Parts of every camper and counselor stayed on over the years, but some simply left bigger pieces. Snarl probably left no major pieces to anyone, except to me. The Vacuum left multitudes of pieces to scores of boys. Lou and Renee were in the middle of leaving pieces everywhere, and there were boys and grown men all over the country and world hanging on to those parts.

• • •

Lou was pretty logical, having certain counselors retain their campers the following summer, and sometimes for several summers. I had a great group of boys during my middle staff years, and all of us looked forward to being together each summer. I still delighted in going to the mailbox for the camp newsletter to see the list of who was returning. As a camper I remembered all but praying to find The Vacuum's name and my other staff favorites on the list. Did campers look for my name on the newsletter list? Did they rush out to see if The Bulk and Moose were returning?

Supplecheck hadn't lived through camper days like the rest of us. It was impossible for the non-camper to understand what it was like to feel the excitement of the monthly newsletter.

I thought about my first staff orientation, when a new counselor insisted that former campers who became counselors had an advantage, and he was right.

I lived through little boy camp obstacles, times of homesickness, being picked on, getting accepted, making friends with a twenty-year-old, making friends with lots of older guys, having The Bulk become my best friend from the first moment, lighting my first campfire match, coaching the Merry Fairy House, and catching The Vacuum's curveball. I wanted Mom and Dad while looking up at cobwebs—I couldn't have explained that to anyone who'd missed the camper experience.

My brother and Lou being hoisted on shoulders for futility—it was amazing, but Lou got it from day one. He understood that futility would be a big part of camp life. I remember wondering how my brother could have liked camp. How could camp ever have gotten into my blood system? It was a question I answered shortly after those first few days as a camper. I finally came to the conclusion that my campers indeed were happy to see my name listed in the newsletter, and I was sure that a lot of campers skipped by my name in search of their personal favorites. I missed my camper days; I cherished my memories.

· · ·

Lou called me into his office one day and went through his throat clearing and pipe cleaning routine. He called me in often, usually to discuss an upcoming program or a camper problem, but I sensed that something was different. Lou's eyes welled up and his lower lip began to quiver. He sadly told me that he'd received a call from Sherman's mother, telling him that Sherman had passed away. He had died in his mother's arms. Lou paused for a moment, then told me that Sherman's mother had wanted me to know. Lou's son was still in an institution at that time, with no hope of ever living a normal life, so the news of Sherman's death was very hard on Lou and Renee.

I sat motionless and Lou handed me a Kleenex. I visualized Sherman sitting on the bench, staring at nothingness. Then I visualized Sherman sitting in his mother's arms, staring at nothingness, with no idea of what was happening. Finally, I visualized Sherman running to first base the first time he ever hit a ball. There were no fielders, Sherman! There was no way I could have thrown you out! You didn't have to run to first base!

I visualized him in full Sherman-like glee on top of the world—on first base—a place he'd never been before.

Lou said softly, "Sherman's mother wanted you to know that they buried him with his ball and glove, with the ball firmly secured in the pocket."

I mumbled, "I bet his mother knew to place the glove at the level of Sherman's armpit."

Silently, I added, "So long, Sherman. Thanks for teaching me a few things."

. . .

Soon thereafter, Ramona entered my life. Some boys on a horseback riding overnight trip found a battered little dog. It looked like she'd just had pups and had been left in the woods to die. They brought the dog back to camp, much to Lou's dismay. Lou understood why young boys wouldn't have wanted to leave the dog, but allowing strays in camp wasn't good policy.

My life was fine outwardly, but my campers had no idea that I was in constant turmoil about where my life was headed. My brother tinkered with the idea of working for Steve Jobs before landing a position with Hewlett-Packard. Bulk and Moose were teachers; and most everyone my age was doing something constructive. After three colleges, Dad bribed me with a new car if I'd settle down and get a degree. That wasn't Dad's normal way; he just wanted me to get a degree.

I was feeling as much like a stray as that dog must have felt. That dog wasn't going to last long at camp; she'd soon be sent to a pound. What else could Lou do?

"You could let me take care of her, Lou," I told him. "I've named her Ramona."

Maybe taking Ramona had something to do with Sherman. Maybe I was a lost soul. Nothing appealed to me—no nine-to-five job, no fast food industry, no chemical or plastic company, no retail business, no tire store, not even the junkyard. (Sorry Dad, but not even the junkyard was for me.)

Playing centerfield for the Yankees—or for any pro team—appealed to me. Actually, in my case, second base would have been more practical, but that job obsession had left a couple years back.

There was nothing out there for me, and there was nothing out there for Ramona, either. So I took Ramona—or maybe she took me. Ramona only needed a few days to get into the swing of camp. She rarely left me alone; maybe being alone frightened her, and who could blame her?

Ramona was at my side the last night of camp, and as I stood with her, my eyes roamed across the gathering during the traditional burning of the camp effigy. Moose and The Bulk were huddled around their boys and Supplecheck stared solemnly with his arm around two boys. I saw The Cubs Kid, no longer a kid, walking quietly, searching for and then finding and putting his arm around a new camper.

I looked at Lou, with his arm around Renee. Renee loved camp, but she devoted her life to Lou. Lou was camp, and Renee was Lou. The last night of camp was Lou's last night of the year. He savored every living camp moment and he always had a lot of camping to do. He rode the buses with the campers back to Milwaukee and then to Chicago. He didn't want to let go. Lou's game was camp, and he was best suited to being the pitcher.

Some of the counselors remained to sing to Lou and Renee. Another camping season had passed by for Lou. Ramona was by my side, and Charley would have been proud. Jack's presence was at that ceremony, too, although The Cubs Kid had no idea. I had nowhere to go; yet I had to leave before post-camp families arrived. I remained a purist; Ramona and I would be gone as soon as Supplecheck gave the word.

The burning of the camp effigy was a beautiful ceremony. No one ever put his arm around Sherman. The Vacuum had an extra arm—if only he had known.

Learning to canoe at Boys Camp

Batting instruction at Boys Camp

 Campingly Yours

A pick-up game at Boys Camp

Little Tom with his older brother, Mark.

Campingly Yours

Lou (on the left) as a counselor at Camp Nebagamon

My brother (Flash) at Boys Camp – "Get it, got it, good"

 Campingly Yours

My cabin at age 11 – The Bulk (top left), Brillo (top middle), Moose (top right) and me/ Kid Flash (middle of first row).

Ramona resting by the lake at Boys Camp

Campingly Yours

Left to right – Counselors Farb, me,
Casey (Greenman), Bulk, and Moose

Left to right – Counselors Casey, Pep,
and Leb

Ramona and me at Boys Camp

Dad with his bulldog Bulky, and me

My first dog Charley

Mom and Dad

My brother and Dad

Charley and me

Campingly Yours

The Cover Photo – Mom, Dad, my brother (left) and me, Charley, the 1960 push-button Plymouth wagon, and my catcher's mask

My brother (left) and me with Bulky

My brother and Mom in the back, with Charley and me

Dad – king of his junkyard

Some of Dad's junkyard crew

20

Finding a Direction

Ramona and I headed out in my '66 Chevy 327. **It was a four-door Impala, so no** one got too excited about it, but I liked it since I could pile counselors in for nights out. Ramona sat in front as I daydreamed my way home. It was an eleven-hour trip for me (hard to compete with The Binder). The Binder was no longer at camp, but we kept in touch often.

Leb had just finished his fourth summer, all as a staff member, and was fully entrenched with camp life. He became one of my best friends and we often stayed up late talking camp philosophy. He had completed college and was working at his dad's steel company, but he was allowed to take summers off for camp.

Leb was probably the most devoted counselor I ever encountered. He gave up time off and fun pickup games to be with campers in need. He was a true company guy and he worked overtime to make sure camp projects were completed. He didn't do it for Lou's sake; he simply was a dedicated person. Leb showed no signs of needing approval from Lou; maybe that was an advantage of not growing up at camp. Leb had no enemies at camp and he created a nice following of campers. No doubt many searched for his name in the winter newsletter. I didn't need to search for his name, since we spoke often during the off-season. There was something camp-special about Leb, not Vacuum-like, not even Jack-like, just a Leb type of uniqueness.

I glanced at a sleeping Ramona, remembering how I'd spilled so many stories to Charley. Ramona knew Leb, so I didn't have to relate Leb stories to her. Maybe I was a bit too old to be reminiscing to a sleeping dog. Maybe no one is too old to talk to his or her dog.

I did let Ramona know one well-kept secret. Lou had told me in confidence that Leb had donated his entire summer salary to the camp scholarship fund. That fund, originated by Lou and Renee, allowed less fortunate boys and girls to attend summer camp. I let Ramona know that Leb would have been upset if I told anyone, but Ramona could keep a secret.

As I pulled into our driveway, I was ready to announce my firm decision to go back to college to earn a degree in education. I wanted to give my summer salary to Dad and have him apply it to Missouri University. Leb must have given me that inspiration, although his donation was for a better cause. Mom opened the door and gave me a rousing hug, and I hugged her back. She loved it when I hugged her, and I knew Dad did, too, since he gave his patented grin of approval. I introduced them to Ramona and noticed Mom faking her dog approval in anticipation of having blond hairs everywhere.

Ramona sat by my side as I announced my college intentions.

I handed my summer check to Dad and said, "No arguments; apply it to tuition."

I let Dad know that a new car sounded pretty good. He said a degree sounded better. Of course, they were glad to have me back for a couple weeks and were also glad to see me scrambling to get everything in place for school. Mom was impressed that I used her Hoover every few days to de-Ramona the house.

Ramona and I loaded the Chevy and headed to Columbia, Missouri. It was easy landing my necessary classes, but a bit more difficult finding a place to stay. I saw an ad for a trailer located on a farm eleven miles from campus at $95 a month. It wasn't exactly the typical college experience, but I was on a mission to get my degree, and it was a great deal—Ramona had acres of freedom.

. . .

College life presented total freedom. In camp terms, it was equivalent to having every night—and every day—off. I went to classes, took a few notes, studied the notes, then took tests every three weeks or so. Most of my friends were in the workforce earning money while I was in school paying money. I hung out at campus taverns, met a few girls, had a few dates, enjoyed an extra beer or two, studied late at night, took Ramona for daily runs, and consistently repeated that pattern.

Then I met Toni who lived alone and worked at a local hospital. She was beautiful, with a model-like appearance. She liked beer and the outdoors, had a great sense of humor, and was willing to see Hank Aaron's return to County Stadium in Milwaukee. Moose, who lived in Wisconsin, bought the tickets and Toni and I took off for a nine-hour ride to see the game.

A fan sitting behind us had a few extra rounds of Schlitz and threw up on my date. Moose all but nailed the guy while I tried cleaning the chunks off Toni's dress. Hank Aaron hit one out, just foul, but that was all I remembered of the game. Moose took me aside and said I should marry the girl.

He said, "Toni is a keeper if she was willing to drive nine hours to see a game she knows nothing about, and got to be the recipient of 'unwanted food.'"

Toni and I dated for a year, I received my teaching degree, and then I took Moose's recommendation. Toni and I had a fun wedding in Missouri with my friends from camp and home in attendance. The song "Ramona" was played as one of the wedding selections.

In a sad moment, I sold the Chevy and all of its memories, and then Toni and I headed out in her 1968 Barracuda. The gauge on her Plymouth was broken and we ran out of gas near Russell, Kansas (no help offered from Bob Dole). Several hours later, we managed to find gas. Then we headed to Colorado for an unplanned honeymoon and arrived the day after the Big Thompson flood. People had been forced out of their homes and all the hotels were full. I slept on top of our U-Haul trailer while Ramona and Toni slept in the car. It wasn't a glamorous honeymoon, but it did have a bit of charm.

The Bulk lived close to where we'd been stranded and he helped us find an apartment. The only money we had was from the sale of the car, so I needed to find work fast. The Bulk was teaching grade school and said he'd heard there was an opening in Denver, about forty minutes away. I called the school, and Blake, the assistant principal and athletic director, said they'd had a late cancellation, so they had an opening for a combination history, geography, and social studies teacher—and coach. He told me to be there in fifty minutes for an interview.

Toni stayed with The Bulk and I took off for Denver in a severe thunderstorm. With the speed and luck of The Binder, I miraculously found the small Catholic high school. Drenched, my curly hair scattered in every direction, I entered the principal's office and was surrounded by Blake and five nuns.

The principal, the head nun, crossed her hands, gave me a deep glaring once over, and asked me, "What do you know about geography?"

I glanced at Blake, who was a dead ringer for Hank Stram. I could have sworn he was the same play-action genius who had frustrated the Vikings. Then I flashed back to the first time I'd introduced myself at staff orientation.

I glanced at all of the nuns, looked directly at the principal, and deadpanned, "Well, I found your school pretty easily."

The nuns didn't seem too thrilled with my response, but Blake thought I was some kind of savior. He must have had pull, too, since he told me to report for class the next morning. On the ride home, I was thinking that they hadn't done much of a reference check on me—but I knew I was okay.

21

Back to High School

A new area, a new job, a new marriage, and living by The Bulk. Toni and I had all the questions; The Bulk had all of the answers. Toni was able to land a job nearby, and together we made a whopping $9,000, which was $8,910 more than Lou paid me my first staff year.

After having made the transition from camper to staff, I found the transition from student to teacher to be a pretty easy adjustment. However, staying ahead of the students in three subjects required hours of late night textbook cramming. Coaching cross-country in the fall and freshman basketball all winter kept me at school until dinnertime. On days of meets and basketball games, I arrived home just in time to get out the textbooks and stay a few pages ahead of the class.

My freshman team played thirty-one games, and later I learned that they were supposed to play a maximum of fifteen. Oops! The principal called me in for a reprimand after the last game. She must have checked my game schedule as promptly as she checked my references.

However, Blake loved the fact that my team had played all of those games. So much so that he said I'd take over his undefeated junior varsity program the following year. He was thinking of making me head baseball coach, as well. I asked the jovial and ever-dapper Blake if anyone had ever checked my references.

Blake said, "No. I knew you were a good kid. You looked like a quarterback type who could one day lead the school in athletics."

I told him the high school wasn't Purdue and that I wasn't Len Dawson. He laughed and said he wasn't Hank Stram, but he sure seemed to act like the head Chief to me.

• • •

Danny was flunking my government class. He had little interest in school, let alone the House of Representatives. Out of all of my classes, he was the only one flunking. I hated the thought of not getting someone through.

I wondered how the canoe instructors could have allowed anyone to become a canoe flunky. As far as I was concerned, that never should have happened. It seemed scary and a bit humorous when I was young, but no one should have had the embarrassment of becoming a canoe flunky. I thought that Lou had missed the boat on that one. I was pretty good at canoeing and I would have been glad to work with potential flunkies.

I kept Danny after class and set up extra time to work with him. That extra time meant before school. He was hesitant, but he agreed. I met with him for two weeks. Danny was a troubled kid who hung out with a tough crowd, and I could tell he appreciated my help, but he wouldn't have admitted it.

Once in a while, I'd take a quick break in the teacher's lounge. I didn't hang out there often, since the smoke was too much for me and I hated the constant faculty complaints. So many teachers were just putting in their time and waiting for summer. They moaned about the administration, unruly students, nagging parents, low pay, and long hours. A few had been teaching at the school for more than twenty years. That was a depressing thought to me, doing something for twenty years while complaining the whole way.

I asked the math and science teachers how Danny was doing in their classes. They both cringed and let me know that he was an awful kid. Each said he was flunking, but they were going to barely pass him so they wouldn't have him again. Wow! I immediately turned my thoughts to Jack.

Later that week, I happened upon a fight in the hallway. Fights were pretty common at the school, but they usually happened outside. That fight involved two students from well-off families against Danny—and Danny was wielding a knife. I had all three boys in my classes.

Using instinct or stupidity, I stepped between them and asked Danny to put the knife down. The action paused, and I could tell they didn't want me to get hurt. Danny taunted the boys and screamed for me to get out of the way. I started to grin and just stood there, Dad-like, and continued to grin. Danny called me a crazy m-f, put his knife back into his pocket, and said he'd see me in the morning.

Sure enough, Danny was prompt the next morning, and I jokingly frisked him for weapons. I knew it wasn't a laughing matter, but I wanted to keep the situation as lighthearted as possible. He let me put his knife in the top drawer, but Danny didn't want to talk government that morning. He said he might have stabbed those boys and asked me how I possibly could have grinned at him when he might have accidentally stabbed me in the scuffle. With that comforting thought, I let Danny know that his waving of the knife had reminded me of my dad.

"Your dad? What did my knife have to do with your dad?"

I told him that I'd tell him the secret—and return his knife at graduation—if he earned a passing grade in government. I could tell that I was one of the few people Danny actually liked, but I had no visions of altering his life or behavior. I also knew that it probably didn't matter if I could help him pass government. He was going to pass all of his classes, since no one wanted him around. I decided that next year I was going to ask Jack to lead the faculty orientation meetings. I knew that Blake would approve.

B lake asked me to be one of the faculty chaperones for the spring prom. I was sure that assignment hadn't come from the principal. I knew most of the 250 seniors and most of the juniors, as well. The camp atmosphere had taught me to learn everyone's name in a short period of time, so learning names over the nine-month school year was easy.

The boys wore tuxedos and the girls thought they were dressed to the nines, but I really didn't see it that way. I always thought prom dresses were the ugliest concoctions invented and that bridesmaid dresses took a close second. All those pastel colors made the Baskin-Robbins display of ice cream look like a well-decorated freezer. Who designed those dresses? Maybe the dress design teachers also refused to fail their students so they wouldn't have to view those lousy colors again the following year.

Watching the dance brought back memories of girls coming to the camp for a social. I wasn't part of the social my first summer, since it was reserved for the older campers, but I remembered being at the dinner table during a rainstorm when a band of fifty or so girls walked into the lodge.

We were in the middle of raucous singing, and WHAM—the whole building fell silent. Girls in our dining hall! One would have thought Lou had just canceled camp! The guys my age thought the girls were some alien life form, what with their make-up and combed hair. Living with girls at school was enough for me, and I saw no need to have girls at my camp.

I really had no idea camps even existed for girls. I assumed, without thinking much about it, that camps were for boys. Anyway, what would girls do at camp? The Bulk and I were curious, so we snuck to Mike Hall and peeked through the window. Our senior village guys were lined up on the far side, and the "intruders" were hovering on the near side.

The music was pounding and Snarl was at the microphone yelling, "Snowball!"

The flakes remained scattered, though, since no one was listening to Snarl. Some of our counselors gathered the female staff members and did the twist.

 Campingly Yours

"Snowball!" yelled Snarl again, and both staff sides grabbed an opposite.

Pretty soon, the dance floor was filled, but the campers didn't do the twist. Instead, they did a boy-girl combo of left hand on the opposite's right shoulder, right hand on the left shoulder, two steps to the left, two steps to the right, all with their arms stretched to keep each other a couple feet apart. The Bulk and I figured that was the standard camp dance, so we gave it a whirl. I couldn't reach The Bulk's shoulders, so we headed back to the cabin.

Apparently, my prom students hadn't learned to dance from camp socials. The kids couldn't get much closer to each other, and the punch had a lot of punch. The nuns didn't attend, and Blake must have thought he heard Snarl's cry of "Snowball," since he danced with as many girls as possible. I had a feeling that Blake knew about the *punch*.

The prom queen was announced and the boys pushed me to the middle of the floor to dance with her. I put my hands on her shoulders and had her do the same with me. Then I showed her the camp two-step. The boys booed me off the floor, and Blake took over. He sure looked like the "dapper one" to me. I'd only watched Hank Stram coach, but I bet he once was the first one on the dance floor after the Minnesota game.

The next morning, I received a call from Lou, asking me to be the CIT director. Earlier, I'd written Lou a letter letting him know that returning to camp would be difficult, since I was a newlywed and fully entrenched in my teaching position. I felt that I'd run my course at camp and needed to place myself in the category of *alumni*.

Lou said he could really use the help and would be happy to give Toni and me the married couple cabin. Being married at camp, heading the CITs, and in charge of a cabin group— that sounded like overload to me. I told Lou I'd get back to him, since I knew he needed a quick answer.

The Bulk called to say that he was going back for one more summer. He also had a teaching career, but he had no other obligations. He thought Toni and I should also go back for one more summer, and he said we'd all have a great time. The Bulk always knew best, so I called Lou and gave him my confirmation. I was heading back to camp for one last summer—with Toni, Ramona, and The Bulk.

The school held its own form of banquet for the graduating class that spring. Blake emceed and numerous academic and athletic honors were given. It was bittersweet for me, since the outgoing seniors wouldn't be returning in the fall.

Two boys took the microphone and gave out the most popular teacher award—to me! I was sort of embarrassed and figured that maybe I had been too easy at giving out grades. As I stepped down from accepting my award, I fell off the podium. The nuns thought I was seriously injured, but I didn't fool Blake. He had a few of the seniors carry me away.

I returned all healed a few minutes later, just in time to say goodbye to my closest students. There was no burning of an effigy, but it was a pretty sweet evening. Danny was at the graduation ceremony. He received a D+ from me; he'd earned it. He shook my hand and said thanks. He never asked for his knife back, so I let my dad's story lie.

Blake said he looked forward to seeing me in the fall, and told me he'd let me know over the summer about my coaching promotions. My first year of school completed, The Bulk and I were headed back to camp for our final summer.

22
One Last Summer at Boys Camp

We crammed Ramona into the loaded car for the two-day drive to camp. Toni knew nothing about camps, especially a boys camp. She wasn't overly excited about going, but I was taking her into my world. Renee had privately told me that she'd entered the camping world to help Lou, but it hadn't been her first choice. Lou had a dream of starting a boys camp, and Renee had agreed to enter his world.

Sometimes ballplayers hang on a little too long. They get standing ovations everywhere, but mainly in remembrance of past heroics. The Mick was a classic example, and so was Willie Mays. Maybe the two best center fielders ever, they just didn't want to let go, and who could blame them? The anticipation of seeing them hit one out just once more was well worth the hope for most fans.

I hadn't planned to go back to camp; I just wanted one more summer of memories. Lou placed Toni in the office part-time and he didn't give her very much responsibility. She seemed okay with the no-pressure assignment. It was hard for her to adjust to many of the

Campingly Yours

camp traditions and all the ins and outs that came naturally to me, and it was difficult for me not to hang around the guys all the time and live in my cabin's staff quarters.

I wasn't devoting enough attention to the CITs, and those sixteen-year-olds were pretty disappointed in me. They were counting on me to help guide them, but I was doing a fair job at best. My cabin group probably thought the same, since most of my extra time was devoted to Toni. Halfway through the summer, I performed a self-evaluation and decided that I'd earned a D+, the same as Danny. He was happy with that grade, but I wasn't.

I thought about past summers and several staff members who had reached the Mantle-Mays syndrome. They were great guys who returned to camp one summer too many. Unfortunately, their last summer was what a lot of us remembered. All those summers of positive impact—but their last weeks of camp were foremost on many of our minds.

My self-evaluation left me in the dumps, depressed, and thinking of leaving early. No, I wouldn't leave—all my years of devotion to camp would have been lost in that one irrational act. I was looking forward to teaching and coaching again, but I never really believed that I'd be doing that for more than three or four years. The complaining faculty members in the teacher's lounge had gotten to me. I didn't want to be fifty years old, griping about the errant ways of the school.

My cabin was on a trip when I made my decision to stay at camp. Toni was running camp errands in town, and Lou asked me to sit at the staff table for lunch. All those summers and I couldn't recall ever sitting at the staff table, which consisted of Lou and Renee, the visiting doctor and his wife, Supplecheck and his wife, and sometimes several visitors. I had also never seen anyone from that table with pudding in their face.

I was a little nervous, knowing that Lou and the others were aware of my lousy performance. Renee had her way of soothing bad situations, but couldn't always soothe Lou, so I was prepared for the worst: a lecture from Lou in front of the others.

Lou cleared his throat as usual (there was no pipe during the meal), and said, "Flash, there's a big need for a girls camp in our area."

Then he reminded me of the day he'd told me that I'd make a good camp director.

"The time is right for you to consider that option," he added. "I spoke with your dad this morning. Your dad's a pretty smart guy."

I was thoroughly confused. There I was, in the midst of what I felt was my worst summer performance, and Lou was verbally shaking me like a rag doll, letting me know once again that it was time to tie my shoes and get my life in order. I liked teaching, and especially coaching, and I could see myself in that position for a few years—maybe even for a lifetime—but what if that meant being stuck, never achieving my goals, and going to work for years on end just to make ends meet?

Toni and I stayed up late that night talking about our options. I was wired, since Lou had put an amazing possibility in my head—and I was feeling it. However, Toni wasn't feeling it. She wasn't against the idea, and that was good enough for me.

We had a day off two days later, and I made several calls to area girls camps. One owner from a camp about fifty miles away was glad to hear from me, and she told me to bring Toni to her camp for lunch. She implied that the time might be right for her to sell, and she was glad I had called. She also acted as if she knew all about me.

I asked, "How could you possibly know *anything* about me?"

She said, "I'm the aunt of The Cubs Kid!"

Suddenly, my mind was made up. It was a fast, crazy, furious, mind-boggling, scary, exciting, irrational, spur of the moment, life-altering decision, but to my amazement, Toni said it sounded exciting to her, too, and the decision was made. I was going to be a *camp director*—and so was Toni. No, that wasn't quite right! We were going to be *camp owners*!

That immediately brought up an important point. How the heck would we be able to buy a camp? It was going to require some thought and planning, but we didn't focus on that part as we got in the car and headed off to meet the aunt of The Cubs Kids.

• • •

We drove county roads, all of them designated with letters—County A, B, F, and FF—but even as confusing as it was, we finally managed to pull onto the road to the girls camp a little before noon. That gravel road led us into a gorgeous park-like 100-acre setting. We passed a lake within the camp and several rustic buildings, then followed an arrow that directed us to the office.

An elderly woman carrying a large wrench greeted us as we got out of our car. She hugged Toni and shook my hand. Her handshake was quite firm—stronger than the one Blake had given me when I was hired at the school. In fact, her handshake was stronger than any my dad or Lou had ever given me and let me know for certain that she could handle whatever task she'd been performing with that wrench.

She led us to the dining hall, where all the girls were standing as the camp director said grace. No one made a sound or moved while she spoke. It was a very military-like atmosphere. I did a quick count and came up with sixty campers. Lunch was pretty light: lettuce, tuna salad, egg salad, some vegetables, and cantaloupe for dessert. Renee would have taken extra heat at the staff show for serving a healthy meal like that, but the girls seemed content with the food and sang in orderly manner after the tables had been cleared. They even carried a melodious tune and harmonized. It was all very controlled—there was no organized chaotic craziness.

After lunch, the camp director crammed Toni and me into a golf cart and took us on a detailed tour of camp. Toni sat in front while I bounced around in back, facing backward. She pointed out two miles of shoreline, including a full lake at the far end of the grounds. Horses roamed in a pasture and there were buildings scattered throughout the camp. It was run down compared to the boys camp and it was apparent that a lot of physical work would be needed to bring it back into top condition. The director said that times had changed and her rigid way of running the camp was considered outdated. Her enrollment had consistently been 120 until the last several years. She showed us nearly every inch of the camp, and I was sure that she saw us as the perfect ones to take over and restore her beloved camp to its former glory.

We said our goodbyes, shook hands again, and headed back to the boys camp. Toni told me she loved the camp, and so did I. We sent the camp director a thank you note the next day and let her know that we were ready to take over—with her help. We offered to work with her for two summers, pointing toward ownership after that. She had all but offered us the camp during our tour, so Toni and I both knew that our search was over before it ever began.

What a beautiful setting! The girls camp was every bit as pretty as the boys camp. I'd been to two other boys camps for athletic meets when I was a camper, but I'd never really paid any attention to their setting, and I really had no opinion about the looks of other camps or the philosophies of their directors. I had always just looked at my camp as the standard bearer for all camps, and I'd always considered Lou to be the Master of All Campers, including campers from other places. That meant that since girls camps did indeed exist, I had also assumed that Lou was the master of all girl campers, as well.

· · ·

My attitude at camp immediately became more positive. I was excited about becoming a camp director and worked hard the last two weeks. I didn't want the campers, and especially Lou and Renee, to remember me as someone who had hung on too long. It turned out just the opposite, and Lou and Renee spent extra time teaching me all sorts of behind-the-scenes director information.

Bob, the assistant maintenance man, known as The Colonel of the Urinal, was spending his second summer at camp. He and I became friends, and I mentioned to him that one day I might own a camp, promising that I'd let him know if it ever happened. I had also checked with Lou first to make sure it was fine with him. Lou said there was no chance for Bob to advance at the boys camp, and it would be a good opportunity for Bob.

Toni and I anxiously waited for a response—but when it came, it wasn't the one we had expected. The director of the girls camp said that she wasn't ready to commit to us, but thanked us for dropping by for a look. It was short, but not sweet, and it came as a hard blow to both of us. I had been so sure that our search was over.

It was puzzling. She had practically offered us the camp during our golf cart ride. Toni and I were willing to spend two summers under her wing, gaining valuable on-the-job experience while I continued to teach and coach during the off-season. However, all of our plans had been shot down by one terse letter. The camp director simply wasn't ready for us—or for anyone, for that matter.

I called her a few days later, hoping that she might have reconsidered, but she told me that she had other family members involved with ownership, and they weren't ready for her to sell. She did say that she'd get back to us if anything changed, but encouraged us to keep searching for another camp.

I spoke with Dad and he recommended I take a position at the junkyard. He said I could earn a decent salary and take off for a few days if a camp possibility arose. After all, teaching and coaching wouldn't allow me much time to search for a camp.

Lou encouraged me to work with Dad, save money, and keep looking for the right camp. He let me know how disappointed he was that the girls camp hadn't worked out, but he told me to stick with my search, since it might take a few years.

Blake wasn't happy to accept my resignation. I could tell he felt let down, but he gave me a full endorsement on my quest to find a summer camp. It was lousy of me to give him only two weeks to find a replacement, but Blake was a decent guy and I appreciated his encouragement. I told him that I was going to miss the students and the school atmosphere.

He told me, "You would have been excited to take on the coaching promotions I had lined up for you."

 Campingly Yours

I said, "Don't tell me about it. It's hard enough moving on."

Our final conversation ended when Blake told me that he had to go, because he needed to hire a new geography teacher who could locate the school.

• • •

My final days at boys camp were over.

"I was here in '77, '77, '77. I was here in '77, where is '76?"

I stood for fifteen years, with two omissions before my final bow in '61. As the effigy burned that last night, my mind drifted to the past. I visualized a nerdy kid with a mask, Sherman using me as a flotation device, The Flash lining one past the left fielder, The Flash hoisted onto shoulders, Lou and my brother standing in the distance as I caught a curveball, staring at those cobwebs, wanting to go home, The Bulk always a step ahead, Snarl's farewell speech, Moose's never really losing his mother, smoke rising up from the ridge, learning where those staff members had gone on my first canoe trip, The Vacuum not taking over camp, the Merry Fairy House, buying Supplecheck whiskey with a beer chaser, my $90 salary, all those U.N. Day rivalries, Jack's wisdom, the multitude of friends I'd made, Sherman's mom placing a ball in his glove, a tattered Ramona being given a second chance, Lou and his wife Renee eating Mom's kugel, my brother splicing the film, and knowing that Dad's fondness of Lou had been good enough for me.

During the closing ceremony, before everyone stepped outside, Lou gave me the honor of delivering the counselor farewell speech:

Sometimes I get embarrassed when I have something serious to say.

It's hard for me to express myself on a topic such as today.

Campers, I hope I can relate to you and make you understand,

that it is your presence and no one else's that makes our boys camp the finest in the land.

The staff is indebted to you campers for the great summer we've had.

You gave us many emotions; you made us angry, you made us glad.

And tomorrow when you board the bus, you'll make us very sad.

In my fifteen summers at boys camp, I've seen what camp can do.

It has changed both campers and counselors; I know it has changed me, and

many of you.

I've witnessed introverts gain self-confidence, and unhappy losers develop sportsmanship.

I've seen those who once hated the outdoors beg to go on trips.

I've seen non-athletes learn to hit a ball and swim that extra lap.

And watched athletes make lanyards and learn to use stars as a map.

But most important, I've witnessed men and boys learn to live, work, and play,

and achieve cooperation and understanding in a manner unique in the world today.

Whether you know it or not, campers, your problems become our concern.

And although we can't always solve them, through our attempts we can surely learn.

The differences that do occur, that cause you anger and make you feel alone,

should only be solved verbally, not by fighting, or casting stones.

And for those who insist on fighting, maybe we should build them cells,

so they can leave the rest of us be and fight among themselves.

As the summer comes to a close, remember your boys camp friends.

Remember we created unity, to form a lasting blend.

When you are home and your friends ask you where you have been,

just tell them, well, I was in heaven, and I hope to go back again.

 **Campingly Yours**

• • •

Goodbye, boys camp; goodbye, Lou and Renee; so long, Vacuum; keep saving the land, Wolf; a shove back to you, Snarl; hang high, cobwebs; sweet tears, Dea Quay; smooth sailing, Flash; need to learn more from you, Jack; take it slow, Crash and Binder; thanks for all those summers, Bulk; thanks for everything, Supplecheck; see ya around, Leb; stay close to the pier, Sherman; no need to visit camp, Mom and Dad; no need to cry, Cubs Kid. Somebody throw a key log in for me. Keep those fires burning, campers, and soon you'll be returning. So long, Master of All Campers; and hello, girls camp someday, wherever you may be.

Campingly Yours

23
Heading Home

When I was young, most kids looked forward to their birthdays and the holidays when they'd receive all the latest toys, plastic guns, government-issued fighting men, or the slickest transistor radio Panasonic had to offer. Kids couldn't wait to rip the wrapping. Overindulgence was the rule as parents battled their neighbors and relatives for the top gift-giving trophy.

Birthday girls would go to school wearing the latest and cutest outfits and jewelry, and birthday boys would show off their Swamp Fox book or BB gun. Most kids fit into that category, but not my brother and me. For every occasion to be celebrated, we received several bona fide, purely authentic, American-backed government savings bonds—with the numbers $25, $50, or sometimes even $100 printed vividly on those rectangular notes. Also printed on the lower left side of each was the name of the donor. Thanks, Grandmas Anna and Fannie, and Grandpas Sig and Jake. Thanks, Uncle Louie. Thanks, Aunt Thelma and Aunt Lucille. Thanks, Uncle Calvin, Uncle Lee, and thanks, Dad, for starting that tradition.

Mom made sure my brother and I sent notes out right away or made a personal call of thanks, but we hardly had a chance to look those bonds over before Dad put them in a safety box for us. My brother and I had no idea where that safety box was located; The Flash assumed it was somewhere in the basement. Dad said not to worry about the bonds, since they wouldn't mature to their face value for several years. My brother had told me that the word mature was supposed to refer to the time of our first shave, but Dad's bonds seemed to carry a whole new meaning. Dad also warned us that the bond-giving tradition would probably last through our high school years.

Toni and I were welcomed back to St. Joe with open arms, and Dad reunited me with the boys at the junkyard. He assigned me to work outside moving steel, and he watched to see how long it would take me to develop permanently black fingernails. The main core of guys was still with Dad and the same customers kept coming in—a testimonial to the fact that Dad was still king of the area junk world. I noticed that Mom and other people no longer called it the junkyard. It had become a scrap yard or an iron and metal yard—but I always thought Dad was happier with *junk*.

Sometimes it was hard to read Dad, and I couldn't tell if he was hoping I'd like the junkyard well enough to stay. I became pretty entrenched with the lifestyle, and the pay was higher than teaching. The men at the yard treated me as if I was the heir apparent, and Dad taught me about the behind-the-scenes business, banking, and even how to lose money on stock market options.

Burlington Northern was my first fiasco. I heard Dad talking to a steel salesman from Manhattan, Kansas, who told Dad that if he invested in nothing else in life, he should buy stock in a company called Nucor. That was my first stock tip, and I'd heard it accidentally.

Dad encouraged me to buy a home, since he said that renting was a waste of money and time—but why had he brought up the subject? Did he want me to feel settled in and forget about becoming a camp director? Maybe he wanted me to become the next king of the junkyard. I couldn't read him. It was time to discuss my future; it was time to have an adult talk with Dad.

After work, Dad and I headed to the driving range. I rarely played golf, but it was fun watching him hit an occasional good shot. He was constantly trying new swings and was never content. No matter how poor his shot, he never got upset, and I'd never heard him say a swear word—not one, ever.

I asked why he thought I should buy a house, and how I'd save money if I bought a house.

"And how can I buy a house without a savings account?" I added. "I'll need to save as much money as possible for a down payment on a camp."

Dad grinned his seal of approval at my comment about saving money for a camp. That grin still got to me, and it especially got to me at that moment.

"I'm relieved to hear that you still have the desire to seek your dream," he said. "You know my dream was to be a writer, but I ended up in the junkyard. My dad needed my help, and I never left."

The next morning we headed to the bank, where Dad took me to the mysterious safety box—which killed my brother's long-standing basement theory. A lady attendant asked for Dad's signature, although their conversation was on a first-name basis. Everyone seemed to know Dad. Maybe the bank gal frequented the junkyard.

Dad helped her pull the box out from the vault and then we went into a small room with a desk and a door lock. Dad opened the box in a Silas Marner fashion and I gazed in anticipation of magical findings—jewels, sparkling diamonds, wads of thousand-dollar bills? No, there was nothing like that. Nothing shiny appeared. In fact, there didn't seem to be much there at all.

Dad proudly displayed his marriage license, a 1938 coin proof set he'd won in a poker game, a pair of tarnished Tiffany cuff links, several oversized one-dollar bills, a 1930s Missouri University degree, and an early 1900s bill of sale for the junkyard. Wow, that was pretty good stuff, but why did he need to pay for a bank box to store those items?

Finally, Dad pulled out a large pile of envelopes bundled in a rubber band—all of our U.S. savings bonds. He said he wasn't sure what would have happened if he'd ever lost them, so he kept them in the safety deposit box. There were a lot of bonds—more than I remembered receiving. I knew that I hadn't sent that many thank you notes.

Dad lined them up on the table and we added the total, reading each relative listed and the year of the gift. When we were done, there was $8,025 in bonds. Yikes! That was the equivalent of a year of teaching, all in one swoop!

Then Dad threw down an additional batch of notes. The donors were all marked *Mom and Dad*. They'd matched each bond we'd been given over the years. I was looking at $16,050 I never knew existed! Dad recommended that I spend half on a house, a little on Nucor, and let the rest ride.

One month later, we purchased a brand new three-bedroom home with a nice yard for Ramona and a cute baby's room. Toni was pregnant—soon there would be four.

The American Camping Association published a book listing all of its members. I scoured the Wisconsin, Michigan, and Minnesota listings, made forty or so calls, and came up with three promising leads. Each director asked me to visit in early May, so I took a week off and drove to the North Woods to see two girls camps and one boys camp. I wasn't particularly looking for a boys camp, but it seemed premature to be picky.

All three directors were gracious and each camp displayed a unique beauty. Unfortunately for me, all three directors were looking for a full-time employee without making any commitment to the future. One camp director offered me the equivalent of a teacher's salary and a winterized cabin on the campgrounds. The job entailed recruiting campers and staff, winter mailings, spring maintenance, and being the head counselor during camp time. If I'd been single with no obligations, I would have quickly grabbed that opportunity to get my foot in the door.

I drove to the north central part of Wisconsin on a random search and literally knocked on camp doors. Only a few of the directors were around, and none of them could offer me any future opportunities. I felt a bit like Barney Fife selling vacuums, minus the bow tie.

As I was heading out, I noticed a boys camp sign and figured I had nothing to lose. No one was around except for a maintenance man. He mumbled that he'd heard a nearby girls camp was being sold—he thought it was to a real estate company. That maintenance man turned out to be a pretty noteworthy someone.

I located the maybe-for-sale camp and walked the grounds uninvited, but I didn't find anyone. The leaves were ankle high, with fallen branches scattered about. The roofs were full of pine needles, screens had been pushed through, and the sailboats, two ski boats, a truck, and loads of tables and chairs were crammed into various buildings. The lake had patches of ice with snow still on its banks, old cobwebs hung everywhere, and there was a beautiful 1920s Cape Cod log home in the middle of the camp with a full lake view.

That maybe-for-sale camp was all I could think about as I drove home. I stopped several times to make phone calls, but each call went unanswered. Those cobwebs were what did it for me; I had to somehow make contact with the owner.

Missouri summers were typically long, hot, and humid, but even more so for me that summer. Toni's pregnancy was on target for October, we regularly attended birthing classes, and all of it was foreign to me. I bought a small catcher's mask for our upcoming arrival in anticipation of having a boy.

Working with Dad was a daily pleasure and it enhanced what I already knew about him. He was a god to all of the area junk dealers, new steel salesmen, battery haulers, copper plants, and small-time thieves. It was Dad's world, and I liked it. He also liked his world and never complained about not becoming a journalist. I didn't mind heading to work six days a week, but my goal wasn't iron and metal. My mind was occupied with the girls camp. I finally made contact with the owner a week after my first visit to the camp. I explained my situation, and she told me there was a possibility of working something out.

That was all she said—no details—but she told me to contact her in the fall after the camp season. The last time I was home during the summer, my mind often drifted to what was happening at the boys camp—but things had changed. All I could think about now was the arrival of the baby and making a phone call in the fall.

24

Friends Are a
Special
Commodity

For most people, a home is the biggest purchase of their lives, and having a baby, especially the first baby, is the most exciting event in a couple's life. Those are magical experiences, forever memories. That should have been enough for me, but not at that time in my life.

The camp director said she'd be willing to sell the camp to me, although a local real estate company had made her a solid offer. However, if I could beat that offer, she preferred to see her place continue as a camp. Then she told me the price, take it or leave it. I had only guessed what a camp would cost, but when I found out the exact amount—gulp!

I was told to hire a Wisconsin lawyer, so I contacted Napoleon in Milwaukee who had been my counselor when I was fourteen years old. He was thrilled to help and referred me to Phil, a senior partner in his firm.

Phil was very professional and exuded the utmost integrity. Although lawyer jokes have been plentiful over the years, none of those jokes could have applied to Phil. He explained all

Campingly Yours

sorts of lingo to me, since he could tell I was a novice. Tax talk, forming a particular type of corporation, and proper insurance and liability coverage were just a small part of my foreign language lesson. Dad let me use his phone at work, since Phil called often.

Phil drafted a thirty-page offer to purchase, and most of it read like an extension to my foreign language lesson. Dad looked it over, but even he was a little perplexed. He reminded me that he'd only bought their house, a few cars, and two dogs in his lifetime. I was pretty sure Dad understood the language more than he admitted, but the price seemed overwhelming for both of us. How was I ever going to pull it off?

Negotiations went back and forth as the number of pages in the purchase agreement kept growing. The lawyers told me it was important to have all the details exact, but I really didn't know enough to have an opinion. I just wanted to sign and be done with the haggling.

A close friend from camp handled all of the accounting projections and worked closely with my lawyers. It wasn't long before I received my first bill—another gulp—and Phil and the accountant were both giving me a friendship break on it!

Speaking of bills, it was also time for the baby to arrive. How could I have made it on my teacher's salary—lawyer and accountant bills, a mortgage, baby expenses, gas, electric, water, the vet for Ramona, health insurance, groceries, car payment, auto gas, and other fun surprises? I wondered if everyone had the same kinds of bills.

My junkyard salary was decent, but not that much higher than the year before. I kept thinking about what Farb had taught me, somewhat in passing. He had a master's degree in business and was working at a bank in Chicago.

"Flash," he said, "hang in there, and remember that *possession is nine-tenths of the law.*"

I wasn't exactly sure what he meant, but I was hoping it was a good thing.

A nurse threw scrubs and a mask my way and sternly told me to put them on in a hurry. Both grandmothers-to-be were in the waiting room as I darted into the delivery room. Toni, two nurses, and I were awaiting the arrival of our first child—but no doctor.

All those baby classes had left me with little confidence and for the first time, I realized why husbands were asked to boil water. Then suddenly, the baby's head was coming out! I decided to forgo any boiling of water for holding Toni's hand.

The doctor popped in just as the baby popped out. No hours of labor had been needed; the baby was simply born. I looked closely, twice—and verified that it was a girl!

There were several wonders of the world, manmade and natural, but seeing that baby being born, slipping into the world so peacefully, opening eyes not yet smart enough to see, suddenly crying for help and assuming there *were* helpers, jiggling her hands and feet in no particular order, and settling into the arms of a father she hadn't picked was truly a wonder to me. That sequence of events was a life-changing awakening. Other people could have the pyramids, the Grand Canyon, and Victoria Falls. The birth of our little girl was the most amazing wonder of the world as far as I was concerned. And the genuine U.S. savings bonds began to pour in for Abigail.

The camp owner's lawyer and Phil battled it out for two months. What if some of the small detailed stuff had ruined the deal? My lifelong career was at stake! I knew that twenty years down the road, I was going to kick myself if some leaky septic tank had canceled the negotiations. I was too nervous and probably acted in haste when I called Phil, claiming that the price was fine and so was everything else. Phil claimed that he might work another $20,000 off the price and encouraged me to be patient. He was more than just a smart lawyer—he was also a father and he told me he'd take care of things.

Most everyone said the girls camp was a bad deal. They tried to reason with me, telling me that the price was too high, the camp needed a lot of work, and the enrollment was only at thirty-five. They said I wouldn't be able to make a living and would go bankrupt. Most everyone said to wait—and that something else might come along. Most everyone said don't do it—except Mom, Dad, and Lou. And those three were good enough for me.

Phil called and said he needed $10,000. My heart sank, thinking that was his fee, but he congratulated me, exclaiming that the camp owner had signed the papers, so I needed to send the money right away for the deposit. I had $2,000 saved from work, so it was time to grab Dad and head for the safety box—and there they were, $8,000 in U.S. savings bonds. All those years of birthday and holiday disappointments had finally paid off. The cumulative gift of joy from all of my relatives prompted me to pause for a moment to say thanks—and to say thanks to Mom and Dad for matching those bonds.

Thirty-five campers wouldn't be enough to sustain a camp program and I was soon to have a large mortgage. Interest rates were at more than fourteen percent; no bank would consider me, so Phil negotiated for the owner to carry an adjustable loan at a lower rate for twenty-five years. I wasn't clear what all of that meant, but Phil reassured me that it was the best—and only—way for me to take possession. At that point, I had no idea how or where I was going to come up with the remaining down payment, and I'd need to increase the enrollment somehow, some way. It also was time to make the announcement that the camp was changing hands.

• • •

Toni and I flew to Chicago, rented a car, and drove to a suburban Sheraton, where the big announcement would take place. The camp owner had arranged everything and had sent notices to everyone connected with her camp. I also made a few calls to my camp friends from the Chicago area, but I didn't want anyone to feel obligated. I was nervous, had no speech planned, and I had no idea how many people were going to show up.

We met the camp owner and she led us to a small banquet room that had already been

set up with folding chairs, sweets, coffee, and soft drinks. I hadn't thought about that sort of stuff, but the camp owner was tuned in, since she'd hosted camp get-togethers for many years. In swarmed lots of people, way more than I'd expected, including about twenty-five of the enrolled campers and their parents, eleven junior counselors, several alumni, and a few recent campers and their parents.

We stood on a small stage as the camp owner quieted everyone down and introduced Toni and me. There had to have been at least a hundred people there to meet and grill us, and they went after us with an overwhelming array of questions.

The tone of some of their questions wasn't all that comforting. How would we be able to run a camp with such a small enrollment? What improvements were we going to make? What did we know about running a camp? What did we know about girls, since they'd heard I had only been at a boys' camp? Since we were from a small town, how would we handle big city girls? Were we firm in taking over the camp or would their daughters be left with no place to go in June?

After all the effort to find a camp—that camp—I was left standing in front of that gathering, feeling small. Maybe the naysayers had been right in predicting disaster.

I tried answering each question with a positive response, but I knew I was getting beat up, and I felt bad that I'd put Toni in front of everyone, too. Then, in the middle of that question-and-answer debacle, in came a posse of people.

One of them yelled, "Right on, Flash!"

It was Rooster, and the room soon became inundated with people from my boys camp past. I fought back tears as Little Tom's parents, The Cubs Kid, my accountant, Napoleon, and The Vacuum followed Rooster into the room. Little Tom's parents knew practically everyone in the room and they spread the good word about Toni and me. Then Lou and Renee walked in, accompanied by Sherman's mom—and I pretty much lost it. After a few moments, the room quieted down again and the questions resumed, but their tone wasn't as harsh, and I was asked one question that I could answer with a solid affirmative.

"Yes, there will be camp in June, whatever the numbers."

One of the fathers then took the podium. He had a gruff voice that matched his south Chicago mannerisms. He said that two of his daughters had attended camp the previous year and that his third daughter was almost ready to start. He let everyone know that he was connected to iron and metal people in Chicago and he'd had them check out my dad's junkyard in Missouri. He said he never heard a single bad word about the guy who owned that junkyard.

The gruff-voiced parent then added, "Junk dealers always have enemies, but not that guy in Missouri, and if this young man is anything like his dad, that's good enough for me."

He firmly announced that his daughters would be returning to the girls camp in June. I glanced to the back of the room, the same glance I'd made many times over the years at the boys camp, and I saw Lou looking at me with a grin. It was almost Dad's grin.

• • •

Having only thirty-five campers was a pretty good reason for some of those parents to be suspicious about the camp's viability. I obsessively went over the operating figures. Renee sent me materials about food expenses, menus, and an expenditure list for activity supplies and office materials. She was most insightful and really had a tight handle on the boys camp budget. Lou sent me staff orientation information, a staff-hiring guide, general information they sent out during the year to parents, and some recruiting tips. Lou and Renee were both helpful, and it was apparent that they wanted me to succeed. All I could do was thank them, as I had nothing to give in return.

The meeting at the Sheraton turned out to be a big success, despite my early frustration, and it was nice of those friends to show up with their moral support. They turned the tide, and I wasn't sure what would have happened without their support. All I could do was thank them, as I had nothing to offer in return.

The reunion with Sherman's mom was especially sweet. She said Sherman had often mumbled the name *Flash*. I told her that I often thought of Sherman. I thought about when he'd hit that ball and ran to the base, and when the ball landed squarely in his glove for the first time—his happy expression was a permanent fixture in my memory. Sherman had taught me that not all children have it easy, and his mom had showed me that not all parents have it easy.

Sherman's mom wished me luck with the camp and thanked me for everything. I told her that maybe we should just thank each other, and said goodbye.

Several parents at the reunion gave us other names to contact, and it was time to hit the road and visit with the prospects. Toni and I left Abigail and Ramona with my parents on several different weekends so we could meet with those new families. We stayed in inexpensive hotels, rented compact cars, and ate sparingly. I wore a sport coat with a button-down shirt and no tie, and Toni dressed in a nice pantsuit.

Most of the parents lived in large homes in upscale neighborhoods, but dressed rather casually. The home visits were actually enjoyable, and the parents got to know Toni and me. Home visits also gave us a chance to get a read on each potential camper. I was given a movie to show from the previous camp owner; it was old, but the film never broke. I kept things rather homey and tried to stay away from sounding like a salesman.

On one particular visit, a grandfather advised me never to use the words "to be honest" when referring to something about camp. He told me that using those words in a sales pitch implied that maybe I was holding back something dishonest. He told me to substitute those words with "frankly." I told him I'd remember that, and then he gave me a deposit for his granddaughter.

That winter and spring, we visited at least thirty families, all from referrals, and twenty-one girls signed up. Fifty-six and counting—I was hoping to find a few more, but at least there were enough to run a program. I still wondered if Lou had purposely had his film break. It sure worked with my brother.

···

I called the Colonel of the Urinal and told him I needed a maintenance man. Bob had been wondering if he'd ever hear from me and was thrilled to accept the job. He'd take a leave of absence from his truck driving position and spend four months at the camp. With fifty-six campers and one employee, it was time to hire more staff.

I flew to Chicago to meet with several seventeen-to-twenty-year-olds who were former campers. They needed a lot of coaxing, since they were pretty skeptical about the camp's future. I had them write down all of the programs and traditions they loved about the camp and to suggest any changes they thought might make it stronger. They were a great group of girls and I could tell they would be an invaluable help to me.

Those girls brought back memories of my first staff orientation and the new counselor who told me I had an advantage growing up at camp. Those girls had grown up with the program and would know all the ins and outs, so I needed them to give it a try. They indicated that change wouldn't be hard; it would actually be exciting. They knew each other well and I could see it was going to be an all or nothing, make it or break it situation. The girls were great, the meeting went well, and I asked them to let me know as soon as possible. As we said goodbye, the girls told me to call a woman named Doc.

While in Chicago, one of the girls gave me a name of an interested family from Flossmoor, a far south suburb. I called the family, they invited me for dinner, and we discussed camp— and I used the word *frankly* a couple times. I let them know that frankly, I hadn't spent a day at the girls camp and only had boys camp experience, but I was going to do the best I could to help their daughter have a wonderful summer. The Flossmoor mother served a great chocolate cake, I had two pieces, and she signed up her daughter— fifty-seven.

The camp owner informed me that she wasn't going to stay during the summer. Toni and I would be on our own—no former director's guidance, just us. I followed up all potential camper leads and hit the road several weekends that spring. I continued working every day at the junkyard and stayed up late working on camp programs and the budget. It was expensive to travel just to see one family at a time, and only two more campers signed up out of five individual visits. It didn't matter how many numbers I crunched, there was no way the camp could make a profit that first summer. I'd put down $10,000 to date, but I needed a lot more before the closing date on June 1.

The junior counselors all came through. They were excited to be part of a new regime and I was happy to have them. Several senior staff committed as well, bringing the old-time staff member total to fifteen. Five new counselors were needed to complete the roster, plus a trip leader and a nurse. I also needed to find two cooks and two kitchen helpers. It was all a little unnerving and there did not seem to be enough hours in the day, but it was also incredibly exciting. Find the down payment, locate five nice girls for staff, work five days a week at the junkyard, head out on weekends to recruit, change Abigail's diapers whenever I was around, and mail out information for parents and staff.

Mailings to parents included medical forms, equipment lists, information about transportation to and from camp, visitation weekend, and a general questionnaire. The staff received contracts, arrival information, and a detailed letter outlining what to expect. I also used a lot of the literature Lou and Renee had sent out over the years.

I called Doc, and it turned out that she had been waiting to hear from me. She had several PhDs and was a professor in South Dakota. Doc had spent twenty years at the camp as waterfront director and was quite willing to help us out. She sounded businesslike on the phone, but she let me know that she'd help wherever and whenever she was needed. Her salary was three times that of any senior counselor, but I told her I'd see her in June. It was all exciting and a bit overwhelming, but I still needed the remaining down payment by June 1—yikes!

I placed an advertisement at Missouri University, seeking counselors and cooks. A sorority cook called and was interested, and she had a friend who might also like the opportunity. A tennis player also called, so I headed to Columbia that weekend and hired all three. I had no idea what to offer a cook, so I contacted Renee. Her head cook had been at camp for years and was highly compensated. Maybe that was why the coffee cake carried the cook's name. The sorority cook told me her weekly salary, so I upped it twenty percent and offered the same amount to her friend. Fifty-nine campers had enrolled and I was seeking two kitchen helpers, four senior staff, and a nurse—but I still had to come up with the down payment. It all felt magical to me.

• • •

In mid-April, the camp director called and gave me the bad news that excessive snow and ice had collapsed the theater building. The news that she hadn't been carrying snow insurance brought me down, as well. Phil had explained the basics of insurance to me, but he never mentioned anything about snow insurance. The original contract became null and void, and Phil sent the camp owner an amended contract to compensate me for the theater. She wasn't happy, and I couldn't blame her for being upset, but Phil insisted that I shouldn't be forced to pay for a theater that was only a heap on the ground.

A nurse from my hometown answered my ad and took the job, and two college girls called for positions, as well. They'd heard about the openings from boyfriends who attended a neighboring boys camp. Their references checked out, so I hired them.

I had promised the campers and staff members that there would be camp in June, but by late April, I still had no signed contract. What if the camp owner didn't sign the new agreement? She had a real estate company that would buy her place, and they'd probably tear everything down anyway, so a collapsed theater wouldn't matter to them. I would have been obligated to pay the staff, since they were under contract—and what was worse, I would have lied to all those families.

The theater was on the ground, I had no signed contract, my reputation as a camp owner was at stake, a real estate company could subdivide the camp with condos and remove years

 Campingly Yours

of memories, and I didn't have enough money for a down payment. I thought about my years at the boys camp, of everyone's time spent there, and all of the history Lou and Renee had created.

What if some company had demolished the buildings of the boys camp and put in a parking lot and a bunch of cheaply-made condos? People would have driven in without the help of The Binder, jumped into a lake with no Pumpkins, tossed a ball around with no Vacuum, capsized a boat with no Flash rescue, and the campfire area probably would have been bulldozed to create a condo basement. The rec hall and lodge would have been wiped out, and all those funny skits and crazy songs obliterated. Condo dwellers probably wouldn't have attempted pudding and whipped cream or have ever heard of a beanie weenie.

I envisioned Lou in the far distance, looking at me—no grin, and tears rolling down his face. I thought about all the alumni coming back to visit their camp. Condos would have destroyed all of their memories.

Sure, things were looking bleak. Without a signed agreement, the girls camp would have become a mass of destroyed memories. Life was all relative, and I took the attitude that many people had it much worse. Hospitals were full, handicapped parking places were full, people lost friends and relatives to war, fathers stood in unemployment lines with hungry children to feed, poverty prevailed in many countries—but all I was trying to do was take over a girls camp. What a lucky guy I was! I had a goal and a purpose.

25

Everyone Needs a Purpose

As much as I hated to sell our house, I realized it was the only logical choice. **Toni** and I put the house on the market in early May, with the thought of heading to the girls camp later in the month. We had an immediate offer—$7,000 more than we'd paid! With $8,000 already in equity, minus the selling expenses, we had $13,000, which increased the camp down payment total to $23,000.

Dad and I met at the driving range and between swings we talked about the remaining down payment. Dad insisted that whatever I did, I shouldn't take on a partner. At all costs, he suggested that I do it myself, with no partner.

We headed to the clubhouse and ordered a vodka gimlet. I had introduced that drink to Dad, and for some reason it was special when we had one together. We also ordered oysters on the half shell, which Dad had introduced to me.

That gimlet-oyster get-together was extra special. We discussed the down payment, and Dad knew that I'd accumulated $23,000. He reminded me that the camp owner had already collected deposits and payments in advance for thirty-five campers, which we concluded would probably be around $20,000. Next, Dad pointed out that I had twenty-four deposits and several advance payments, which I told him added up to another $18,000.

He slurped an oyster and calmly told me to give all the deposit money back to the camp owner, including the portion she'd taken in, and add it to the down payment. That seemed like a pretty simple plan and it had never occurred to me that I could use her deposit money as part of the down payment. However, I wasn't sure that I could sign an agreement and simply hand back her $20,000. Our original agreement had stated that I needed a full down payment, but it never specified where the money had to originate.

It was all pretty cloudy to me, but Dad thought it was my best bet—my only bet. Even with that, however, I was still about $19,000 short.

I explained to Dad that I was going to contact several friends and try to round up whatever money I could—but Dad said, "No partners, and no obligations."

I sat there as Dad explained to me that he and Mom had discussed borrowing against his life insurance. I, of course, had no idea what he was talking about, although I was pretty sure it had nothing to do with snow insurance. He said that he had several old paid-up policies dating back to World War II and that he could borrow $20,000 against them at a rate averaging less than four percent. He explained that it was basically borrowing against his own money at a really cheap rate. The payback would be around $750 per year.

"If I get run over by a truck," he said, "Mom will receive $20,000 less on the face value of the policy, so you'd have to pay her back someday."

I was amazed. Those oysters and gimlets had somehow produced a quick $40,000! I could give the camp owner her deposit money back and then owe $750 a year against a $20,000 insurance loan. I wondered how long Dad had worked on that plan.

Next, Dad reminded me that my gross summer income would be minus all the deposits and advance payments—a total of about $38,000. He let me know that the pressure would be on to have a great summer and that I'd need the campers to spread the good word to increase enrollment as much as possible. He told me to pay all the immediate bills during the summer and then finish paying whatever bills were left over using the following year's

Campingly Yours

deposits.

He finally added, "At all costs, pay every bill, and never be a deadbeat."

I'd spent all winter trying to figure out how I could make it work, but Dad had known all along that it *would* work—and he had been one of only three people who had told me to go for it.

. . .

Phil called and once again congratulated me. The camp owner had integrity and wasn't going to sell her soul to build condos. She had signed the agreement and the price had been reduced by $15,000—but the theater was now my problem. The down payment had also been reduced by $3,000, leaving more for Mom if a truck ever found Dad. Handing the owner's deposit money back was the last loophole, but I decided not to tell Phil. He might have frowned at me, or maybe at Dad.

Mom was very supportive through the whole ordeal.

She said, "A lot of people have no purpose in life. They go through each day without asking questions and not caring if they've really made any difference. Think about Lou and Renee. They have a purpose: creating a second home for thousands of boys. Those boys can leave the city and all their so-called complications for eight weeks and head to the North Woods. No phone calls, no television, no nagging parents, no matching socks, no movies or malls—just learning to enjoy nature and one another."

She added that at Lou's camp, boys were given the opportunity to adjust, think, interact, wear old clothes, make mistakes, cry, grow, become independent, and overall, just be boys. She knew I'd had a tough few days my first summer, but she trusted Lou and Renee to guide me—and all the other boys.

"Your dad and I were impressed with Lou and Renee the very first time we met," she said. "I could tell right away that their hearts and souls were in their camp and their mission."

Then Mom looked at me, smiled, and said, "Girls have the same needs as boys—and you've just acquired the same purpose as Lou and Renee."

Mom was quite intelligent, and she had a great way with words. She lived in a small city, but she possessed big world smarts. I detected a bit of sadness when she talked about purpose. Maybe she didn't think she had fulfilled a purpose. I wasn't sure, and I possibly was reading too much into it. She had fulfilled a huge purpose for me; maybe I needed to let her know more often.

The third week in May was a genuine happy sad time. It was time to overload the car, to leave a space for Ramona, to latch the baby seat, to say a final goodbye to our house, to drive to Mom and Dad's, and then to watch them wave from their top step until we were out of sight. Their son, daughter-in-law, granddaughter, and grand-dog were driving away, headed for a big adventure. Mom and Dad were happy for me, and I was happy for them. After all, they still had each other.

26
Not Enough
Down Payment

Driving onto the camp road was a magical moment, yet I inwardly stayed reserved because the final papers had yet to be signed. Toni hopped out of the car and was anxious to see everything. It was apparent that Ramona would love camp, since she quickly darted into the woods, deer-like. We couldn't find the camp owner, so we took the liberty of walking the grounds.

The ice and snow had melted, leaving fallen branches and leaves everywhere, and I knew that each spring would require a huge cleanup. The theater building was sitting in a pile on the ground, every building needed a thorough cleaning inside and out, and it was obvious that the raking and overall ground maintenance could take several weeks. The word *overwhelming* was taking on new meaning, yet the experience was still magical to me.

We finally met the camp owner as she pulled into the driveway. She was happy to see us and showed us our quarters, the cook's cabin. She was congenial but businesslike as she asked us to leave everything in place until the final papers had been signed on June 1. The staff was due to arrive on June 14 and the campers would arrive a week later. Office work alone would take up most of each day and with all the outside preparation and a building on the ground—yikes! The word *magical* had been joined by the phrase *nerve-wracking*.

The cook's cabin had a shower, heater, cubbyhole bedroom, and a small sitting room. Ramona was fine, but the rest of us were a bit cramped. Since we had no access to the office, we made our calls from town and did our paperwork in the cabin. I could tell that the camp owner was uptight about us touching anything. I assumed she was worried about liability should something go wrong. I asked for her permission to rake leaves, and though she was reluctant, she agreed. That set the stage for the week.

I raked leaves from dawn to dusk while Toni organized the paperwork. That included organizing camper medical and personality forms, making a Rolodex file of addresses and numbers, creating menus, reviewing activity needs, and making master lists of everything we needed to complete before the arrival of the campers. Lou and Renee's information was very detailed and proved to be an invaluable help for our initial organization. Toni and I thanked Lou and Renee; that was the best we could offer.

I contacted a local construction company to repair the theater. They said it would take two to three weeks, so I told them to start on June 2nd. I never quite felt that everything was fine; I just wanted June 1 to arrive and the camp owner to take back her deposits. Phil was flying in that day from Milwaukee.

Finally, leaves were stacked four feet high and the piles lined the entire camp, since I wasn't allowed to use the camp truck to haul them to the dump. The wind blew off the lake every day, causing the once-raked leaves to scatter. I felt as if I was raking upstream.

Our cabin heater didn't work, so we wrapped Abigail in extra blankets and put her on our bed. Ramona loved frolicking in the leaves, running in the woods, and getting her feet wet in the lake in the cold May weather. We had little contact with the camp owner. She was packing and made it clear that she wasn't available to assist us with the startup process. Through all the obstacles, the experience remained magical to me—and to Ramona, as well.

Phil hopped off a commuter plane wearing a three-piece suit and carrying a briefcase. I picked him up at the Rhinelander airport and together we headed to meet the camp owner and her lawyer. Phil was concerned about several points and told me to let him do all the talking. He embodied charm, brains, and organization, but also managed to be very father-like in his manner. I put my complete trust in him and kept my fingers crossed that using the deposits as part of the down payment wouldn't destroy his trust in me.

Phil greeted the camp owner, her lawyer, and her accountant. They were all well-dressed and businesslike, and I felt totally out of my element sitting at that corporate table. Phil was correct in having me keep quiet. He had several points to change on the agreement, all in my favor, and her side agreed to everything. Then it was time for the deposit check to be written—my moment of truth.

Would the camp owner be upset that I didn't have the full down payment and nix the deal? Would that cause Phil to lose faith in me? An overwhelming emptiness washed over me. I sat numbly wondering if the last two years had simply been wasted. The camp owner would sue me for false promises and claim that I'd wasted her time and money. Then all the camp parents would tie me up and swing me from a tree. They'd hold a public mocking of me while their daughters threw pudding and whipped cream at me until my body was completely covered. Finally, a Snarl-like father would put an old catcher's mask on me and they'd leave me dangling forever with the very items that had made me hate camp that fateful first day.

Suddenly, Phil shook me out of my reverie by saying, "Congratulations, camp owner!"

She had turned over her deposits—and my down payment was complete. It had all happened while I was dangling from the tree! A huge weight was suddenly lifted from my shoulders, although a heavier weight had just been added—The Girls Camp.

I thanked Phil profusely as we headed back to the airport. He told me that he'd put together my bill, but not to worry about paying him all at once. He knew that I'd take care of it. Phil had a lot of father in him.

I asked Phil, "How did it turn out to be so easy to get her to give back her deposits? Why didn't she complain or say anything?"

Campingly Yours

Phil just smiled and said, "Your dad called me last week. He said that if any problems arose with turning over her deposits, he'd wire the money and I could send the deposit money back to him the next day."

Phil told me that he'd already discussed it with the camp owner's lawyer and they were fine with having the camp owner keep her deposits. Again I'd been worrying for nothing—not knowing that Dad had quietly taken care of any potential problem. Phil knew, as well. Those two liked and understood each another. I, too, was a father, and I'd been given an advantage.

All I could do was silently say, "Thanks, Phil and Dad."

27

A Girls Camp Owner

Driving onto the camp road took on a whole new meaning for me yet again. I grabbed a rake and realized for the first time that I was raking my own leaves. If the feeling of owning a house for the first time had been huge, owning the girls camp was gigantic.

I sat by the lake and stared at the whitecaps. I rolled onto my back and marveled at the height of 200-year-old white pines. Squirrels were darting in and out of the oak trees and a bald eagle gently landed on a budding white birch. Ramona leaped like a deer, having the time of her life frolicking in the woods. I sat there for a long time, just staring, thinking, and appreciating, but finally it was time to get up, since there was six weeks' worth of work to do in just three. The campers were arriving all too soon. My moment of reflection was over. It was time to get to work, Flash! There was no time to waste—although I never considered that moment of reflection as wasted time.

Soon afterward, a car pulled onto the camp road—my first official visitor. A father with twin daughters hopped out and introduced himself. The girls talked a mile a minute, letting me know that they were fourteen years old and had spent several summers at the camp. I couldn't keep up with their verbal pace, but the father handed me a deposit and told me to count them in. The girls claimed that they knew everything about the camp and told me it was going to be a great summer. I became somewhat dizzy listening to their ramblings while the father rolled his eyes, lovingly saying that they'd be all mine for the summer. Judging from those twins, I could tell that there wouldn't be a dull moment at the girls camp—and they made sixty-one!

Toni, Abigail, and Ramona were fast asleep, and as usual, I lay awake, my mind racing in multiple directions. Ramona was in dog heaven; Abigail cried, ate, pooped, crawled, checked out bugs, and slept; the camp transition was pretty easy for her. Toni worked long hours at all sorts of behind-the-scenes jobs and was learning by doing. She was smart and quick, but it was hard for me to tell if she shared my emotions about the girls camp.

There were no cobwebs in our bedroom, but the doorway to the main office had plenty. I needed to make certain that they'd stay in place. The staff was due in two weeks for orientation and I wanted to make a good impression through well-organized meetings. My first newsletter needed to go out soon to show families the new format. The campers would be arriving in three weeks, and all the necessary information needed to be accurately presented.

The twins would be my first listing of campers returning. After camp, I wanted the campers to get used to rushing to the mailbox, ripping open the newsletter, and urgently checking all the camp happenings. I wanted them to get lost in those monthly newsletters and digest all the "campingly yours" gossip.

I tried to fall asleep, but continued savoring my first night of camp ownership. Scores of "what ifs" kept popping into my mind. What if I hadn't pulled into that boys camp on my way home? What if the maintenance man hadn't been around? What if Mom and Dad hadn't hit if off with Lou and Renee? What if my brother had tied his shoes? Was I a nerd wearing that catcher's mask? Was Dad a nerd?

"I think Dad is kind of nerdy, on purpose, but he has gobs of people who like and respect him…zzzzz…The camp owner is gone, so there's no one around to tell me things…Where's The Bulk? How did he have all those answers?…I need to start raking leaves at five in the morning…then hit the office and make parent calls at eight…type the newsletter…learn how to use the mimeograph machine…zzzzz…I owe Mom a letter…she had a purpose… maybe she just needs to hear that once in a while…120 newsletters to be mailed…IBM Selectric…nice machine…the junkyard never had electric typewriters…zzzzz…Jack sent some information for staff week…he's got so much to do to get his camp going, but he thought of me…zzzzz…Lou and Renee called and said, 'Congratulations, Flash.'…zzzzz… How much food had to be ordered?…What about crafts supplies?…zzzzz…Will I be going down to pick up the campers?…Are there any archery targets?…zzzzz…Where could I find some tetherballs?…Three weeks of hauling leaves out…Why didn't I hire some help…I couldn't afford help…zzzzz…Dad and Phil plotted those deposits for a week…I would have paid Dad back the day after closing…zzzzz…What if Dad wasn't so smart?…What if Mom and Dad didn't care?…I got lucky…Thanks, Dad, for that catcher's mask…you, too, Mom, since you helped buy it…zzzzz…Thanks, brother Flash for telling The Vacuum I could catch a curveball…zzzzz……..Thanks, Lou, for looking over my shoulder…over everyone's shoulder…the Master of All Campers…zzzzz…Dea Quay cried at that campfire…I'll bring him here someday…zzzz…'This camp is your camp, this camp is my camp, this girls camp was made for you and me'…and Mom and Dad…and Phil…and The Flash…and Sherman's mom…and Moose's mom…and sixty-one campers…zzzzz…"

• • •

Toni and I hustled morning, noon, and night for two weeks. It was tiring, but a fun kind of tiring, at least for me. The construction company came through and rebuilt the theater in record time.

Bob, the Colonel of the Urinal, revved in one morning on a Honda motorcycle, the first employee of the new regime. He was excited to be part of the new adventure and wasted no time hauling piles of leaves to the dump. Bob and I stayed up late reminiscing about our time together at the boys camp. I handed Bob a huge list of projects that needed to be completed before the campers arrived. Bob showed a genuine interest in the camp and I could tell that he was going to be more than just an employee. He was excited to be on the ground floor of reviving the girls camp. I got the sense that Bob and I would become close friends, and that he'd be sticking around for a long time.

The girls camp was a peaceful and serene place to work those first two weeks in June, despite all that had to be completed. The only noise was the wind off the lake, mowers now and then, workers putting up the theater, and Abigail screeching at a high pitch. With the lake bordering half the camp and acres of forest comprising the remaining boundary, the noise from all the work was minimal.

Then the time had come for the staff to arrive—twenty or so high school and college girls, most of whom knew each other from camp. Next came Doc, driving a yellow Cadillac, and the noise level rose to a fevered pitch. Doc could be heard over all twenty girls as they screamed and hugged. Abigail's loudest wails could never have outdone that staff reunion. The lake, trees, and all the ensuing acres couldn't contain the noise level. The serenity of the North Woods had just been put on hold—welcome to camp, girls staff.

Everyone was in place for orientation to begin, including the cooks, kitchen staff, and nurse. The staff had one night to get unpacked and settled, since meetings were to begin in the morning. Bob spilled his motorcycle early in the evening, and one of the girls thought that he was pretty macho, so The Colonel of the Urinal acquired a new name—Macho Bob.

Macho Bob made a campfire and we held an impromptu gathering at the center fire circle. Songs, stories, and laughter filled the evening, and I took the time to explain a new tradition, the key log ceremony. I wasn't expecting anything that night, but Macho Bob grabbed a piece of wood and threw it into the fire, thanking me for bringing him back into the camp world-- and he became a bit teary-eyed as he spoke.

Doc stood up, threw in a piece of wood, and orated for several minutes. She was very articulate as she spoke of camp, past, present, and future. She concluded by saying that only good things were in store for camp.

Other old-time staff members then joined in and expressed their hopes for a great summer and for a bright future for the camp. A new staff member then threw in a key log, saying that she already felt at home.

The old-time staff members broke into "Friends," a song that had originated at camp, as one of our college girls, Patti, strummed the chords.

"I think that I shall never see, the kind of true friend you are to me. I think that I shall never find the kind of true friendship that is yours and mine."

The girls harmonized the sweet tune with Patti, who was an accomplished musician and singer and had studied at the Berklee College of Music. Patti far surpassed Sheriff Andy Taylor; she was the real deal. I was used to rowdy songfests, but I could tell that singing would have a different flavor at the girls camp.

The girls formed a circle and sang the camp creed, which ended with "Taps," a tradition after each campfire. What a beautiful ending to an unplanned campfire. I learned that the girls camp could become quite serene, even with all those female counselors. I thought about reciting the Master of All Campers, but held back. Lou was the Master; I was just an apprentice.

• • •

I had put together a staff orientation folder loaded with information that had been sent by Lou and Jack. I incorporated what I thought would suit girls more than boys, but a good portion of the material was universal. Doc chaired several meetings, including ones about understanding campers and about staff members working together as a unit. Doc rarely used notes; she was a gifted speaker. She probably was in her fifties, but she could easily outwork the younger staff members. She was the waterfront director, but offered to write the camp newsletter during the summer with the help of camper volunteers.

Jack attended our orientation in spirit. I led a session emphasizing that there was no such thing as a bad camper. I liked group involvement, and the girls were eager to chime in. I redirected questions, as I really wanted to hear what others had to say. The small staff made it easy for me to get to know them quickly. There were no slow thinkers in the group. They all were well-educated and took a deep interest in doing what was right for the camp. They were a great bunch, full of spirit and know-how. They were willing to rake leaves, paint buildings, clean cabins, and wash windows—without complaining.

I made a point of having individual meetings in the office with staff members to let them know the importance of their roles. Dad also attended each of those meetings in spirit. He treated his employees like gold, and I wanted to be like Dad.

Doc cleaned the waterfront daily, starting at dusk. She was relentless in her effort to have the camp ready on time. She washed rowboats, cleaned sailboats, hand-sickled the tall grass and weeds, and made sure the piers were spotless. Girls who had never picked up a rake before worked furiously to load leaves onto a flatbed truck. Then they piled onto the back as Macho Bob drove them to the stump dump.

Seventeen loads were hauled on the two-ton truck to the dump by a bunch of high school and college girls. The girls had arrived at camp with make-up and brushed hair, and it was fun to watch their appearance transform into ratty hair and dirty fingernails. It was even more fun to know that they didn't care what they looked like; they were having a great time.

Meetings, work, more meetings, more work, early hours, late hours—the girls never complained. Toni and I could feel their emotions, since the staff was truly excited to be an integral part of our first summer. It was time to reward them with a night out—the first all-staff fellowship sponsored by Toni and me.

We reserved a room at a restaurant, which was a local landmark. We ordered finger food for everyone and supplied pitchers of soda pop. The girls reverted back to their "going out" clothes with combed hair and rouge. It was nice to watch them mingle and get to know each other away from the camp atmosphere. Toni and I made sure to move around to various groups. Patti brought her guitar and we sang camp songs, including "Friends." The customers and waitresses gathered around to join us.

Bill, the bartender, let me know how impressed he was with such a nice group of young ladies. We sent the junior staff back to camp, but five or six of the college girls stayed behind. They were all of age, so I innocently told Bill that I'd buy the girls a drink. I was used to going out with the boys staff, which usually meant a pitcher of beer accompanied by seven-ounce glasses—costing three dollars at most.

However, the girls requested Bill's famous ice cream drink, a Banana Banshee. Bill stared at me, and I nodded in approval. Patti strummed more songs, the girls finished their drinks, and then they all said thanks as they hopped into the van, driven by the non-drinking Macho Bob. Bill smiled as he handed me the check: $45 for seven ice cream drinks! The tip alone would have covered two pitchers of beer.

Bill shook my hand and said, "Welcome to girls camp."

Dad would have registered a formal complaint if he had known I'd paid that much for anything that had to do with ice cream. Forty-five dollars—welcome to girls night out, Flash.

· · ·

There was only one more day until the campers arrived. Toni and Doc headed to Chicago to escort the campers the following day. I gave the staff a much-deserved day off, and Macho Bob and I remained behind to finish everything we could. We hauled another large load of leaves, and several piles were still scattered throughout camp, but Macho Bob and I prioritized and figured the leaves would just have to wait.

We moved beds, furniture, boats, tables, and chairs, and tried to complete jobs the staff hadn't quite been able to get done. The staff members had worked hard, but there was just too much to accomplish with too few people. They needed their time off, and it was important for them to be fresh when the campers arrived.

Macho Bob didn't mind—he was just proud to be part of our first summer. I left Abigail with a sitter and took Macho Bob to the local pizza place for a quick bite. We returned to work until midnight or so. Good night, Macho Bob. Get some rest. See you at 5:30 a.m.

Abigail was fast asleep, with Ramona by her side. Both of them lived in a carefree world, unaware of what was about to happen. Sixty-one screaming girls were due to pile off the buses the next afternoon. It was easy for Abigail and Ramona, and I was almost envious that they had no worries. On the other hand, they had no idea of the excitement running through my veins. When those sixty-one girls piled off those buses, I'd instantly become Lou. Well, not really Lou, but I'd assume the same profession—a camp director.

Two years in the making: searching for a camp; stumbling into the boys camp and running into a maintenance man; waiting all summer to hear from the camp owner; finally getting a "yes" from the camp owner; hiring Phil; learning about legal jargon and tedious negotiations; meeting everyone at the Sheraton and promising parents that there would be camp; persuading staff members to return; recruiting new girls on weekends; buying and selling a house; borrowing against life insurance; hiring new staff members; having no snow insurance; Dad talking to Phil; signing the agreement; working dusk to dawn and then some; having the staff members arrive; seeing the Colonel become Macho; experiencing our first impromptu campfire and key log ceremony; buying ice cream drinks; hauling leaves—and it would all come together in just one more day. There was no way that I envied Abigail and Ramona as they slept peacefully.

"Good night, Mom and Dad. Thanks for everything. Camp will start tomorrow, so bring them back safely, Toni and Doc—and the Master of All Campers."

F ive-thirty came none too soon. I needed the three hours of quiet time before breakfast to catch up on the huge stack of neglected mail. I rummaged through payments and bills and came across a letter, written not so laterally in pencil, with the return address of only *Melanie.*

"Hi, my sister talked me into coming to camp. I'm not afraid. I know it will be a fun time. Can I go water skiing? See you soon, your new camper, Mel."

Wow, that letter brought back memories of my first anxieties of camp. I hoped Mel's sister would be to her what The Flash was to me. I knew I'd make it a point to find Mel right away and thank her for the letter.

Macho Bob was milling around, finishing up odds and ends. I put down the mail and tweaked my outline for the evening friendship fire. I wanted the campfire to combine spirit with a toned-down edge. The campers could go a little crazy, but they also needed to see their first key log ceremony.

The theme was "getting to know you," and several staff, including Doc, would be assigned to say a few words on the topic. I wanted the campers and staff to feel the moment and to appreciate the beautiful lakeside setting. I wanted them to grasp what I had once felt at boys camp. I wanted everyone to bleed camp; I wanted camp to run through their veins. It had happened to me, so it could happen to every one of the girls. It could even happen to Macho Bob.

Abigail and Ramona joined me in a silent moment by the lake as I thought about Lou and Renee and the influence they'd had upon me. After World War II, Lou had found land and borrowed money from Renee's family to achieve his dream of opening a boys camp. It wasn't Renee's dream; it was Lou's, but Renee had promised Lou that she'd help in any way, and she proved to be smart, caring, and devoted.

Lou had envisioned a camp that included boys from all over the world who would laugh, cry, compete, sing, play, wear old clothes, and learn to live together in a peaceful environment. Lou taught his version of right and wrong, and he ran his camp the only way he knew—his way. Although I felt he had paid special attention to me, in reality, he was really watching over all the campers. He watched over The Flash, Snarl, and even the smokers. He knew who the smokers were, but felt camp was the best place for them to eventually learn right from wrong.

Lou had made sure that no one picked on Sherman. Lou had asked Jack to speak to the staff because Jack understood the value of camping. Lou gave second chances and he valued a child's ability to improve. Lou rarely showed up in cabins; but if he did, it was because something was wrong. Lou could at times be intimidating, so no one wanted to be on his angry side. He was gentle, but a cross look from Lou was enough to set a camper back a few days. I admired Lou for doing things his way—and only his way.

I put one arm around Abigail and the other around Ramona, and we watched a bald eagle soar across the lake. I wasn't sure how I was going to run the girls camp or how the campers and staff would view me. I planned to pop into the cabins often to get to know the girls and have them feel okay about me. I didn't want to intimidate anyone. I wanted to incorporate some of what I'd learned from Lou, but not everything. Lou was a father figure and mentor to thousands of boys. It was his way, and it worked for him—but Lou's way couldn't be my way. I'd have to figure out my own way as the summer progressed. I silently thanked Lou and Renee for bringing camp into my life and for steering me into a career in camping.

Dad never intimidated anyone, and he never gave me a look of disappointment. Dad would have been a great camp director. I couldn't be totally like Lou, but I wanted to be all Dad—and both of them would be hard shoes to fill, even if they were untied.

28

And So Begins My First Camp Season

Inhe staff gathered at the entrance and practiced a welcome song traditionally sung to the campers as they got off the bus. I had my camera around my neck and waited in anticipation as the staff bubbled with excitement. The first ever campers for Toni and me were entering the camp road.

The screeching sound of the bus brakes was heavenly music to me as Toni and Doc jumped off the bus, followed by sixty-one girls. Some hugged, some screamed with joy to be back, and some looked scared to death. I probably was just as afraid, but I tried not to show it.

Doc asked everyone to head to the center fire circle for cabin assignments. Just like boys camp, counselors and their campers were called to the middle, starting with the youngest group. Everyone cheered as names were called, and each group was then whisked away to their cabin.

Mel's name was called, and I gave her a Snarl-like shove while welcoming her to camp. She laughed and shoved me back. She was kind of a tomboy and I could tell immediately that

Campingly Yours

she'd fit right in.

The cooks had set out brownies and lemonade, and the campers indulged during their tour of camp. The afternoon turned hot and I thought the girls would enjoy a short swim before dinner. Doc put on her blue tankie (one-piece bathing suit—a girls camp thing) and was ready for the onslaught. She said she'd keep a close eye on the beginners. The lake was almost two miles long and Doc probably could have lifeguarded the whole circumference. I trusted her completely.

Macho Bob and I decided to join in on the open swim and play King of the Raft. We swung girls three times and then hurled them into the lake. The campers were having fun, as were Macho and I. From the corner of my eye, I noticed a small girl sitting on a bench by herself. I swam to shore and let Macho fend for himself.

The little girl was pouting, claiming she didn't like camp. Yikes, my first homesick camper, and she was so small. I signaled for her counselor and whispered that she should bring the little girl out to the raft. Then I swam back out and rejoined Macho as girls tried in vain to push him off.

I mumbled to Macho that the little homesick girl was on her way. Macho and I tossed dozens of girls off, then they climbed back on and tried their best to push us into the water—but no go. After several minutes of domination, Macho and I declared ourselves kings of the raft. We stood on the edge, wrestler-like, with our hands in the air declaring victory.

Suddenly—poof—the little homesick camper had sneaked up behind us and pushed both the Macho man and the Flash into the water. Everyone cheered the homesick girl and several staff members on the raft raised her onto their shoulders for a victory dance. For a brief moment, I looked through that little girl and visualized my brother—and I quietly thanked Bob for not being so macho.

We served about eighty-five people at each meal, including staff members. The dining hall was a beautiful rustic wood structure, ninety feet long and forty feet wide, built in 1945, sitting just a few yards from the lake. Years of plaques and camp nostalgia covered the walls and rafters. We used ten round tables, though the building could accommodate twenty-five. The campers piled in for the first meal and they all stood for grace.

I felt compelled to say, "I once felt sorry because I had no shoes, and then I met a man who had no feet. Be seated."

Memories of Lou and my first few days of camp passed through my system.

I assumed the noise level of eighty-five girls would be pretty mild, but I was wrong. Boys were rowdy with mid- to low-pitched voices, but less than half that number of girls raised the decibel meter to a whole new level. The cooks were a little slow putting out the meal, but that was fine with me. The girls sang cabin songs, team songs, and even "John Jacob Jingleheimer Schmidt." I started "Mrs. O' Leary" and pranced around the dining hall with a bunch of staff chiming in, "Fire, Fire, Fire!" I wasn't Lou, but I sure felt as if I was dancing in his shoes.

The cooks had prepared a fantastic spaghetti dish with garlic bread, fresh vegetables, sweet potatoes, and a tossed salad. No pudding for dessert, just ice cream bars. It was obvious that the girls loved the meal, since the noise level remained high. At the boys camp, if the meal wasn't very good, the noise level decreased. The better the food, the louder the dining hall; I silently thanked Renee for the menu.

It was imperative that the first evening campfire be special. Several staff spoke about "getting to know you," and their speeches were intertwined with fun songs, group games, and a non-scary campfire story. I introduced the key log ceremony and it was inspirational listening to half the camp offering some form of thanks. Several girls thanked Toni and me for saving the camp. I hadn't expected any thanks, and it brought back the exact feeling I had endured when Snarl threw a key log in for me.

The most inspirational moment came when the little homesick girl stood in front of everyone, tossed her key log (which missed the fire completely), and thanked her parents for sending her to camp. She should have thanked Macho for not being so macho.

The ceremony concluded with the forming of a circle and the singing of the camp creed.

 Campingly Yours

We put our right hands over our left, and I squeezed the opposite hand of the person on my left. Each girl continued the squeeze until it came back to me. The squeeze symbolized the circle of life as we all became a unit of one. We sang Taps, the circle unwound, and we said our first goodnights. No "Master of All Campers;" that was Lou's thing.

Toni, Abigail, Ramona, and I visited every cabin to say goodnight. I entered more cabins that night than Lou had during my whole career at boys camp. I liked the concept, and maybe Lou would have liked going into cabins more often. No, that wasn't Lou's thing, but it was my thing, and the girls loved it.

My family was fast asleep, but I stayed in the office to catch up on a nasty stack of mail. Several staff members came in to shoot the breeze. We talked about life until one in the morning, and though I got nothing accomplished with the mail, without trying, I accomplished a lot with those girls. They left the office that night feeling great about camp. The mail could wait another day or two.

I lay in bed thinking about that magical first day. It was nice of Macho Bob to play along and take one for a homesick camper. Macho wasn't worldly, but he understood camp. It was already in his veins—one down and sixty-one to go—plus the staff.

"I called Mom and Dad to let them know that everyone made it to camp safely…zzzzz… I'm exhausted but anxious for tomorrow to begin. Swim tests, riding tests, visiting the nurse for physicals, signing everyone up for activities…zzzzz…the same as boys camp…but they're girls…zzzzz…Girls camps definitely exist…Morning wake up, no bell…a loud speaker system…don't have anything planned…I'll wing it…zzzzz…Boy, Patti can sure sing…not a camp voice…a Broadway voice…Got to learn every camper's name in two days…they all know mine…zzzzz…Ramona loves camp…Abigail has eighty babysitters, but mainly Doc…zzzzz…Supplecheck and Doc must be related…zzzzz…Why didn't Lou go into the cabins?…I loved it…so did the staff and campers…I could tell…zzzzz…Maybe do a quiz in the morning and give out a prize…zzzzz…Hope Toni likes camp…I think she had a great first day…the kids loved her…zzzzz…Please be sunny tomorrow…zzzzz…The squeeze made it around the circle…we became one…'This camp is your camp, this camp is my camp, this camp was made for you and me'…and the homesick camper…zzzzz…so small."

· · ·

The boys camp had a bell and a loud siren to signify meal time and activity changes. The girls camp came with an intercom system, with speakers throughout the grounds and cabins. I hated the thought of having to wake everyone up with my voice, and the bell system had been so easy, but that was the procedure I had to take over, and it was time for my first wake-up announcement.

I deadpanned, "Good morning, everyone! It's a bright sunny day in the North Woods." It was a staff member's birthday, so I announced, "The first one down to the office to correctly name the staff birthday girl will receive an amazing prize."

Doc, who was already in her second hour of cleaning the waterfront, popped in right away. Then I heard thunderous steps running down the hill. I thought the horses had gotten loose! Fifteen to twenty girls raced to the office door, and together, the mob scene sang a camp version of the birthday song to the lucky staff member.

Everyone screamed things like "Good morning! Happy camping! Wake up everyone, time for breakfast!" while I scurried around to find twenty amazing prizes. Toni came through with crazy bubbles, pens, boxer shorts, pencils, and stickers. She saved the moment, and I knew it was time to head to the Ben Franklin to load up on gobs more amazing prizes.

My disappointment at no bell system had ended abruptly. The simple fun and resulting bonding that took place that morning was priceless—except for the cost of the amazing prizes. At that moment, I realized that the intercom system offered all sorts of fun possibilities. With that one simple question, a new era of announcements had begun.

Watching the campers hustle to their physicals and various activity tests brought back many mixed feelings. Our nurse didn't have the same worries as the boys camp nurse; it appeared that the girls took showers pretty regularly. When I checked to see how the nurse was doing, I chuckled to hear a camper ask what the heck athlete's foot was. Where was The Bulk when I needed him?

Doc was a great swim instructor—no microphone needed. I was happy to have her. She was very efficient and everyone would be safe with Doc in charge of the waterfront. She was to water what Supplecheck was to land, all-knowing and all-seeing. Doc was everywhere.

Horseback riding tests were pretty fun to watch. Our head riding instructor wasn't a typical camp counselor. Horses were all that mattered to her, and developing riding skills and proficiency were her goals for the campers. I could tell that she wouldn't be rushing down for morning announcements, but the campers would definitely learn how to ride.

Just before lunch, I took a call from a mother who had heard that camp was off to a great start. She asked if we had room for two fourteen-year-olds: her daughter, who had attended before, and a friend. Boy, news traveled fast at the girls camp, as well! I paused and ruffled some papers around to let her know I was checking to see if we had room, but I didn't fool her. She laughed with me as I confirmed the enrollment for the two girls.

"Sure, send them our way," I said—and we had sixty-three.

The cooks were off to a delicious start, the campers were eating well, and the noise level remained high. I could only imagine what the noise level would be with a full camp! I'd need to borrow earplugs from Willie the crane operator.

Several mothers and a couple fathers called to inquire about their daughters. They asked pretty much the same questions: How is she adjusting? Is she homesick? Is she in a cabin with friends? One mother let me know that she had told her daughter that she'd pick her up if she didn't like camp. Yikes! I only remembered hearing about my mom calling one time, and that was to inform me of my Vietnam War lottery number! All those years at boys camp, and Mom only calling one time. Maybe times had changed. I couldn't imagine Lou taking a call from a mother saying she was going to pick her boy up if he didn't like camp.

I had pleasant conversations with all the parents and let them know I'd get back with them with an update in a couple days. I explained to the "pick my daughter up" mother that she might be in danger of setting a negative precedent for her child. I encouraged her to write positive letters to her daughter emphasizing how proud she and her husband were of her. Not so surprisingly, she was the mother of the homesick camper, the small one who had thrown Macho—and me—off the raft, the same small camper who had thrown a nice key log in the fire, the same small camper who was no longer homesick. I found it interesting that after only one day at camp, that little camper had become taller than her mother.

Camp has always been a hard place to describe to those who have never experienced it, and in only my second day as a director, I realized that it was equally hard to describe to parents how their daughter was adjusting. If only there could be a way for worried parents to become part of the hanging cobwebs. Then they could see for themselves that their daughters were becoming independent for the summer. They could watch their daughters move from swimming to riding, from riding to crafts, from crafts to soccer, and from soccer to sailing—all without anyone holding their hand. They could watch their daughters hang around the playground area during free time with ten and twenty-year-olds.

The "pick up my daughter" mother would have made a perfect hanging cobweb. She could have learned independence from her daughter. I would have loved to see that mother's reaction as her daughter was being hoisted on the staff members' shoulders, and to watch her become teary-eyed during her small one's key log thank you.

If only there was a way for parents to see true camp. It wasn't their fault, I realized. It just was hard to explain to parents on the telephone how their daughters were adjusting to camp life. I'd always tell parents the truth, good or bad, and I could only hope that they'd believe me.

It was a good thing that Jack hadn't spoken to the "pick up my daughter" mother. On the other hand, maybe a lecture from Jack would have been good for her. I made sure some of the cobwebs hung around for good measure.

$\bullet \ \bullet \ \bullet$

The entire camp was divided into two teams, Tan and White. I wasn't sure where those colors came from, but the long-standing competition needed to stay in place—once a Tan, always a Tan; once a White, always a White. A few of the girls were second-generation campers, and their mothers made sure their daughters were placed on the proper team. Sisters and cousins had to be on the same team, as well.

By tradition, it was called the *Color War*, but I didn't think the term "war" belonged in the camp vocabulary. Simply calling it Tan and White sounded good enough to me. Doc was all for that, as well, and together we made a decision to wipe one negative phrase off the girls camp books.

The second evening of camp was devoted to the start of Tan and White. It was a perfect time to bring back the spirit of Dea Quay, the Native American who had spoken at a campfire during my first summer at camp. The Tan and White teams were told that the games couldn't begin without the approval of the spirit of Dea Quay. I taught the Quay two-step and chant to both teams, and the entire camp was soon shouting to the skies to bring back the spirit of Dea Quay. The Bulk was two-stepping with me that night, at least in spirit. One of the staff played the role of Quay's grandmother, and with enough campers prodding, Grandma Quay finally made the official declaration that the games could begin. The spirit of Dea Quay would always remain alive. Maybe the ceremony was a little corny, but I gazed into the skies and I could almost see Dea Quay smiling through his tears.

$\bullet \ \bullet \ \bullet$

Toni and I again traveled through each cabin that night. We didn't plan to do that forever, but doing it the first few nights seemed logical, and we knew every girl's name by the end of that second evening. By eleven o'clock, I was again playing around with the mail. I knew the camp was a business, but somehow that part kept getting shoved onto the back burner. I remembered Dad emphasizing that the best thing that could happen was for the campers to have a great summer, and then the rest would fall into place—so far, so good, Dad.

Five staff members walked into the office to shoot the breeze, and a pattern seemed to be taking place. I was glad they felt comfortable, and it was good to learn more about them. I think they looked at me as a somewhat nerdy guy, which of course was fine with me. I liked acting a bit naïve and keeping the girls a little off guard. It was better if they didn't quite know what to expect. As they sat in my office at midnight, I did inquire about who was watching their cabins. Each of them responded with "My co-counselor." Hmmm, maybe it was a not-so-good pattern that was taking place.

I finally stood and said, "Goodnight, girls. Get some rest. Be ready for tomorrow morning's wake-up quiz."

Another one a.m. bedtime, and there weren't enough hours in the day to run our camp of sixty-three girls. A full camp would mean I wouldn't even need to own a bed! Yet somehow Lou always had 140 campers and managed to go to bed around ten. How did he do that? Were girls different than boys? Was I that much different than Lou?

"How did Lou do that?...zzzzz...Are parents going to call every day?...Did Lou get calls like that?...Sixty-three sets of parents...zzzzz...what if the camp was full?...I could hire Jack and he'd alleviate those parent calls...all camp for Jack...no griping, interfering camper-sick parents allowed...zzzzz...Dea Quay was smiling...This place is exhausting, but fun...Please, no one get hurt...zzzzz...No more Color War...No more war...I need to write Mom about her purpose...zzzzz...The old-time staff members seem to like the new camp...and I like them...zzzzz...Only three homesick ones left...I'll work on them tomorrow...first full day of activities...maybe I should help teach tennis...zzzzz...see you in a few hours, Doc...zzzzz... Good night, Dea Quay...'This camp was made for you and me'...zzzzz...and maybe Mom someday."

29

Do the
Right Thing

Sixty-three campers was a perfect number for running camp, but not great
monetarily. No one complained, since there was plenty of space in each activity.
There were no lines for water skiing, and every girl could ski twice in one period. Horseback
riders were receiving close to private lessons. Doc was able to advance the beginning
swimmers at a fast pace. Patti and her dancing counterpart, Syd, drew almost every camper
for theater. They already were choreographing a song-and-dance show for parent visitation
weekend. I taught tennis first period each morning, and for that hour, I happily felt more like
a counselor than a director.

A week into camp, and each day was sunny and warm. Maybe Dea Quay had an in with
the weather gods. Sunny days coupled with good food and fun activities made for happy
campers. Homesick campers were a thing of the past, and even the "pick up my daughter
mom" called with compliments. Toni and I could do no wrong, or it at least appeared that
way. The staff and older campers viewed us as saviors because we had revived the camp and
I actually felt like I was wearing Mantle's old number 7. Dad's comment about everyone
having fun was firmly planted in my mind. One week down, Dad—so far, so good, Dad.

The mail had been neglected long enough. I asked the staff to give me a reprieve, and they stayed out of the office for two nights so I could finally treat camp as a business. I paid the stack of bills and sorted the remaining tuition money for deposit. The camp would be in the red, for certain, but I couldn't tell by how much. I needed to have enough money on hand to pay all the summer bills, including staff salaries. I couldn't worry about the next year's deposits. Seven weeks of the summer remained—and there was still a whole lot of camping to do.

The second night of paying the bills didn't go as well. The bills were fine, but some of the staff was not. At about one a.m., I heard loud voices coming from the parking lot, and the loudness continued to the staff retreat. I called Doc on the in-camp phone system. Her cabin was close to the retreat and I knew she'd still be awake typing the weekly newsletter.

She checked out the problem and came back to the office with a lousy report. She surmised drinking, and maybe underage drinking. Using her years of authority at camp, Doc had quieted the girls and sent them back to their cabins.

I asked Doc, "What form of discipline has been used in the past for this type of situation?"

"Well," she said. "The original owner, the previous director's husband, founded the camp in 1946 and passed away two years ago. From day one he ran the camp with strong authority. All of the drinking girls would have been fired—not just the underage ones. They would have been shipped home before morning wake-up."

Wow, one week of sunshine, and my so-far-so-good had come to a screeching halt. Doc didn't necessarily agree with the past policy, but she said that no one ever walked on the old director. It was his way or the highway. I asked Doc if she thought I should use the highway. She said it wasn't her call, but she'd support whatever decision I made.

I couldn't wait until morning—another night of little sleep. Doc rounded up the girls and brought them into the office—five staff members, all great girls that the campers loved. They all came from good homes and I knew they weren't normally troublemakers.

Doc said goodnight and then whispered, "Good luck. I'll support your decision."

 Campingly Yours

The girls were crying before I even said a word. The late night meeting in the office had already had a sobering effect on all of them. I asked how many were drinking, and all of them raised their hands. I asked how they had obtained the liquor, and they said the bar served anyone. I asked what would have happened if they had caused such a problem in years past, and the girls reluctantly mumbled that they probably would have been sent home.

One of the girls remembered that when she was a camper, her counselor left mysteriously in the middle of the night. She said the campers believed the rumor that the counselor had gotten ill, been sent to the hospital, and couldn't return to camp. However, that "drinking" staff member now realized that her counselor hadn't gone to the hospital. She'd been sent home for the very reason all five girls were sitting in my office at two in the morning.

The girls kept crying and apologizing profusely. They reminded me of Charley the day he'd made a mistake in the house. Charley never boo-booed in the house, but on that day he was sick and left traces of his diarrhea all over the living room. Dad had walked in and almost got mad, but he found Charley in the corner, his head on the ground, making dog-weeping noises. Charley knew he was in trouble and had no idea what Dad was going to do to him.

I instructed the girls to compose themselves, head back to their cabins, and to be at breakfast as usual. I let them know that my decision would be made in the morning. Jack would have reminded me that all the girls were good kids, and good kids sometimes made stupid mistakes. What a tough call.

I had the rest of the night to come up with an appropriate decision. What a mess. If I sent them home, there'd be a huge hole in our cabin and activity coverage and there'd be crying campers throughout the camp. I had spent the entire spring encouraging those girls to give the new camp a try, and now they were hoping I'd give them a second chance.

At the boys camp, if a counselor was sent home, his name became negatively fixed in camp lore. I couldn't remember all the guys who filtered in and out of the boys camp over the years, but I could name on one hand those who had been booted out. Being kicked out of camp became a lifelong brand that was nearly impossible to erase. I had until breakfast to make my decision.

Dad never used an alarm. His eyes popped open every morning at 5:03 a.m. I called that morning and explained the "camp crisis" in detail. He asked if I'd ever drunk beer when I was underage. Then he asked if I thought he'd ever drunk beer when he was underage. I knew the answer to both questions. He reminded me that I was in an unusual position, since I was a father figure to eighty-five girls. Then he calmly told me to treat those girls exactly like I'd treat Abigail, and then to do the right thing.

"Thanks, Dad," I said as I hung up the phone, "and say hi to Mom."

After breakfast, the girls quietly came into the living room of our camp house. I didn't want to make a big scene and had avoided the office. The girls started crying and apologizing again.

I asked, "How would you feel if you were sent home?"

One answered, "It would ruin my life. I'd always be remembered as a staff member who got fired from camp."

I asked if she'd considered the consequences of getting caught. She said no, but added that she probably would have done it again if she hadn't been caught.

I had each girl call her parents and explain exactly what happened. The girls were then sent back to teach morning activities. I asked them, for their own sake and for the sake of the camp, to hold their problem within. The campers didn't need to know.

Before I could contact their parents, another staff member ran into the office, saying that a camper had fallen off a swing set and wasn't moving. Someone shouted on the intercom for the nurse, and then the whole camp ran to the playground area.

Doc, as usual, beat everyone to the punch and was already attending to the fallen camper. Doc was certified in first aid, CPR, and everything else, for that matter. She placed the camper on a medical backboard and traveled with the nurse to the local emergency room. Toni notified the girl's parents and all of us waited on pins and needles, hoping the prognosis was favorable. There was only one phone, and I didn't want to tie up the line until news came

Campingly Yours

251

from the hospital. All the drinking counselors were waiting to hear from me, and I had no opportunity to speak to their parents.

Then crisis number three entered the office. Three campers from the fourteen-year-old cabin claimed they were missing several belongings. Stamps, some clothing, and several pieces of their jewelry were missing. Jewelry! I had no idea that girls brought jewelry to camp! The girls started accusing one of their cabin mates, but I slowed them down and assured them that their problem would become a priority right after lunch.

Did Lou have those types of problems? Probably, but I never paid much attention. I was pretty sure he didn't have to worry about missing jewelry.

I recalled one day when a popular staff member dove into the shallow end of the lake and injured his neck. He was carried off on a stretcher and rushed to the emergency room. It turned out that he had sprained his neck, but at that moment I realized how worried Lou must have been. What if the counselor's neck had been broken and he became paralyzed? The very thought of it was horrific. I'd never realized the pressure of Lou's job until that moment. I had looked to Lou as a mentor, but not as a crisis manager. I had three camp crises, and all had to be dealt with—sooner rather than later. What if I couldn't solve any of those problems? Parents would be unhappy with the camp, no deposits would come in the fall, and camp would have to close.

"Come on, Flash," I thought. "Campers and counselors first, business fifth or sixth. Snap out of it and do the right thing."

Doc called just before lunch and reported an iffy prognosis. The injured camper had hurt her back and the attending physician had admitted her to the hospital. Doc said that she was going to stay with the camper and send the nurse back to camp. The physician had gotten in touch with the camper's parents and they were satisfied with the medical supervision.

I ran to the dining hall to say grace and get the meal started. During the meal, I went back to the office and spoke with the parents of three of the drinking girls and then rushed back to the dining hall to give the noon announcements. After lunch, I spoke with the remaining parents and scheduled a meeting with the campers in the cabin where the stealing was taking place. I also asked the five drinking staff members to meet me immediately following the afternoon activities.

The girls missing their belongings were certain that the items had been stolen and not just misplaced. Their counselors concurred that there was a thief in the camp. I let the girls know that no one should be accused and that every effort would be made to solve the mystery.

The five drinkers entered the office. They were done crying, but they were still on pins and needles, waiting to hear my verdict. I apologized for taking so long, but they understood. I reminded them of how happy I was when they signed up for camp. They wanted to be a part of the new camp and keep the camp traditions alive. I reminded them of the key log ceremony and how each one had said some form of thanks in front of the whole camp. Each of them had made a statement about camp being their home away from home. I pointed out that most of their best friends were at camp and that their closest lifetime friends would probably be camp friends.

Then I asked, "If camp means so much to you, why did you put the camp's reputation at risk?"

Each girl said she'd acted without thinking about how it would hurt the camp. I told them all that their parents would totally support my decision if I sent them home, which caused all five of them to start crying again. Yikes, that crying stuff sure made things more difficult! I asked if they'd ever consider getting into such trouble again, and each assured me that they'd learned their lesson.

For a long moment, I stared through the girls and imagined Abigail at their age. I couldn't stand the thought of my daughter being booted out of camp. I would always give Abigail a second chance to prove herself. Finally, I told the girls to go back to work, but always to remember that they'd been given a second chance, and someday I hoped they'd pass a second chance on to someone else. They tried hugging me—but no go.

I remembered watching Dad carry Charley out of the living room while I cleaned up the mess. Dad didn't yell at Charley. He just put Charley on his lap, and they took a nap together. I had cleaned up Charley's mess, but Dad had helped me clean up my mess with the drinking counselors when he told me to think of Abigail and do the right thing. Dad would have made a great camp director.

* * *

The injured camper turned out to have only a bruise, and the doctor released her late that afternoon. According to the doctor, the camper had been pretty dramatic when she arrived in the emergency room, and he explained to Doc that he felt obligated to err on the side of caution. Our nurse picked up Doc and the injured girl, and they arrived back just before dinner. The bruised girl received a hero's welcome and two of her cabin mates acted as her crutches, assisting her to the dining hall. The bruised camper was eating up the attention, and the dinner, as well.

Boy, I recalled never purposely letting anyone know I was injured. I never wanted to come out of a game.

I thought it was manager Eddie Stankey of the White Sox, who once said, "If the bone's not showing, you're playing." Maybe it was Durocher?

However, being injured at a girls camp appeared to be a desirable thing, thanks to all the attention. I concluded that none of the campers were destined to play for the White Sox.

The evening activity was an all-camp lip synch show. Each cabin had to perform, which meant that everyone would be in the theater for more than an hour. I snuck out halfway through the show with the senior counselor of the fourteen-year-old cabin. The two of us took a quick look through shelves and drawers in the cabin. I wasn't into invading privacy and didn't have a warrant, but the search ended rather abruptly. We found t-shirts, jewelry, stamps, stationary, and three stuffed animals wedged under some clothing in a drawer occupied by the camper the three girls had originally accused. It was too easy and too obvious. She must have *wanted* to get caught—but why?

I planned a meeting with the fourteen-year-olds immediately after the evening activity. I kept them in the office while Doc and the senior counselor held the troubled girl back. However, at that moment camp crisis number four took place.

The cooks called and said they had lost all power on their end of camp, which included the whole younger village. Macho Bob rushed in and announced an electrical wire—possibly live—was down in a potentially dangerous location. I put the fourteen-year-olds on hold, notified Doc to meet Macho, and made sure that all the campers stayed in their cabins. The senior counselor stayed with the troubled girl.

Doc rushed to the office, quietly let me know that she'd gotten a confession from the girl, and then headed out to join Macho. The cooks were worried that the food would spoil in the refrigerators and freezers, and all they could do was keep the doors sealed. Toni stayed with the fourteen-year-olds.

A tree branch had knocked the wire down. Doc gathered a bunch of flashlights as Macho found the appropriate circuit breaker to deaden the wire. Then they wound black electrical tape on the severed ends. When Macho finally announced that the hazard was over, I had Doc call the emergency number for the local fire department.

Then I headed back to my house, where I found the fourteen-year-olds having a great time. Toni had made them a treat of pizza and pop. Soda pop and pizza weren't a big deal to the girls at home, but at camp, those items compared favorably to gold.

The girls were informed that one of their cabin mates had confessed to stealing, and all the girls instantly started crying. It was a touching scene, since they obviously liked the troubled girl and didn't view her as an enemy. I asked them to return to their cabin, and I let them know that the troubled girl was going to stay with us that night.

Those fourteen-year-olds weren't at all what I would have imagined going into the summer. They were an intelligent, caring, and understanding group of young teens. They had a wild side, especially the twins, but their caring side took over at the right time. They were a lucky gift for a first-year director. I appreciated those girls and knew that someday they'd make fine counselors.

Doc brought the crying camper to our house, where Toni and Doc gave her a warm hug. She told us she had wanted to get caught, and it was easy to tell that her problems hadn't originated at camp. She said her parents stayed up late, and she wanted to talk with them. I agreed to let her phone her parents, but told her I wanted to speak with them first.

The parents explained that their daughter had gone through major difficulties at home, including schoolwork and social adjustment. She'd been accused of shoplifting, but nothing had come of it. She cried a lot and stayed in her room most evenings. Although the girl was on prescription medicine and was receiving professional help for depression, the parents hadn't informed the camp. We all agreed that their daughter was in need of help greater than anyone at camp could offer.

The parents asked if they could pick their daughter up the next day. It was a tough call for me, since I thought camp might help their daughter, but she was in the midst of severe depression and in obvious pain. We arranged for a noon pick-up, and I felt it was the right thing to do. I also told them I'd refund her tuition, which also seemed like the right thing to do.

That girl wouldn't be considered a camper who was booted out of camp. She'd stick in my memory as a sweet girl, a camper who was ill, a camper who had caring parents, and a camper who someday would find her own way to happiness. Her cabin mates would always be remembered as campers who cared, and they were a great group of fourteen-year-olds. No one was booted out of camp that day, not even the drinking counselors.

• • •

I remembered walking a shopping mall with Dad one day. He pointed out retail stores with just a few customers. He hated the thought of sitting around with no action; one or two customers, with no guarantee that they'd buy anything.

Dad said, "The good, the bad, and sometimes the ugly pass through the junkyard every hour. There's seldom a dull moment, and I love the action."

As I finally took a deep breath after weathering four crises at the camp, I understood Dad's point of view for the first time in my life. So much had happened in one day, along with the normal everyday activities, including three meals and an evening event in the theater. For most of the campers and counselors, it was just a typical day at camp. They were unaware of the difficult events. The ugly had passed through camp—an injured camper, a troubled girl, and five drinking counselors; the bad had passed through camp—a dangerous electrical wire; and the good had passed through camp—a group of caring fourteen-year-olds, Doc's remarkable presence, a clean bill of health for the injured camper, a troubled camper's understanding parents, and five second chances to good girls who had made a mistake.

As I lay in bed that night, exhaustion took over.

"I hated the problems but I loved the action...zzzzz...Dad was right...no sitting around...action...zzzzz...Will the staff take advantage of a softy?...zzzzz...Did I do the right thing, Dad?...Did those drinking counselors laugh at me because they got away with it?... zzzzz...No sending Abigail home...those girls are all my summer daughters...zzzzz...I love this camp and those girls...I won't let the girls know...zzzzz... I couldn't send them home... zzzzz... Dad and Charley on the couch sleeping...zzzzz...Goodnight, Ramona...zzzzz... 'This camp was made for you and me'...but not the troubled girl...zzzzz..."

30

Why Are Babies So Delicate?

Patti and Syd had the theater rocking with song and dance. The parents were coming, and the show was ready. The campers had talent and I was excited for their parents to see the production. I was a little nervous for visitation weekend, but not too nervous.

The sun kept popping out every day, activities were running smoothly, the staff members were getting along nicely, and camper spirit remained high. Camp crises were normal; not as bad as the four-crisis day, although campers and staff members always had their share of issues.

Various staff members consistently visited my office after hours and we'd talk more about life than about camp. They spewed about school, peer pressure, parents, divorce, happiness, and depression. They forced me to become an amateur psychologist and sociologist, along with being a summer educator. Macho became a camp character and the girls adapted a Village People song to "Macho, Macho Bob, I've got to be a Macho Bob," thus setting his legend in stone.

The cooks also had many needs: more knives, warming trays, different utensils, a larger mixer, a bigger walk-in cooler, and more counter space—just to name a few. How had the camp managed to serve meals in years past? Our cooks put out quality food despite the deficiencies and we had a beautiful meal planned for the parents.

Visitation weekend and dealing with all the parents wasn't what was bothering me. Lou and Renee had called and invited Toni and me to bring the song-and-dance show to the boys camp. I was nervous, more than on the day of U.N. Day baseball finals, more than when I sat at the table with the nuns hoping to be hired, more than at the Sheraton introduction gathering, and even more than waiting with crossed fingers for the camp director to officially sign over the camp.

It was Lou. I wanted his approval and I wanted him to see me as a solid camp director. I didn't want to disappoint him. The day after parent visitation, our camp would travel to the boys camp. A road trip, finals, the championship game, everything would be on the table—and Lou's stamp of approval would be at stake.

Parents lined up at the front entrance, Doc handed out the visitation edition of the newsletter, the gates were unlocked, and mounted riding instructors slowly led the cars through the wooded paths to the north field to park. No Binder was needed; just the horses. Campers rushed to their parents as if they hadn't seen them in years. Just for the heck of it, I checked the makeshift parking lot to see if by chance a push button Plymouth wagon had pulled in. Actually, I should have looked for an all-leather 1967 Marquis coupe, but I knew that neither car was due that weekend. The owners of those cars still had never seen summer camp.

Toni and I greeted as many parents as we could and eventually we were able to speak to everyone. Some parents apparently didn't realize there were children other than their own at the camp, since they dominated a lot of our time. The cooks put out a remarkable meal—barbecued chicken, baked fish, all sorts of veggies, a huge fruit dish placed inside a cut out watermelon, coleslaw, homemade potato salad, homemade rolls, brownies, carrot cake, and chocolate chip cookies. Good food made for happy campers, which made for even happier parents.

The song-and-dance show was a huge success, and almost every camper participated, either on stage or behind the scenes. Bulbs were flashing from all angles, and one would have thought it was premiere night on Broadway. A few parents offered positive criticism, which I found to be most helpful.

A couple mothers thought the camp could have been cleaner, and they especially commented about all of the cobwebs hanging around. I told them I'd take note, but secretly made no immediate plans to remove any of my sacred webs. All in all, it was a great visitation weekend, and the parents were pleased that their daughters were having a great summer. Four weeks down, Dad—everyone was having a fun summer, Dad—four weeks to go, Dad. There was still a lot of camping to do—and the song-and-dance show was headed to the boys camp.

Macho cranked up the camp's red school bus and along with two vans, the whole camp was soon on the road. My stomach was churning; the moment of reckoning was near. We were an hour away, near the Flambeau River, when the girls started complaining about needing a bathroom break. I couldn't recall boys having to stop, so I said we'd arrive in about an hour, and then they could do their thing at the camp. I didn't want to make a bad first impression with a late arrival. The girls went berserk!

"We can't make it! We'll wet our pants. We have to stop. Macho, stop the bus!"

Macho pulled the bus to the side of the road and the girls piled out. There were no public waysides along the route, but I thought their pit stop would go quickly, since they could just duck into the woods.

I had thought wrong.

The girls literally lined up, one at a time, to go into the woods. No doors to lock, no toilets, no outhouses, no nothing, just woods, but for some reason, the girls lined up systematically and waited for the girl in front to come out of the woods. I couldn't watch, of course, but I suggested to one of the counselors that the girls could all go at once since the woods were plentiful—but no go. Macho and I just stared at each other and thought, "Welcome to girls camp." Due to the long line, we were destined to arrive late.

Macho guided the bus slowly along the boys camp road. Campers were playing ball and shooting baskets, and canoes and sailboats were making their way through the bay. There was no Snarl, no Vacuum, no Pumpkins, no Bulk, different canoe instructors, and no Flash. Most of the names had changed, but camp looked the same and time hadn't warped the character of the place where I had first set foot eighteen years earlier.

The girls piled off the bus as Supplecheck strolled from the office to greet us. He looked at his watch, noting that we were an hour late.

I shrugged my shoulders and said, "Girls."

The guy counselors and some older campers greeted us, as well, and Supplecheck announced what activities were available for the girls. He emphatically instructed the boys to show the girls the way and then announced that dinner was at six.

As everyone dispersed, Supplecheck laughed and asked, "How do you handle all those girls?"

I answered, "I guess not so well. We are an hour late."

I entered the office and received a huge hug from Renee.

Lou stood up, gave me a firm handshake, and said, "Welcome back, Flash."

We talked about each other's summer and he was glad to hear that things were going well at the girls camp. I told him I'd never realized how much went on in one day of directing a camp.

He laughed again and said, "Wait until you have a full camp!"

I caught up with some of my campers and staff and showed them my old stomping grounds. They were full of questions about my past, but I didn't reveal too much. Mystery was a good *shtick* for me with the girls.

The bell rang signifying dinner, and I thought, "Please, no pudding and whipped cream!"

The boys upped their craziness, singing and carrying on in front of the girls. The atmosphere was loose, typically organized chaos during the meal. All had been good so far, and I saw no evidence of a possible dessert disaster.

There was a short free period after dinner, so I grabbed a few of the older girls and showed them the ball field. I found several gloves and an old mask in the ball shed. Then I put on the mask and had the girls pitch to me. No Vacuum curveball—just twenty-mile-an-hour fastballs. The girls thought I was a bit nerdy wearing the mask, but they had a great time throwing balls to their camp director. I missed a few on purpose, took one on the shin, and pretended to be hurt. The girls weren't too concerned and all of them proceeded to throw balls at me at the same time.

One hit my mask and I acted as if they'd knocked me out. They dragged me off the field as I feigned injury. As I was being dragged, I could see Lou standing on the top step to his office, grinning. Time stood still at the boys camp.

A short time later, everyone piled into the theater; it was time for my moment of truth. I wanted the girls to be on their best behavior and I wanted the show to be fun for the guys. Lou introduced me and asked me to come to the front stage. I received loud alumni applause, but tripped on the first step, hitting my head on the fall.

A few of my boys camp friends and Macho Bob carried me off the stage as the room became silent. A moment later, I reappeared to loud applause with a bloody bandana wrapped around my head. Lou looked confused, as did some of the crowd, as I extended my thanks to Lou, Renee, and the guys for inviting the girls to perform.

I took a seat in the back as Lou led a chorus of "Keep on the Sunny Side." After a rousing chorus, Lou called on anyone in the crowd to share a good joke. A few of the boys had goofy jokes that made everyone groan.

"Hey Lou, do you know what the fish said when he hit the wall?"

Lou said, "No, I don't know what the fish said when he hit the wall."

The camper followed with, "Dam."

Mock laughing followed, and that was as off-colored as the jokes ever got. After several jokes and another loud chorus, Lou called on Lacey, one of my female staff members. She was a new counselor, blonde, very cute, and I noticed some of the boys had strategically managed to sit by her.

"Hey, Lou, do you know why babies are so delicate?"

Lou replied, "No Lacey, why are babies so delicate?"

Lacey shouted back, "Because they're made with only one screw."

There was silence—it seemed to last for an hour. I sank down in my seat. An off-color joke from the girls camp! What had I been teaching the girls? Fifteen summers of Lou's approval had been shot down with one racy joke from a trampy blonde counselor who needed to be fired.

My hour of agony actually lasted about eleven seconds. Lou stood motionless during that span and finally broke out in full laughter. Maybe it had taken him that long to get the joke; I didn't care. He laughed, and suddenly everything was fine again. There was no need to fire cute, sweet Lacey.

The girls entertained the boys with a great show and Lou let me know how important it was to have such talented musical directors. After a short dance and some ice cream bars, the girls boarded the bus for the trip home. I made sure they did all the bathroom stuff they could, since there'd be no stopping in the woods after dark.

Lou shook my hand and told me to keep up the good work. As he said goodnight, he asked if my head was okay from the fall.

My head was just fine. I had Lou's approval.

31

Be Well, Girl Campers

The second half of camp flew by. The sun gods were good to us all summer and we had the best weather I could remember in all of my camping years. Daily traumas were normal, as were late night staff talks. Eighteen-hour days were par for the course, but each morning, I rose with as much enthusiasm as the previous action-packed day.

Girls stormed the office for amazing quiz prizes; it didn't take much to make them happy. Once in a while, I'd hand out a Hershey bar as a prize, and that was the ultimate gift to make me their hero. Girls continued to give thanks at key log ceremonies, Doc passed almost every swimmer to at least intermediate level, Macho's legend grew larger each day, Tan and White games were competitive (but not too much so), the cooks whined all summer but continued to prepare great food, the nurse complained that the campers complained too much, and though the riding director's "horse only" behavior seemed odd to me, she ran an efficient program.

A major boys camp in our area wouldn't have us over for what was a traditional social because their director said we didn't have enough campers. I told the director that our whole camp had traveled two hours, including a full bathroom stop, to visit a much larger boys camp, and that camp welcomed us with open arms.

It was a classic case of the big guy snubbing the little guy. I only knew the ways of Lou, Renee, Jack, and Supplecheck—I wasn't prepared for having a camp director snub anyone, much less a whole camp. I had grown up watching how Dad treated the mighty and the small. Dad would have made a great camp director, and as far as I was concerned, there was a nearby boys' camp director who could have used his guidance.

I loved the way the final night used to end at boys camp, so I modeled the ending of our girls camp in similar fashion. The last three nights consisted of a final staff show, a request night, and a banquet. Camper and counselor farewell speeches were equally as touching as those from the boys camp, and the end-of-the-year song was very special for me.

"I was here in '79, '79, '79, I was here in '79, where is '78?"

Several of the girls stood till the early '70s, and Doc stood for nineteen years. I knew that, almost simultaneously, Lou and Renee were standing till 1945 at the boys camp.

The staff continued with a past tradition of elaborately decorating the dining hall for the last night, but the theme was kept a guarded secret from the campers. The staff chose "The Wizard of Oz." The dining hall became unrecognizable. The walls were decorated with murals of the yellow brick road, munchkins, scarecrows, witches, and the Emerald City. The staff members all wore Oz character costumes and the campers entered the dining hall with wide eyes and smiling faces.

Our last three nights, as it turned out, were much more elaborate than at the boys camp. Girls cried each night, but I kept reminding them there was still a lot of camping to do. Toni and I were the brunt of several staff skits, and for the first time, I could relate to how Lou and Renee had felt during all those ribbings. Toni did well with the campers and staff, but I still couldn't tell if her heart was really into the camp.

Camp had been in my blood for sixteen years, and even more so with the girls camp. I didn't want the girls to go home. I was exhausted from long hours with no days or nights off, but I didn't want our magical first year to end.

As everyone formed a final circle to sing the camp creed, I realized exactly how Lou must have felt as he watched the camp effigy burn. He didn't want to let go of his boys, and I didn't want to let go of my girls. A burning sensation crawled through my stomach; Mom couldn't help with that one. I knew that Lou and I were both saying goodbye to our campers that night.

"Goodbye, boys, goodbye, girls, see you next summer."

For that brief moment, I felt as if I was standing in Lou's shoes. I looked down and noticed that my shoes were tied. I was standing in my own shoes.

The early morning bus scene was one big cry. Though no one wanted to leave, the girls were ready to see their parents. It was a perfect happy sad situation. Doc coerced the campers onto the bus and took roll. Then the doors closed and the wheels slowly began to roll out onto the camp road.

Toni, Abigail, and I waved goodbye.

Everyone had fun, Dad. Mission accomplished, Dad. The campers are gone, Dad, and there's no more camping left to do.

I held back my tears and listened to the quiet. The stillness was overpowering.

"Goodbye, girl campers; be well, girl campers; be good, girl campers; say hi to your parents, girl campers; have a nice school year, girl campers; don't leave me, girl campers; come back, girl campers; how about one more week, girl campers? I'll miss you, girl campers; read your newsletters, girl campers; till next summer, girl campers...we still have a lot of camping to do."

That night, I called Mom and Dad to let them know that the girls had all arrived home safely. Dad spoke first and asked if I thought the girls had had a fun summer.

"I think so," I said. "They appeared to enjoy themselves."

"Do you think the parents were pleased?" Dad asked.

"I think so," I said. "Some griped a lot, but they admitted that their daughter was happy."

Dad said, "Those girls will be back. Parents can gripe all they want, but the child carries the upper hand."

"Did I carry the upper hand growing up, Dad?" I asked.

Dad said, "Probably, but I've always avoided griping to those in charge of my children."

"I think camp went well, Dad," I said. "Most everyone had a magical summer, including me."

Dad said to expect enrollment to double the next season.

"How's Mom doing?" I asked.

"Hang on," said Dad, "she wants to talk to you."

"Hi, Mom," I said when she came on the line. "Camp went well. I'm exhausted, but I'd like to start the summer all over again."

Mom said, "I knew you'd do well at camp."

I told her, "That's exactly what The Bulk told me my very first summer. How did you know I'd do well, Mom?"

She said she knew about my shoe thing—and about my brother's shoe thing. She told me my shoes were never untied. She also said that she was going to visit camp the next summer.

"Thanks, Mom!" I said. "I can't wait for you to make your first visit to camp—and thanks, Mom. You were the reason my shoes were always tied. You fulfilled a purpose—for me."

She said, "Don't forget about your father."

No worries, Mom. Dad would have made a great camp director.

32

Overwhelmed, but Happy

Two weeks had passed, and silence presided at the girls camp. Sometimes late at night, I thought I heard camper noises coming from the lakefront cabins or cheers from the dining hall echoing mealtime madness. I enjoyed thinking about all that had gone on during the summer, and it was therapeutic to listen to those imagined noises.

The September edition of the newsletter was ready for the mail. I opened with: "Greetings from the girls camp—we trust all is well with you and your family." I then mentioned that the girls should always have their parents read the newsletter, as well.

Philosophical thoughts followed in the next two paragraphs and then I moved on to camp events. The first letter after camp was a perfect opportunity to reflect on the previous summer—happy times, sad times, times spent together. Information on each staff member was then listed—and where they were headed in the fall, from work to school. Reunion dates were given, monthly birthdays were acknowledged, and information was given about next season's enrollment forms.

I closed the newsletter, and every letter, for that matter, with *Campingly Yours*. The newsletters were dropped off at the Eagle River post office, and I realized that I had rushed them into the mail as fast as my brother and I had once raced to receive our monthly newsletters.

The camp lost money, and I owed bills, but several of my creditors were gracious enough to extend their payment due dates till the fall. It seemed a bit early to send out enrollment forms. I felt there was a fine line from appearing too pushy, and I didn't want to imply any form of desperation.

When Dad asked how much money the camp had lost, I said, "Plenty," but I could tell he'd already figured it pretty close to the penny. He told me that he and Mom were sending $2,000 so Abigail could eat.

Then he added, "And throw an extra bone to Ramona."

Emphatically, I said. "I'll only accept it if I can pay you back."

He agreed, and though I felt guilty, remorseful, shamed, incompetent, and dependent, I knew well that there would have been no memories from the girls camp if it hadn't been for Mom and Dad's generosity. For my own satisfaction, I needed to pay them back, and not just monetarily. Maybe Dad would come up with the bases loaded someday, with Mom on third base.

By mid-September, enrollment forms and general information had been mailed to the families. We asked for names of potential new families, indicating that word of mouth was our best way of advertising. Two weeks later, we received fifty enrollment forms and twenty new prospects.

Toni and I drove to Missouri to drop Abigail and Ramona at her parents' home, and then we headed to Chicago, Milwaukee, Cleveland, and Cincinnati to visit interested families. Several of those new families also gave us other names to visit, and in a ten-day span, we visited more than thirty-five families.

During the summer, I had snapped hundreds of photographs—from bus arrival to bus departure—and I put together a fifty-one-picture slide show. I hauled a large screen, slide projector, and briefcase full of camp literature into each household. I liked the briefcase, since

 Campingly Yours

it made me feel lawyer-like and gave me a bit of a false feeling that the families might think I was smart. I also liked the fact that there was no film to break, although that would have been a bad deal in my brother's case.

We drove a 1973 twelve-passenger Dodge van that had lots of rust on the driver's side panel. I made sure to park with the driver's side facing away from the house entrance at home visits and if possible, I parked in the street. Night visits hid the rust pretty well, but daytime visits made for nervous times when parents walked us out to our van to say goodbye. We stayed at inexpensive motels, ate the Denny's Grand Slam often, and used a pay phone constantly to make contacts.

I flipped the slides and pointed out events and names. The parents were impressed that Toni and I could highlight particulars on all the girls and staff members (thanks, Lou). Each visit lasted about two hours and by the end, the families knew us pretty well. We also had a good handle on the daughter's personality, likes, and dislikes. I carried a notebook and scribbled down bits and pieces of information about each home visit, such as:

- Parents were from Boston, father asked question about how much candy he could send.
- Daughter likes sailing, has bright red hair.
- Father wore gold chain and likes Chinese food.
- We only met daughter and mother because father was watching Bears game upstairs.
- We got lost in downtown Chicago and had no place to park, half hour late, but family was understanding.
- Daughter did handstands and watched slide show while upside down.
- Every time we asked daughter a question, mother would answer.
- Daughter on 4,000 medications, none of which I've ever heard of.
- Girl has Crohn's disease.
- Girl is diabetic.
- Girl cried the entire visit, announced that she didn't want to attend camp, and stormed off to her room—father wrote a check in full.

- Family cat bit me and blood poured from my hand, but no one seemed to notice.

- In Cincinnati, I gave entire presentation to five families with my fly open.

- All five signed up.

- Mother asked if daughter would learn to pick and roll. Fortunately, I understood basketball. No promises made about turning daughter into a Larry Bird.

- I walked into house and became suddenly ill with stomach and diarrhea problems. No toilet paper in the bathroom.

- Father said if daughter was homesick, he'd personally fly up and take her home. I gave him the phone number of the "pick up my daughter" mother.

The notes proved to be great reminders of the various individuals, since all of the home visits, fathers, mothers, and daughters, became muddled in my mind after awhile.

Toni and I picked up Abigail and Ramona and drove eleven hours back to camp. The huge stack of mail was an overwhelming but welcome sight. Twenty-five enrollment forms, including fifteen new campers, were part of the pile. Even the no toilet paper family signed up! That meant acknowledgments needed to be mailed out right away, and I was able to pay off all the summer bills. Later, fifteen additional family prospects came in. It was time to make calls and hit the trail again.

Toni stayed at camp, but I was on the road again the following week. It was too tough dropping Abigail and Ramona off in Missouri each time. Prospective parents preferred seeing both husband and wife, but most understood the concept of raising a baby.

I hustled to Milwaukee, Chicago, Cleveland, Cincinnati, Dayton, St. Louis, and then back to Chicago as more names came in during the trip. By mid-November, it was time for reunions. We visited old campers and potential new ones in each city, the same routine that brought Lou and Renee to see my brother and me.

Abigail made some of the trips, but Ramona stayed in a kennel. I hated the kennel part of recruiting, and so did Ramona. By December holiday time, we had put thousands of miles

on the van, four newsletters had been mailed, staff invitations had been sent out, all birthday people had received a personalized camp greeting, hundreds of calls had been acknowledged, all bills had been paid in full, and the enrollment had nearly doubled. Toni and I were exhausted, but for me, it was a happy exhaustion. I wasn't sure about Toni—about the happy part, at least. Best of all, I sent a check for $2,000 back to Mom and Dad.

. . .

Winter school break meant absolutely no business for the girls camp. Most families vacationed, so Toni and I could travel and not be missed, but we opted to stay at camp and catch up on odds and ends. I ran budget projections, and it appeared that with the doubled enrollment, all our bills could be paid on time, some money could be put into building improvements, and Toni and I would have a little left over.

Lou reminded me to expect about a five percent cancellation rate, so more recruiting was needed to cover the possible loss. It was a great feeling of satisfaction. The campers were happy and were spreading the word to their friends. Staff members were returning and had their friends contact us. It appeared that 120 campers would be enough to make a respectable living. I never thought to take any of it for granted. One major camp injury and enrollment could head downward in a hurry.

After the winter holiday, an official-looking piece of mail arrived from A.G. Edwards addressed to Abigail. She had mysteriously opened a stock account—$2,000 worth of Hershey and Disney stock!

33

Welcome to Camp, Mom and Dad

Double the enrollment also doubled the amount of office work. By early June, we were receiving twenty-five needy calls a day from parents, campers, and staff members. Our larger creditors were hot on our tail as they began to see bigger dollar signs.

I did my best to use the local milk company, hardware and grocery stores, plumbing and electrical suppliers, lumberyard, wholesale food company, and office supply store. There were several other area companies that greatly appreciated the camp's business, helping to secure the good name of the girls camp in the community.

Most of the sixty-three campers and the staff members were returning, and several additional alumni staff also signed on to return. Those people, along with new campers and staff, made for a well-rounded mix. Macho Bob and a small crew spent long days preparing the grounds and cabins for season two.

Rooster, my baseball partner from the boys camp, volunteered to lead several staff orientation meetings. He had graduated from Chicago University with a master's degree in psychology and his background as both a camper and counselor made for valuable meetings. The staff appreciated his insight, and the fact that he was single and good-looking no doubt contributed to the staff's rapt attention.

I started my days at six a.m. and concluded them around midnight, since late night staff visits continued to be the norm. Camp was in place, the staff looked great, enrollment was nearly at capacity, the buses were due to arrive soon, and I was nervous. Not nervous for the coming season, but nervous because Mom and Dad were planning to make their very first trip to camp—any camp.

. . .

The noise level in the dining hall also doubled—deafening, but fun organized chaos, with girls cheering while standing on chairs, staff members doing pyramids, and cooks personally serving homemade brownies and being mobbed. Cabin songs and Tan and White cheers seemed to last forever, but I loved the spirit and by no means wanted to curb it.

Our camp was near several other girls and boys camps, and I scheduled multiple intercamp get-togethers, including soccer, basketball, baseball, tennis, archery, riding meets, and socials with the boys camps. The boys camp director that had snubbed us the year before decided that our enrollment had grown large enough to warrant our participation in a social. If it had been just the director, I would have waved goodbye, but I knew that our girls didn't deserve to be punished for his rudeness, and I also understood that it wasn't the fault of the boys. An additional plus was that the boys from that camp would recommend our camp to their sisters and friends. What a great deal! Our camp managed to get snubbed one year and recommended the next.

Crises were also the norm, and a day seldom went by without some type of scratch-the-head situation. During the second week of camp, two counselors came to the staff table during lunch and pointed to a friend who consistently wandered off during meals.

274

At that same moment, two homesick campers were sitting on Toni's lap, crying their eyes out. They were sure they were going to be sent home after two weeks of tantrums. The girls were ten years old, and every time they started crying, their cabin would join in. During that particular meal, a whole cabin of ten-year-olds had their heads on the table, sobbing up a storm. Even brownies didn't help.

It was raining for the third day in a row, so everyone was asked to stay in the dining hall for an extended songfest. The continual rain put the staff on edge, since their campers were restless. We scheduled rainy day activities, but it was hard to please that many girls with indoor activities. Rain, restlessness, lots of homesick campers, and a frustrated staff made for tough times.

The wandering staff member took off during the songfest, in the rain. The nurse and Doc discreetly followed as she headed to her cabin bathroom. Later they reported that the wandering girl threw up, brushed her teeth, and then quietly slipped back into the dining hall. The campers were singing, "Fire, Fire, Fire!" but without much enthusiasm. The ten-year-olds cried through the entire songfest, and the wandering staff member sat quietly at her table looking tired.

Phone calls poured in from not-so-happy parents. Some were sympathetic about the lousy weather, while others somehow blamed the camp for the downpour. However, the "pick my daughter up" mother from the previous summer phoned to say how pleased she was with everything. I told her to send Macho Bob a thank you card, but she didn't get the drift. It was hard for parents to get it, simply because they didn't live at camp. They didn't see the fun times, sad times, and hugging times, but they did receive the take-me-home letters.

Sometimes a camper would have an argument at rest period with one of her friends, after which she thought the whole cabin—or sometimes the whole camp—was against her. Then she'd instantly write a take-me-home, everyone-hates-me letter to her parents. The parents would receive it three days later and then would immediately call. Their daughter would be fine by that time and only vaguely remembered why everyone seemed to hate her. I chuckled at the parents inwardly, but not outwardly, since I'd been taught that the customer was always right. That cliché might have been accurate in the retail industry, but it didn't always apply to the girls camp.

Another call came in from an angry father who had been waiting for however long it took for me to get to the phone. I explained that sometimes I was at the other end of the camp and that he could have left a message to call him back. It was his fourth call, and each time he screamed that his youngest daughter was being mistreated by her cabin and demanded that she be moved.

He had an older daughter at camp, as well, and she caused quite a few disturbances. The angry father never mentioned the older daughter; he just squawked about his little one. The reality was that the younger daughter was having a fun summer. I brought her into the office and asked how she liked her cabin, and when I brought up the possibility of moving to another cabin, she started crying. ("Great job, Flash, smooth talking—way to think that one out.") I finally comforted her and told her not to worry; she would stay with her group. She left smiling, but then I called her father, who screamed at me, believing nothing about the meeting I'd just had with his precious little one.

I told him that his older daughter had a foul mouth and was causing some cabin problems, but he shouted, "I don't care about her g**damned mouth" and insisted that she was fine.

The wandering staff member threw up her dinner, as well. She was a wonderful counselor, very sweet to her campers, and quite wholesome, but she had a problem, and her type of problem was new to me. Doc brought the counselor into the office and I asked her point blank if she was throwing up food consistently.

When she denied it, I told her that Doc and the nurse had witnessed her throwing up after both lunch and dinner. She sheepishly said that was an invasion of her privacy. I asked if I could call her mother, and she started sobbing.

Just as I was handing her a tissue, the phone rang. It was the screaming father again. I'd never thought that anyone could have made Dad look even better, but that father accomplished the feat. As he was screaming gibberish about his "unhappy" daughter, my thoughts drifted toward Dad.

I thought about Dad's grin whenever I made a big play or when my brother was carried on shoulders for his home run. I thought about seeing Dad lay Bulky on the front seat of the Plymouth the day he died. I remembered how Dad had never called to complain to Lou, and how Dad was always there to help Mom with every step of her agoraphobic journey. As the tirade continued, I actually started to appreciate the screaming father, because he was reminding me of how lucky I was to have Dad.

The wandering counselor returned from the bathroom just as I was finally hanging up the phone. She was still sobbing, and tearfully let me know she was bulimic. She also said that her mother had suspected, but wasn't fully aware of her condition.

I was pretty clueless when it came to medical stuff, but I tried to act as if I knew what *bulimic* meant. She asked to speak to her mother in private, so I left the room as she made her call.

After a short time, the counselor called me back into the room and said that her mother wanted her to come home. What a sweet girl. It was so sad; she would have made a great counselor for many summers. I spoke with her mother, who was frightened but very understanding.

She apologized for her daughter's behavior, but I said, "There's no need to apologize. It's a pleasure to speak to a mother who truly cares. I also want you to know that your daughter will always be welcome here at camp."

It was all confusing to me. The bulimic counselor was very pretty, popular, smart, and appeared to have the world at her feet, yet she needed to go home. On the other hand, the daughters of the screaming father were staying, even though I thought about sending them home just to get rid of the father, but again it didn't seem fair to punish the girls for their father's behavior.

Later that night, I heard screams coming from the south field, where the younger cabins were located. One of the counselors called the office from the in-camp phone system to report that she'd seen the shadow of a man walking the field carrying a big bag. I rushed out with Ramona as screams came from all the cabins in that area.

The girls were relieved to see me, and they dramatized the situation by catching their breath and skipping words as they told me about the intruder. Suddenly the shadow reappeared, and Ramona took off, barking. To everyone's relief, the intruder called Ramona by name and then knelt down to give her a hug.

It was Macho Bob, hauling trash!

I asked Macho, "Why in the world are you carrying trash bags at midnight?"

"I was awake," he said, "and know we've got a big day tomorrow, so I figured I'd get a head start."

As we talked, I noticed that the stars were out, gazillions of them. Tomorrow would be a sunny day—and Mom and Dad were due at the end of the week. They were also bringing Aunt Lucille.

The sun came out the next morning and the following day, as well. The bulimic counselor went home, the dining hall cheers were again at peak level, the homesick campers stopped crying, Macho hauled the trash during daytime hours, Mel (the tomboy letter writer) was learning to slalom, the twins were as wild as ever, Patti continued to entertain at campfires and in the theater, key log thanks were pouring out in record numbers, and the angry father kept calling. I was exhausted at the end of each night, but I was having the time of my life.

• • •

D ad was lovingly holding Mom's hand as they descended the commuter plane steps. Aunt Lucille, all five feet of her, was right behind them. I could sense that Mom was shaking inwardly, but she'd made it! As they came through the airport door, Dad spotted me and gave one of his patented grins. That grin did it for me, as always, and I felt my body tingling with giddiness. Mom and Aunt Lucille each gave me a hug. Lucille commented on how well dressed I was, even though I was wearing old sweats, a T-shirt, and a ball cap.

Dad had reserved two rooms at a motel near the camp, and we dropped their bags off before heading to camp in time for the evening meal. Toni, Ramona, and Abigail were at the top of the hill to greet everyone. Mom claimed first right to hold her granddaughter, and Dad broke out with that grin.

Campers and staff members were just entering the dining hall, and I rushed down to say grace. As my family entered the hall, everyone broke into a traditional welcome song: "We welcome you to girls camp, we're mighty glad you're here."

Dad didn't miss a beat as he began to perform an impromptu soft shoe, much to the delight of the crowd. The meal noise was deafening, since the campers tended to up the level to show off for visitors. I also hammed up the announcements a little more than usual before declaring that the canteen would be open immediately after the meal. That announcement raised the noise level even higher. I wanted Mom and Dad to see real camp—true camp. I wanted them to understand why they never needed to call Lou to complain. I wanted them to understand why camp was in my veins.

Abigail led the way as Toni and I showed my parents around camp. Several campers were playing catch on the ball field. Dad instantly migrated that way while I rushed back to our house to pick up a couple gloves, and, of course, the catcher's mask.

I got behind the plate as Dad tossed a few to the girls. They hit almost every pitch, since he placed the pitches right down the middle. Mom and Lucille sat on the bench, laughing and having the time of their lives. It didn't take much to make Lucille happy, and it sure was nice to see Mom sitting comfortably. At least, she appeared to be relaxed. Dad was sixty-three, but at that moment, he could have been mistaken for a twenty-one-year-old staff member.

A fourteen-year-old girl stepped up to the plate, and Dad announced that he was going to throw his famous roundhouse curve. At the same time, I received notice that the angry father was on the phone again, wouldn't leave a message, and would be waiting until I picked up the phone. He was upset, really upset, I was told.

The girl at the plate was a good athlete, and I knew she was going to whack Dad's not-so-curvy curveball a long way. A nice crowd had gathered and was loudly cheering for Dad.

"Come on, Mr. Flash, throw it past her!" someone shouted.

Dad wound up and threw his patented roundhouse curve, and it actually broke downward. Swing and a miss! No one was in more shock than I when Dad then threw the same pitch for a swinging strike two. Playfully, Dad tipped his golf hat to the crowd as they went wild on the sidelines.

"Come on, Mr. Flash, strike her out."

I signaled for a third curveball, but Dad shook it off. I signaled again—but again Dad shook it off. Dad threw a fastball right down the middle of the plate, and the older good-athlete girl ripped it long and fair down the left field line. She ran the bases, hero-like, her arms raised, and jumped on home plate into the arms of the jubilant crowd that had gathered to greet her. The girls then hoisted her onto their shoulders and paraded her around as Dad sent a small grin my way.

No one rushed Dad, but no one needed to. Dad would have made a great camp director.

That night, Mom explained that visiting camp was the best therapy she'd ever encountered. All those years of living vicariously through the stories of my brother and me, she'd been saddened by the thought of holding Dad back. She was amazed at how independent the campers were, how they knew where they were going, and that no one held their hands along the way. She had sensed the value of camp that first night she met Lou and Renee.

She also noted that while I probably could have been a ball player, most ball players wouldn't purposefully throw pitches down the middle to help the other team. She said that most ball players wouldn't take time to throw to Sherman or allow themselves to get pushed off a raft by the smallest camper.

She said, "Most ball players wouldn't take time to befriend the crowd. Most ball players are untouchables, performing on stage—but a camp director can be touched by all of his

Campingly Yours

subjects."

She quietly shed a few tears of remorse because she'd never visited the boys camp, but I told her, "You made up for it today, Mom. You saw Dad throw a purpose pitch—right down the middle."

I let her hug me, and as I hugged her back, she said, "You know, your dad would have made a great camp director."

And the angry father was still waiting for me to pick up the phone.

Sailing at Girls Camp

A "cool" look during the early years at Girls Camp

Campingly Yours

Doc teaching swimming

Jackie the cook with Abby (left) and Anne B

Campingly Yours

Riding at Girls Camp

Morning wake-up quiz at Girls Camp

Campingly Yours

Macho Bob with his daughter Tia (Mini Macho)

Windsurfing at Girls Camp

Campingly Yours

285

Abby (left) and Anne B with Ramona

Ruth and Hudson

Campingly Yours

Grandpa George with his assistant Kevin in the camp workshop

My first 14-year-old group at the Girls Camp

 Campingly Yours

Anne B's first camp ride

Sparky

Campingly Yours

Oscar in his wheelchair (he walked again a year later in front of the entire Girls Camp)

Rose the bulldog

CITs who spruced me up for Mel

Male staff at Girls Camp

Pamela (Mel) and Flash (me)

34

Through the Years

The camper and counselor farewell speakers depicted the beauty of our second summer. There had been headaches, hassles, and daily crises, but the farewell speeches reflected only the positive side of camp. Typically, none of the campers were aware of the behind-the-scenes craziness and only Doc and a few higher ranked staff members had any dealings with crisis stuff. Going to bed exhausted was normal for me, but not the campers. They were at camp to have carefree fun. I had spent fifteen years as a camper and staff member, but I never thought much about the behind-the-scenes problems Lou and Renee encountered. I never had to take an angry parent call or deal with a bulimic camper. None of that had ever crossed my mind.

My second summer at the girls camp had been much tougher, but the campers had never felt my angst. Some of the campers were homesick, some had cabin problems, some felt left out at times, some made fools of themselves on stage, some showered a bit infrequently, some had a multitude of bug bites, some complained about the food, some had pinkeye, some took way too much medicine, some feigned stomach aches so they wouldn't have to swim in the lake, some insisted they were having their period so they wouldn't have to swim in the lake,

292

Campingly Yours

but some loved camp no matter how many of the above complainers were in their cabin.

Lou must have had angst. Lou loved his boys camp and I loved the girls camp. Bring it on—the good, the bad, the strange—all of it. I ate, drank, slept, and spent every waking moment thinking about the girls camp. It consumed me, it gnawed at me, it worried me; it was my life. I was married to the girls camp.

My goal of having camp spread into the veins of every camper and staff member had nearly been met. By springtime, camp was full, and most of the staff members signed on to return. It really bothered me if a camper didn't re-enroll, and I took it as a personal failure. What had gone wrong? Why had the camper dropped out? What could have been done to make her feel better about the girls camp? I had to accept the fact that not all female veins were made for camp, or at least not for the girls camp.

The April newsletter was copied in pink; a precious new camper had been added to the roster.

"We are happy to welcome first-year camper Anne B to camp."

Abigail had a sister. Dad put Mom on her first solo flight, and I picked her up in Minneapolis. A letter arrived from A.G. Edwards addressed to Anne B. It appeared that she also had miraculously purchased shares of Hershey and Disney! It was great having Mom help with the girls as Toni and I prepared for the summer. In fact, it was great having Mom there, period.

• • •

"I was here in '93, '93, '93. I was here in '93 where is '92?"

Another request night, another exhausting summer, but it was all still magical to me. As Toni and I counted the years down to 1979, I drifted back to memories—some good, some not so good, some sad—but all meaningful.

Lou and Renee sold the boys camp after my second summer at the girls camp. I had assumed they'd have their camp forever. I never thought about the boys camp ever being without Lou and Renee. They sold it to Leb, made the announcement in the rec hall, and then walked out. The campers and staff were in shock and sat in silence as they heard the announcement.

How tough it must have been for Leb to sit there without receiving any approval. Lou was the Master of All Campers, the Joe DiMaggio of the camping world, but I knew Leb would be fine. He was a great choice to carry on the boys camp tradition. The boys would soon learn that Leb would take over for DiMaggio and become a Mickey Mantle of the camping world.

Two years later, Moose became the owner and director of a girls camp in Minnesota, one of the oldest camps in the country. The property was beautiful, but the enrollment was close to zero. Moose and his wife worked day and night and finally succeeded in bringing the camp back to its glory days. Moose's mother would have been proud of her son. My hunch was that she had guided her son behind the scenes.

Dad sold the junkyard in the mid-90s. He told me about it after the sale had been confirmed. He named his price, and only one buyer made an offer. Dad said, "Not one dollar less," and that was it. The junkyard had been in the family since the early 1900s and Dad had been king of the junk world since the 40s. No more; he signed on to work for the new owners as long as they needed him. I also assumed that Dad would be at the junkyard forever. I knew the yard would never be the same, and I was right. Although the junkyard remained successful financially, it never was the same without Dad at the helm.

• • •

Jackie came to camp in 1981. Though she was overweight and moved pretty slowly, she was a baker extraordinaire. She took to Abigail and Anne B and snuck them into her cabin for all kinds of sweets. Jackie became a third grandmother to my kids. I hated the thought of all those sweets, but a grandmother figure for the girls during the summer was worth all the dental work in the world. Jackie prepared scrumptious banana bread with nuts for me and sent them special delivery to our camp house once a week. Jackie was a keeper, and I'd never let her get away. I could do no wrong as far as Jackie was concerned.

Ruth came to cook a few years later from a sorority in Tulsa. What a sweet lady, well-mannered, and a fantastic chef. She and Jackie whipped up all sorts of great meals for the girls. Ruth ordered the food and was a master at budgeting. She saved the camp thousands of dollars each summer and kept neat files. She was a very religious person and was a true blessing for me. After six summers of preparing yummy food, Ruth developed heart problems, not overly serious, but enough that her family would no longer allow her to cook for the camp. Ruth recommended Hudson, one of her associates, to take her place. Jackie remained a mainstay through all the changes.

Hudson was a unique individual. He was a former gang member, had never had a checking account, once cooked for golf professionals at a private country club in Denver, and lived with his sister and lots of nieces and nephews. As far as I could tell, the camp became his only job. He never collected unemployment, so whatever he made at camp was it for him until the following summer. He called each winter and asked for an advance, and I usually sent him $500. He was always very appreciative. Hudson was an old-fashioned cook and had no problem rolling out three meals a day for 200 people—by himself, if need be. I gave all of the cooks a special bonus at the end of each camping season, sometimes as much as two weeks' pay. The cooks became family.

• • •

Jennifer was thirteen when she came to us with numerous psychological disorders. She disrupted her cabin daily, so much so that other parents called and demanded that she be moved to another age group. There was nowhere to place her; it would have just been moving from one fire to the next.

I called her mother often, to the point that she complained that I was bothering her too much. Jennifer was an unwanted child. Her mother told me that she had no time for her daughter during the summer; she was simply too busy. I explained that Jennifer was threatening suicide in front of her cabin mates, but she said it was the camp's problem and that her daughter made the same idle threats at home.

Jennifer was a danger to herself and to those around her. The staff members weren't trained to help her, and neither was I. She cried, screamed, threw tantrums, and abused herself—she needed to go home. I called the mother and demanded that she pick Jennifer up, only to get a voice mail saying she was on a cruise for a week. Jack had said that there was no such thing as a bad camper, but he hadn't elaborated much about bad parents.

I placed Jennifer on full watch for a week. Other parents continued to complain, but I had no place to send her. Her mother returned from her much-needed cruise and reluctantly picked up her daughter. The mother outwardly was stunningly pretty, but I viewed her as ugly. I had failed in my every attempt to help Jennifer and never heard from the mother or Jennifer again.

• • •

Our horse program was always top-rated, and we leased the same horses each summer. Anne B loved the horses and hopped aboard by age three. She was a natural, and what a great deal for a little girl to have twelve horses—all pets—in her backyard.

She was feeding and grooming the horses by age six and became a proficient equestrian by age eight. Horses consumed her; they were all she talked about.

I'd never thought about a horse dying during camp until Apollo keeled over one afternoon. It was on a cabin day and fortunately the campers were in town. I called our forever horse supplier Art, and he told me to get a shovel and bury the horse. I thought he was kidding, but he wasn't. Macho and I couldn't exactly move a 1,200-pound dead animal, let alone dig the hole before the campers returned.

I reached a local excavator who said it would cost me double to bring his backhoe to bury the horse. I agreed to pay him if he could get the job done before mid-afternoon. Sure enough, he drove into camp with a big bulldozer, knocked down the main power lines, left live wires spread on the ground, found the horse, dug a huge hole, and placed Apollo to rest.

The campers returned to no electricity and one less horse. They had no clue what had taken place, and riders were told that Apollo was ill and had to go home. Anne B would have been devastated, more so than the other campers. I tried to be an impartial camp director, but I was relieved most of all to spare Anne B from knowing that she'd lost one of her beloved pets.

• • •

A close friend from the boys camp sent his daughter Betsy to camp. By age sixteen, she was a brilliant singer. Betsy was far more advanced than Sheriff Andy Taylor; she was potential Broadway material. Unfortunately, I happened upon Betsy smoking one day—not even sneaking a smoke like my brother's cabin mates. Betsy was a CIT. I wondered if I should tell her father or just be a confidential camp director and not say a word to her dad.

Betsy was counting on my trust, but I hated cigarettes and the thought of Betsy ruining her throat, so I reluctantly called her dad. I lost Betsy's trust for a while and let the two of them deal with the situation. Betsy eventually gave me a second chance as a camp director, returned for several more summers and directed camp plays. Years later she invited me to attend her Chicago performance of *Les Misérables*. Betsy had earned her Broadway role, but maybe her camp experience played a small part in that role.

● ● ●

66 ❚ was here in '93, '93, '93. I was here in '93, where is '79?"

That lively song was sung rather quickly, but the memories of all those years lingered. So many events during those summers, so many people, so many girls with camp running through their veins. Not every camper learned to bleed camp, but those who did knew they'd bleed girls camp for the rest of their lives.

Doc left camp after twenty-six years of devotion. I didn't want her to go, but she felt it was time. She was "old school," and the camp had become more liberal with each passing summer. Doc had helped save the camp and asked nothing in return. I looked at Doc as family and hoped she thought of me in the same light.

● ● ●

T oni was brought into a world she had never known existed. Girls camp wasn't in her veins. She worked hard, treated the campers nicely, and was the go-to person for the homesick girls, but she slipped more and more into seclusion as the summers progressed. Sometimes she stayed in our upstairs bedroom and became less visible to the campers and staff while I was continually front and center, taking all the heat or gaining all the accolades.

Mom asked if I was happy in my marriage. I knew it was a loaded question. Mom was continually receiving professional help for all her fears. She was perceptive, probably more so than most of her analysts. She offered me help, and I accepted.

I called her several times a week and we talked about all sorts of life situations. The conversations weren't always bleak; we talked about fun things, as well. She had a great laugh. Most of all, she understood me because I was her child. Even though I was in charge of all those girls each summer, I was still my mom's kid.

"No, Mom, I'm not doing so well in one of my marriages," I told her, "but my marriage to the girls camp is just fine."

Campingly Yours 🌲

· · ·

The fourteen-year-old group from my first summer proved to be all I'd expected. Most became solid staff members and leaders of the camp. The twins remained high-spirited and great promoters of the camp. Macho Bob announced that he was getting married and needed a full-time position. He had spent eleven valuable summers at camp, and he, too, had become part of the family.

Accidentally falling on the boys camp stage turned into a once-a-summer pattern at the girls camp. Toni and I were annually awarded best directors during a mock awards ceremony, and somehow I'd trip and fall four or five feet to some sort of "injury." The male staff members would carry me off stage, and the new campers were unsure about what had taken place.

One summer, I took my usual fall, and the crowd starting chanting, "9-1-1, 9-1-1."

One little girl in the audience began crying profusely. She was intensely worried about me.

"Daddy, Daddy! My Daddy's hurt!"

Anne B was four, and I had failed to consider that she might be concerned about my possible injuries—another brilliant move, Flash!

· · ·

Televisions were never a camp consideration during the summer. I had one upstairs in our house and tuned in either NBC or a fuzzy ABC in the spring. By midnight the only show on was the Home Shopping Network. One night, one of the staff members caught two campers watching a two-inch Sony TV, the latest in technology. Those campers were Abigail and her best friend, Stacy.

Great, my daughter should have been kicked out of camp, but there was nowhere to send her. It turned out that Stacy had brought the television, much to the dismay of her parents.

I confiscated it and told her that I'd give it back to her at the end of the summer. I became fascinated with that two-inch screen and tried it myself late that night. I dozed off to the Home Shopping Network and left the tiny set on the open windowsill ledge. Naturally, it rained that night and I slept through the storm.

I found the TV on the ground the next morning, soaked and ruined, and Stacy accused me of throwing her TV out the window. Luckily, she was a good sport, and it became a running joke among Abigail, Stacy, and me. Every time I'd run into Stacy, some comment would be made about the TV. Camp had a way of transforming simple incidents into larger-than-life memories.

. . .

D ogs continued to be an integral part of my life, and of life at the girls camp. I bought Rose, a pure white bulldog, thinking that a puppy would help revive an aging Ramona. It did help; Ramona visibly perked up. I also bought Rose because of the memories it would bring back for Dad.

The first day I brought Rose to see Mom and Dad was memorable. Dad's grin was wider than usual, and he and Rose got lost in the yard for what seemed like hours. Dad was in his upper 60s, but I was happy to see him rolling in the grass with Rose. I stared at them from the picture window, remembering the last time I'd watched Dad and a bulldog from a window. I had promised that one day I'd pay Dad back for all that he'd done for me.

A few moments later, Mom joined me at the window and quietly told me that she knew I'd seen Dad carry Bulky away.

"How do you know that, Mom?"

She added, "I also know that you've been worried about never being able to pay your father back, but I want you to know that you've more than paid him back."

"How's that, Mom?"

Campingly Yours

She said, "Abigail and Anne B, but also—"

She stopped speaking and simply pointed out the window.

· · ·

Camp tuition went up each year, the return rate for campers and staff consistently was 80–90 percent, and the girls camp provided a better living than I'd ever anticipated. I moved the family from camp to Milwaukee, then to Kansas City, and eventually to Tucson. Anne B and Abigail adjusted nicely to each move and it was great to see them develop a close relationship with their grandparents during the six-year Kansas City span.

Dad loved taking Abigail and Anne B for ice cream. He continued to gripe about the price of a cone, but he was the only one griping. Living close to my parents was nice for me, as well. I took up golf and the stock market so I could share more interests with Dad, and it was great getting insights from Mom in person, rather than through long distance phone calls.

· · ·

George showed up in 1989, the year Macho left for full-time employment and family obligations. George had just retired as owner of a machine shop in southern Wisconsin, and strolled into camp one day wondering if we might have a part-time position. He was a little grumpy, but he said he could tinker with most anything, told me that he'd just started collecting his social security, and wanted to keep busy.

"Sure, George!" I said. "Do you think you could rebuild the wood fence by the road?"

He said he'd bring some tools and get started in the morning. Sawing noises started each day at six and I often took a peek to see how George was getting along. The fence was being erected in perfect form, and he used a handsaw throughout the entire process. After a week of diligence, George had built a beautifully sturdy hand-sawed fence. Even for an amateur like me, it was easy to tell that George knew what he was doing.

I asked George if he knew anything about plumbing, and he said, "Sure, a little bit."

I asked if he knew anything about septic systems, and he grumbled, "Sure, a little bit."

I asked, "George, could you build an addition to a cabin?"

He exclaimed, "Sure, why not?"

I asked George about electricity, roofs, boat motors, auto motors, tires, clogged toilets, and changing oil, and he assured me, "Sure, all of that's no problem."

"Hey, George, do you know anything about kids?" I asked.

"Heavens!" he shouted. "Get out of here! I have my own kids and have a hard time remembering the names of all my grandkids!"

"George," I asked, "how would you like to work full-time, May through September, and then take the rest of the year off?"

"Sure, that sounds pretty good to me," he said.

"Great," I said, "Let me show you the shop."

George peeked in the shop and said in his gruff voice, "You mean you've got a table saw! Why didn't you tell me you had a table saw?"

As soon as the staff members arrived that summer, they immediately dubbed George *Grandpa*. Welcome to the world of summer camp, Grandpa George!

• • •

In the 80s, I finally woke up and realized that the camp's drinking and driving rule wasn't sensible. Yes, I had driven after drinking as a teenager—and as a boys camp counselor. Lots of people did, thought that didn't make it right. We just didn't know any better. I messed up with a lot of things growing up, but as a camp director and father, I felt that it was important to set disciplinary standards for the campers, staff, Abigail, and Anne B. Several of those standards were based on the very mistakes I had made over the years, so I knew exactly what

Campingly Yours

I was talking about.

The camp drinking and driving rule changed to a very simple format. Absolutely no drinking and driving—not one sip, and it was written into every staff member's contract that violating that rule would mean immediate dismissal. I emphasized it during staff orientation, and everyone was told their first warning was written into their contract.

The fourteen-year-olds were on a two-day overnight on Mackinac Island when I received a nine p.m. call from a frantic staff member. She'd taken campers to an evening movie and as she was leaving, she had seen the trip leaders stepping out of a bar.

She had asked them if they'd had anything to drink and they replied, "Only a couple beers."

One trip leader was also a licensed bus driver and the bus was the only mode of transportation for the trip. I called Grandpa George and he and his wife, Rose, volunteered to sleep in our house and keep an eye on things while Toni and I took off to rescue the girls.

What a mess, a five-hour drive, campers stranded in town, and the need to fire two "what were they thinking" staff members. The police eventually arrived and escorted the girls back to their campsite, so at least the group was in safe hands. Toni and I arrived at two a.m.

The trip leaders knew that I had to fire them, and they rode silently back to camp with Toni. I assumed the role of trip leader and bus driver, since I didn't want the girls to have their trip ruined. I had brought very few clothes, but the girls surprised me the next day with a nice pair of white socks. It was a simple, fun gesture of gratitude, but more meaningful than they could have imagined at the time. When I got back to camp, I washed the socks and placed them in my catcher's mask.

Ramona made it through sixteen summers of boys and girls camp. Dad had once said that the biggest problem with owning a dog is that they don't live very long. He had also said that watching your dog die was gut-wrenching, bringing a sad end to years of joy.

Ramona became listless just after the summer of '89. She sat and stared at nothing for two days, and I knew it was time to have the vet put her to sleep. I sat with Ramona and cried. I cried for Dad and his bulldog; I cried for not being there for Charley; and I cried as Ramona was taken away from me. Ramona had been there from day one at the girls camp and had been a friend to a thousand big and little girls.

I recited Dad's views on dog ownership to Abigail and Anne B as I thought, "So long, Ramona. Thanks for letting so many campers hug you. You never caused an ounce of trouble, Ramona. Say hi to Charley and Bulky. Come back someday, Ramona. Come back someday. I know you will."

35

Not Always Easy

By the mid-90s, trends for camps were changing—except at my girls camp.

Eight-week programs were becoming a thing of the past. Parents were requesting a four-week program, and some even asked about the possibility of a two-week session for first-time campers.

I couldn't stand the thought of change. I had grown up under the summer tutelage of Lou and Renee and only wanted to know "old school" camp. As a camper, I needed the full eight weeks. The first week, campers settled into their routine. Homesickness passed, friendships formed, and old timers had fun reuniting. During the next two weeks, campers learned new skills and honed old ones. Cabins worked on unity and mapped out events for the full summer. A certain amount of continuity was formed going into the fourth week, and then we had parent visitation weekend. The visitation took camp away from normalcy for two days, but shortly afterward, continuity returned.

By the fifth week, campers were becoming more proficient with activities and looked forward to working on skills they couldn't practice at home. New friends became best friends, and the staff became tighter. There was a constant feeling of excitement for upcoming events, special days, and shows. Then came the final few days—whew, what a build up of closeness, fun, arm-in-arm, staring at the burning camp effigy, crying, singing to Lou and Renee, and watching the buses slowly take the campers away from their eight-week home.

That same feeling of continuity was also engrained at the girls camp. At summer's end, I announced bus departure times and the girls chanted at peak capacity, "Hell, no, we won't go! Hell no, we won't go!" It was the only time I turned a deaf ear toward swearing.

Almost overnight, everyone had a computer; I was pressured from all sides to enter the modern age. My camp director friends did all their networking through their computers. They sent their newsletters and other correspondence via email.

The thought of my brother and I not rushing out to the mailbox, not ripping open the much-anticipated news of who was returning, and not jumping for joy when we read our favorite names all but did me in. The girls loved receiving the newsletters by mail, and so did their parents. Their feedback was positive and appreciative.

Then came cell phones. People had to be kidding! I broke into hysterics at the thought of Lou using a cell phone. Information through the media was moving so fast. Ten-year-old girls watched shows I had no idea existed. My daughters were learning things that made me blush. It was all passing me by, but I was determined to hold out as long as possible. The girls camp would be one of the few, if not the only camp to maintain its original format—at all costs. I made a nice living and was willing to forego a few extra dollars to keep the camp "old school," Lou's school—and Dad's school. Dad actually played golf partially to get away from phones. Dad and a cell phone in the same sentence—no way!

In baseball, the advent of the designated hitter really bothered me. Strategy was taken away and American League managers had an easier task—less thinking and fewer maneuvers. The thought of possible inter-league play was disturbing, as well. The mystique of the World Series would be lessened, I thought. Also, pitchers could no longer throw an 0-2 pitch inside without the possibility of having the batter rush the mound to start an all-out brawl.

I couldn't remember many players, if any, challenging Gibson or Drysdale on a high and tight fastball. In my mind, changing in baseball was equivalent to altering holy thoughts. Did baseball need those changes to survive? Maybe, but probably not. Did I need to change the girls camp to survive? Maybe, and probably so.

I visited numerous households where potential campers would ask if they could attend for four weeks; after all, other camps offered that option. When I answered, "No," it all but sealed the deal for families to look elsewhere.

I caved in to a small degree by allowing one cabin of first-year campers who attended camp for only four weeks. I then replaced them with a new group for the second four weeks. That lasted only a short time as the four-week option began to snowball. I ran two years of seven-week camps and even one season of six and a half weeks in a desperate attempt to keep a one-session feeling of continuity. Then the six and a half week families started asking for three weeks. There was nowhere to turn.

• • •

Toni was becoming less and less enthralled with the girls camp, and the campers could tell—news always traveled fast at camp. Parents were growing restless, as well. Eventually, Toni was confining herself for long stints in our upstairs bedroom. I tried to help her and then run down and put on a game face for the campers and staff. The pattern became run upstairs to help, run downstairs to teach tennis, start meals, console homesick campers, say grace, take a meal upstairs, then run back down to give lunch announcements, run up, run down, always keeping my game face on.

Campers continually asked for Toni, but I told them she was in town running errands. I hated lying, and it was an ugly thing to do. She was sick, but I couldn't help her. I had messed up; it wasn't all her fault. I had brought her into a world that was mine, not hers. I was married to the camp, and maybe she saw the camp as competition—and the camp was winning.

 Campingly Yours

Junior counselors were caught drinking and had to be handled accordingly; a cook walked out; a mother called, screaming that her child had been placed in the wrong cabin and demanding that she be moved. I tried to pretend that our marriage wasn't in trouble in front of Abigail and Anne B, but they were both in high school and were no dummies. They knew, but I couldn't let them know that I knew they knew.

I tried to hide everything from my girls, from the campers, from the staff, and from myself. I hated reality, but still loved the girls camp. I hated four weeks, but I'd rather take that than no camp. I hated computers, cell phones, and fax machines, but I loved answering machines, since I hated taking calls, especially negative calls, asking, "What's wrong with the camp and what's wrong with you?"

I loved answering machines.

• • •

After eighteen summers, Jackie was no longer at camp; her knees had given out. One summer, a not-so-campy cook walked out and left Hudson alone. I ran downstairs from our house to the camp kitchen and told Hudson to do his best. He took me aside and said he would cook for the entire camp, the last two weeks by himself. He would have three solid meals ready each day, plus a good dessert. He reminded me that I had sent him money every winter as an advance. He told me no one had ever trusted him before, and then he urged me to go take care of my family. That summer, Hudson used part of his bonus money to buy a leather jacket, his first ever. When he returned home, the jacket was stolen. Life wasn't always kind to Hudson, but he was family to me.

Mom asked me if I was happy with my marriage. It was again a loaded question. She knew I was running upstairs while running myself down. She asked if I was still happy owning the girls camp. I told her that I was trying to show happiness; trying to keep the magic alive. I owed it to the campers and staff. I told her enrollment was slipping, I was slipping, Abigail and Anne B were slipping, and I was facing two strikes with one to go.

Mom was the only one I felt comfortable confiding to; not anyone else, not even Dad. It wasn't Dad's area, and I was embarrassed for him to know that I was having problems. I asked Mom not to say anything to him, but she probably did; married couples have a way of spewing all.

Mom was easy to talk to, analytically smart, but without the need of a couch. She was fulfilling a great purpose in life by helping her son. I had been the director of campers and staff for all those years, but I was still her kid—and I needed help.

Mom asked me, "What happens when a player faces the two-strike pitch?"

I told her, "The Vacuum taught me that after taking two, I should hit the ball to right field."

Mom asked, "What happens when you hit to right field?"

"Usually good things, Mom," I said, "and it's the best way to advance the runners."

After a momentary pause, Mom smiled and said, "Flash, it's time to hit the ball to right field."

• • •

Jack ventured back to the boys camp in his later years to head the CIT program. Each summer, Jack took his group to several camps, and one night he and his boys stayed overnight at the girls camp. I always set Jack up with a doubles game and made sure he had a solid player as his partner. He loved hitting with the girls and was never short of compliments. He loved the girls camp and was happy that the program consisted of old-fashioned traditions. Jack was a purist and had no care for modern-day conveniences interfering with camp life.

I always learned a lot from Jack, starting from the first day I met him at the boys camp staff orientation. I knew there was something special about him, and he was eighty years old when I finally realized just how much camp had consumed his life.

We held a campfire for the CITs, and Jack explained the value of training to become a full counselor. Jack was as enthusiastic as the day he'd led the staff orientation my first year back at boys camp. Our girls loved him and asked why he was still working at his age. Jack laughed and said he had never had a real job. After all, camp wasn't work to him.

The next morning at six a.m., Jack conjured up a few CITs to do a polar bear swim. I jumped in with him; what a thrill for me to swim with a camp legend. Jack didn't see himself that way, but I did. Just after breakfast, Jack popped into the office to say goodbye, since he and his CITs were headed to another boys camp.

As he turned, Jack tripped on the top step and ripped a big gash in his leg. Blood was everywhere, and I learned that he had a medical condition that caused excessive bleeding. Jack screamed in pain for several minutes. It was awful! His screams were frightening and I thought he may not make it.

Our nurse rushed to the scene and slowed the bleeding, but she said that Jack needed to go to the emergency room, so we readied a vehicle. I wanted to go with him, but Jack said no and emphatically refused to go.

"I need to get my CITs to the boys camp by ten this morning, and I don't want to be late," he said.

To him, his boys were more important than his bleeding leg. Jack was special. He had devoted his entire adult life to camping—his camp, other camps, campers, CITs, counselors, and directors. Jack had never made much money and never owned a home. He survived that bad leg day and completed the CIT trip, making sure his boys gained a valuable experience. Jack eventually went to a doctor and received some stitches in his leg, but to him, his leg didn't matter; his CITs mattered.

Several months after his visit, Jack fell into a coma and never recovered. The camping world had lost a legend, but the legend never knew he was a legend. There was always something special about Jack, and I was extremely lucky to have been friends with the man

Campingly Yours

who had never met a bad camper.

· · ·

Toni and I were divorced in the late '90's; it became final one day before parent visitation day at camp. She wasn't at camp that summer, so I was on my own. Enrollment had dropped twenty percent, but the diehard girls who had camp in their veins remained loyal. It was hard finding new campers; most families deemed it safer to send their girls to camps without internal problems. I had finally given in and set up two four-week camp sessions. Without that move, the girls camp just couldn't compete, since all the other area camps had converted to four-week programs years earlier.

I realized that the campers needed an adult female in camp, and I had stayed in touch with Patti over the years. I contacted her in the fall to see if she'd help out. She had just made a career change and was excited at the opportunity to return to the camp where she'd spent most summers during her childhood and teens. I hired Patti full-time as a co-director and she assumed recruiting, parent contact, and countless other duties. Patti brought with her a vast knowledge of camp tradition—and her musical talent. The campers and staff instantly responded to her as co-leader of the girls camp.

· · ·

How did dogs end up being such an integral part of the girls camp? Maybe it was foreshadowing when Dad brought Charley home, maybe it was Dad's view of dog ownership, or maybe it had started the day I watched Dad carry Bulky away. Charley had taught me true friendship and Ramona had showed me pure devotion. Rose was my sidekick at camp for eight years and Dad loved every minute he was around her.

One spring, Rose tangled with a porcupine, and true to her breed, she didn't give up on the fight. Macho Bob had taken a week off his work to help with spring clean-up, and he

Campingly Yours

and I found Rose loaded with hundreds of quills. Rose looked like a porcupine herself, and it took a five-hour midnight operation to remove all those quills. Macho fainted en route to the vet at the sight of the bloody Rose. I was more worried about Rose's prognosis than Macho's image, so I kept the fainting part of the episode to myself. Macho didn't remember any of it.

Rose never fully recovered, and just before camp began, Abigail and Anne B discovered her floating in the lake. I swam from shore to recover Rose's body, then wrapped her in a wool blanket and carried her out into the woods. I dug a hole and gently placed her in it. Then I bought a white rose and placed it on her grave.

I thought about how Abigail and Anne B openly wept as they watched me carry Rose away. There was no window, so I knew they knew—and Dad knew that I knew.

I called Dad to tell him that I'd lost Rose. He paused for a long moment, and then quietly told me to give Abigail and Anne B a hug.

• • •

Sparky the wiener dog dominated our canine scene throughout the '90s. He was a nine-pound miniature dachshund, shorthaired, and brownish-red in color. Small dogs and little girls belong together, and the campers swarmed all over Sparky on a daily basis. Although he was actually Anne B's dog, he became my sidekick during the summer when Anne B lived in a camper cabin. Some claimed that Sparky was literally attached to my hip. He helped teach tennis, performed skits on stage, pinned a few staff members during all-staff wrestling skits, and got lost several times in the woods. When Sparky was missing, it created havoc among all the campers, especially the young ones, so all activities immediately ceased and an all-out search began.

Homesick campers always asked to hold Sparky, and I became convinced that he was the best cure for tears. During winter reunions, the first question asked by campers was, "Is Sparky coming back?" It was hard to keep an exact count, but I was sure Sparky played a significant part in enrollment. He was camp *shtick*, and everyone expected something from Sparky. It was all fun and magical to me, and I suspect to Sparky, as well.

36

Thanks,
Mom and CITs

Hundreds of letters and calls poured in after my divorce. It was wonderful to know that so many people cared not just for me, but for Toni, as well. My friends set me up on dates—but no go. Unbeknownst to me, Abigail had changed the birth date on my driver's license, thinking I might have a better chance at meeting someone. Thanks to Abigail, I had a fake ID, just like all the staff members—great.

Mel left a message on my answering machine, saying she was sorry to learn of my situation. She said she was also living in Tucson, my hometown, where she was a teacher for the deaf. That was the same Mel who had once written a note to me in pencil before my first summer, saying she was looking forward to camp—the same tomboy Mel who had learned to ski on a canoe paddle, become a staff member, and eventually promoted to village director.

I called her back and left a thank you message on her machine. Later, she called again and suggested that it might be nice to meet and catch up with each other's lives.

During my camp director years, I had taken hundreds of girls out for dinner, pizza, and ice cream. It was no big deal; just part of the personal touch I knew the girls enjoyed. It was a

Campingly Yours

kick for the girls to go out with their camp director. I picked Mel up and we had dinner at a quaint restaurant that had live jazz music. During the meal, I was a camp director to Mel and she was a former camper/staff member to me.

She told me all that was going on in her life and how much she enjoyed working with deaf children. I told her a bit about my situation, and when the check arrived, she offered to pay for her part of the meal, but I said no—a camp director would never let one of his girls pick up the tab.

My friends fixed me up with more dates, but none of them worked out too well. I called Mom to let her know that I wasn't cut out for the dating world. She suggested that maybe I should take off my ball cap and spruce up a bit.

"OK, Mom," I said, "but this going-out-on-a-date thing really isn't for me."

I was bouncing around town one afternoon in my red Miata and thought I'd see if Mel wanted to go out for ice cream. It had been a month since I'd had dinner with her. Over many summers, I had often "snuck" staff members out for ice cream. It wasn't really a problem. I was the only one who could have fired them for it, and they were with me.

Mel wasn't home, so I left a note on her door, telling her that she'd missed a convertible ride and a chance to get two scoops of her favorite flavor. She called me later that night and said she was sorry she'd missed out on ice cream, but she said she was only free on Tuesdays, so we set up another dinner meeting. As time went on, we met for several Tuesday dinners, but I was still a camp director—nothing more, just a camp director.

I received an invitation to a New Year's Eve party and asked Mel to tag along. Her mother was in town, so I invited her, as well. The afternoon of the party, Mel called to let me know she wasn't feeling well and would have to cancel. I let my friends know I probably wouldn't make the party, but they started yelling at me, saying that there would be several single women and that it would do me good to let loose a bit.

I said, "OK, I'll try to make it."

I stopped at an Italian restaurant and ordered all sorts of carryout dishes—and then headed to Mel's house. Her mom was overwhelmed by the gesture and the amount of food, but let me know that Mel was sleeping and was too sick to eat anything. I had a great meal with Mel's mother, said hello to a sick Mel, and then headed home. I had no desire to meet single girls at a party.

I called Mom late that night to wish her a happy New Year. She said there was something different about my voice.

"What's that, Mom?" I asked.

"I don't know exactly," she said. "There's just an upbeat, happy tone."

"What do you mean, Mom?"

"I'm your mother and I can tell your moods," she said.

I told her there was a girl I kind of liked, but I didn't think anything would come of it. Mom asked if the girl liked me.

"Maybe," I said. "We've had a few dinners together."

"Well, did you spruce up a bit for her?" Mom asked.

"No, Mom," I replied. "I still wore my ball cap."

Mom asked, "Are you happy?"

"Maybe, Mom," I said. "Her name is Mel."

Mom said, "Keep wearing your ball cap."

• • •

After more than twenty years of owning and directing the girls camp, each summer still offered new and exciting challenges. The crises remained similar—sick campers, cooks not getting along, staff members misbehaving, power outages, continual rain causing cabin fever and extra homesickness, boats not starting, inflatable rafts deflating, camper and staff eating disorders, parents complaining but sending their daughters back each summer, and more camper medicines than any camp nurse should have had to endure.

I finally was persuaded to purchase a computer to modernize the camp. That meant creating a website and sending most mailings via email. Campers would no longer be digging in their mailboxes for the monthly newsletters. The whole thought was depressing. The always-sacred newsletter had joined the ranks of the Pony Express.

I wrote a three-page newsletter, pressed a button to spell check it, and then pushed another button that sent the information instantly. No stamps, no address labels, no licking to seal the envelopes—just an email address list and the push of a button.

I thought about all the campers through the years who had received those cherished newsletters once a month from the mailman. Then I thought about all the modern-day campers who would never know that feeling. That wasn't a happy sad feeling—just sad.

. . .

The summer of '99 was a nervous time for me. Enrollment had increased, loads of staff members returned for their eighth to twelfth summers, Patti was a big help, crises were at a minimum, the weather remained sunny, and all of it continued to be magical to me. However, anxiety still threatened to overwhelm me. I was feeling the same apprehension I had experienced that first summer when I took the members of our girls camp to Lou and Renee's boys camp. It was almost the same feeling I felt the year Mom and Dad made their first-ever visit to camp. It didn't matter that both experiences had turned out better than I could have imagined—I was still a wreck.

Mel was coming to visit!

The preceding February, I had mumbled to her that I wasn't exactly going out with anyone else. She sheepishly and cutely muttered the same words. I asked her if that meant I was no longer just a camp director. She smiled and told me I was still a camp director.

The CITs and I were very close that summer, and they came into my office often to shoot the breeze about anything and everything. They called it *bonding*. I told them about my

Tuesday dinners with Mel, the New Year's takeout food that she never ate, and how my mom had told me to keep wearing my hat. The girls ate up the conversation; they loved being in on their camp director's personal life.

Next, I informed them that Mel would be visiting the camp. They screamed with excitement and quickly started planning ways to fix up my appearance.

I asked, "What if Mel has a bad visit and decides to dump me?"

The girls could tell that I liked Mel a lot, but they also could tell I wasn't too confident. I promised to introduce Mel to the girls and asked them to help me along the way. The CITs loved our bonding session that night, and so did I.

I headed to the Rhinelander airport to pick up Mel, the same airport where Mom and Dad had landed years earlier. I was just as excited to see Mel that day as I was to see Mom make her very first visit. Mom would have understood—the same way Dad understood how I viewed Lou.

After a few moments of waiting, Mel came down the steps, beautifully tan, with hurricane-like curly brown hair that whirled in all directions. Her smile was as wide as a smile could get as I put my hand out to offer my welcome. Instead, she gave me a full-out hug and kiss! I was glad the CITs weren't around.

Mel's stay at camp was phenomenal. She made friends quickly with lots of campers, and the CITs took her in as one of their own. She helped with water skiing and swimming, and the girls appreciated her instruction. She also taught everyone the song "Friends" in sign language.

"I think that I shall never see, the kind of true friend you are to me. I think that I shall never find the kind of true friendship that is yours and mine."

The tune was beautiful, watching the whole camp perform sign language was beautiful, having the campers and staff take to Mel was beautiful, and of course, Mel was beautiful.

Before the week was over, I asked Mel to marry me. I hadn't planned to ask her; it just happened. I had no ring—and I was wearing jeans and a ball cap. I guess I panicked; I didn't want to let her get away.

My proposal caught her totally off guard. She said she had to think about it, but she didn't think very long—and then she said yes!

I phoned Mom and Dad, and Mel spoke to Mom for two hours. I loved every minute of their conversation, even though I heard only one side of it. After they had hung up, Mel told me that she already loved my mom—which came as no surprise.

The CITs were ecstatic at the news, and they took partial credit for Mel's not dumping me. As I put Mel on the plane and initiated a goodbye hug, I asked if I was still just a camp director.

She smiled and said, "Yes, you'll be my camp director forever."

And Mel would be mine forever, too.

37
Don't Leave Me

Mel and I didn't waste any time and set a December wedding date. I took her to St. Joe after camp to meet Mom and Dad. Mel and Mom sat in the living room and gabbed for hours. They were a perfect union. Meanwhile, Dad and I sat in the den, leaving the gals to themselves.

In the past, Dad and I would have gone to the driving range, but he told me he'd quit golf. He said that most of his golfing buddies were gone and he couldn't keep up with the younger guys. Dad wasn't being "poor me" about it; he just couldn't play well anymore. Then he reminded me that he had never played well, although he'd probably had a better fifty years of golf than most low handicappers. Dad never became proficient at hitting a golf ball, but fond memories of his time spent on the course made him a great golfer.

Dad took me to his bedroom and pulled out a jewelry box. Inside was a classic elegant gold bracelet with a small diamond set in each link. He had bought it for Mom in New York several years after they were married.

We rejoined the girls, and Dad handed the box to Mom, who in turn presented it to Mel.

Campingly Yours

Mel cried as she tried on the bracelet and said that she couldn't accept it. Mom said she had cried too when she received the bracelet, almost fifty years earlier.

Mom said, "Wear it in good health and someday hand it down to another person you love."

The bracelet was worth a lot of money, but its real value was Dad's memory of giving it to Mom, and her memory of receiving it.

Later that fall, a month before Mel and I were to be married, Dad suffered a severe stroke—and Mom's world instantly crumbled. She delayed calling my brother and me, since she didn't want us to see Dad in such a dramatically altered state. Mel and I flew in a few days after his stroke and Abigail met us, as well. Mom, Mel, and Abigail all broke down, crying feverishly—as I watched. What an awful spot for Mel, just coming into the family and having to endure such family pain.

I stepped into Dad's room. He sat in a wheelchair, staring Sherman-like out the window.

"Hi, Dad, it's Flash."

No response.

"Hi, Dad," I repeated as I stepped directly into his line of view.

No response.

I just sat there and stared at the man who had thrown countless balls to me; the man who had grinned every time I did something that pleased him; the man who had doubled the savings bonds gifts; the man who had let me borrow against his life insurance; the man who had believed that I could run a girls camp when hardly anyone else did; the man who had always believed in me, no matter what I did. Mom, Mel, and Abigail were still crying out in the hall. I sat with Dad and cried inside.

I wanted to call off the wedding, but Mom wouldn't allow it. She said that Dad would be against it, and it would hurt him to know that he was the cause of hurting Mel and me.

"OK, Mom," I said. "Dad's in enough pain, so the wedding will take place as planned."

Two days later, a nurse took Dad to a gym facility in the basement of a rehabilitation center. Mom and I accompanied them. Most of the patients were in wheelchairs, dressed in hospital gowns with tie strings on the back, and couldn't function without help from a physical therapist. Therapists were manipulating legs and arms, several patients were using resistance bands, some were climbing small wooden stairs, and others were being taught to regain their speech.

Two therapists stood Dad up from his wheelchair and handed him a large red playground ball. One steadied Dad while the other stood in front of him, trying to get him to toss the ball her way. No luck. They tried several times, but with the same negative result. I walked over and stood in front of Dad, a few feet right of the therapist. Out of nowhere, Dad faked a toss to the therapist and threw a red bullet my way. I caught it—barely, but I caught it. I stared at Dad in amazement and he gave me an off-center, stroke-ridden grin.

• • •

Mel and I had an outdoor wedding under the desert sky. Mom and Dad were unable to attend. The glow on Mel's face during the ceremony was a picture I'll always remember. To me, she was Sherman standing on first base, she was Sherman's mom and dad witnessing their son hit a ball, she was Lou grinning at the bonding of the Merry Fairy House, and she was Dad rolling on the grass with Rose the bulldog. Why had Mel chosen me? She could have had a million guys, but she chose me. It didn't matter. I was just glad she said yes.

Two weeks later, Mel and I flew to Missouri to show Mom the movies of the wedding. She loved the wedding shots, but it was apparent that she was having a tough time adjusting to Dad's illness. Mom had always depended on Dad for most everything, and suddenly she was living in the house alone. Dad was fighting his way out of the wheelchair, and I thought he recognized me, since he perked up each time I walked into his room.

We left on Sunday, but I called Mom at least two times daily to check on her and track

Dad's progress.

The following Thursday, I said goodnight to Mom, and on Friday there were several frantic messages on my answering machine, saying, "Flash, call home right away!"

I didn't want to make the call. I didn't want to hear about Dad. I couldn't take the news, so I closed my thoughts to Dad leaving. I stalled, not wanting to make the call, but I finally reached a voice—one of Mom and Dad's neighbors. It wasn't about Dad; it was Mom. The fire department had broken into the house and found Mom in her bedroom. It was Mom. That was it.

It was Mom.

It was Mom.

At that moment, my thoughts went directly to Moose. I slumped onto my desk, trying to get a handle on the shock of losing Mom so suddenly. Moose had been so young when his mother died, but for the first time, I could walk in Moose's sadness. How had he made it through when he was just a kid? I was a middle-aged man and the hurt was the worst I'd ever experienced. How had Moose been able to endure? I felt sorry for Moose, but I also felt sorry for me. Mom had always guided me through. She was my confidant and my voice of reason.

Dad was fighting to get out of a wheelchair and had just lost his wife of fifty-two years— even though he didn't remember being married.

I read Mom's eulogy and Moose attended the funeral, but Dad couldn't make it.

• • •

The May newsletter brought loads of response from the parents. I talked about the upcoming summer, the bus schedule, rules for parents and campers, and ended with the following:

A Mother's Day Comment from The Flash

I was thinking about Mother's Day as it approached this Sunday. I always managed to send

my mom a card, as I never was home for her special day since I took over the girls camp. Lately, I liked sending the flowery kind, since she normally would expect a humorous one with a picture of a bulldog doing something ridiculous. I'd write something nice and mushy, just to surprise her even more. She'd call me and tell me how much the card meant to her. She'd almost cry (maybe she did cry), and then let me know what a wonderful son I've been over the years. She'd brag to me about myself and let me know how much my dad thought the same way (it was Sunday—golf day for Dad). She talked about Abigail and Anne B, how great the camp has been over the years, what a wonderful father and husband I've been, and on and on. I'd say "Thanks, Mom," implying that a mom has to say those things to her son.

Those kinds of conversations went on for years, since we talked all the time, no matter where I was living. She read every newsletter and let me know how informative they were (and also corrected my boo-boos). She loved living vicariously through me and kept up on all my happenings. Did I mention that when I was a few dollars short, she and Dad loaned me the money to help buy the girls camp? Neither of them would accept a payback.

My mom called me Flash, and I called her Millie B. Maybe that's how we arrived at Anne B. I suppose it was unusual for a son to stay so close to his mother. I liked still being a son, since it seemed to throw me back to the old days, when all the responsibility was placed on the parents. During those phone call moments and the times when I visited home, I forgot about reality and just was allowed to become a kid again.

"Millie B, Flash is home!"

Here came the fruit plate, soup, perfectly-made omelet, or anything else gourmet. We told jokes, talked about camp, her antique collection (watches, oyster plates, silver, crystal, and cookbooks), since she was modestly an expert on all subjects. She was a fashion designer, a writer for the blind, and an artist. Few knew any of this about her; she preferred bragging about her son, The Flash. She was my biggest fan and she let me know it constantly.....even when I messed up. It didn't matter. And when I did mess up or became confused with life, I'd always go to her first. Did I mention that she was an amazing analyst and kept her couch open at all times? I used that couch

Campingly Yours

quite a bit.

All of you campers take note. Talk to your mom, listen to your mom, ask questions of your mom, help your mom understand you, and remember your mom this Mother's Day. You don't need to buy her a gift. Present her with a card, write something nice, and wait for her response. Stay in touch with your mom constantly and forever. You'll be glad you did, and you'll have no regrets.

Millie B died a couple months ago…in her sleep. As I was reviewing the above paragraphs, I realized that something special has been going through me my entire life. Millie B was my biggest fan, and I, The Flash, was Millie B's biggest fan—and I will be forever.

We wish you a wonderful May, and we'll stay in touch throughout the spring.
Campingly yours and love,
Mel and The Flash

• • •

My own drive to run camp had inwardly diminished, but Mel was excited to take on the role of camp director. She became a Pied Piper to the campers, as well as to the staff. She was a natural leader and offered much-needed guidance.

She could tell a camper "no" while having her arm around the camper in the process. She was caring, loving, and stern, and she was by far the hardest worker at the camp. Everyone noticed her presence and everyone respected her efforts to keep the girls camp at a high standard. Parents were impressed with her candor; they knew they were speaking to a well-educated, thoughtful director. I was impressed by how she could handle so many aspects of camp and still have the time to teach aerobics, Pilates, and beginning swimming activities. Mel revitalized the girls camp—and me.

Dad had progressed from the hospital to a nursing home, and I visited him just before staff orientation. I hated the thought of a nursing home and Dad would have loathed the idea if he had known where he was living. Some of his functions returned and he was able to walk.

 Campingly Yours

I felt he still recognized me. He had trouble completing thoughts, but he still perked up whenever I walked into his room. He had no recollection of Mom or of being married to her for fifty-two years.

Dad's sister Thelma visited him almost every day and helped care for him the way a mother would care for a son. I felt guilty about having to return to camp; I wouldn't see Dad until the campers left.

Dad asked when I was coming back, and when I said, "Soon, Dad," he grinned. Time didn't mean too much to him. I called him most every day that summer, and he always asked when I was coming to see him.

"Soon, Dad, soon."

. . .

I was here in '03, '03, '03. I was here in '03, where is '02? Where is '79?"

After more than forty years in camping, too many thoughts raced through my brain as the end of the year song wound down to 1979. I thought about Hudson, who had served eight summers of meals, who had helped me in my time of need, yet never had a dime to his name.

Hudson had developed prostate cancer and was living in a nursing home in Tulsa. I called him, and he was excited to hear my voice. He wanted to spend the summer at camp. When I asked if he felt well enough to help out in the kitchen, he said he'd be on the next bus. I talked to his head nurse, but she informed me that Hudson was on morphine and was in an advanced stage. She also said that Hudson didn't understand how bad his condition was. The doctors wouldn't let him travel.

Two weeks later, I received a call that Hudson had passed away. His family asked for money for the burial. I spoke again with his head nurse, who told me that Hudson had wanted to return to the girls camp in the worst way. Hudson had told her that the camp was the only place he ever considered home.

We named one of the cooks cabins The Hudson. I had lost another family member.

• • •

"I was here in '03, '03, '03. Where is '79?"

A quick song, but with long memories. Dad needed brain surgery, and my brother and I had to decide if Dad should have to go through that form of agony. The doctor advised us that the surgery could possibly help Dad gain a little better quality of life—but there were no guarantees.

We hated making that decision. Neither of us wanted Dad to suffer, but we took a chance and said yes. Dad made it through surgery and a few days later was placed in the lockdown center of the nursing home. It was awful—there was no other word to describe it. My brother headed home, but I stayed with Dad. Then I received a call from Mel, informing me that Sparky, then age thirteen, had suffered a seizure. According to the veterinarian, Sparky's chances of survival weren't good.

I sat with Dad, thinking about Sparky. All those years with the Little Man and all those antics at camp—for all those years. Dad needed me, and Sparky needed me. How could I not be there for Sparky? Maybe I could pull him out of it. Charley had looked for me, but I wasn't there. Sparky needed me, but I was with Dad. Dad needed me, Sparky needed me—I stayed with Dad.

Sparky died the next morning, but I had chosen Dad. If Sparky could have talked, he would have told me to stay with Dad. One week later, somehow, some way, Dad perked up and asked me to take him to the casino. He won $165 and grinned each time the blackjack dealer pushed money his way. I shook my head in amazement at my dad.

As the camp mascot for thirteen summers, Sparky had been an integral part of the lives of many girls. I wrote a eulogy for Sparky in the December camp newsletter:

Hi Campers and Counselors,

I want to let all of you know that Sparky passed away today at the age of thirteen. He was known as the Sparkman, the Young Man, the Sparkster, the Sparkmeister, the Little Man, the Three-Legged Man, the Baby Man, and countless other names. Sparky was the girls camp mascot for thirteen summers. Each year, he comforted numerous homesick campers and had a daily line of campers waiting to walk him.

He acted in more than thirty-five performances on stage and appeared each year in the camp video. He was shot in archery many times and dragged away, but always managed to recover. He rode horses, climbed the wall, sailed, chased deer, performed sign language, and always barked on the morning wake-up calls.

He appeared each year in the all-camp photo, and always campers would plead, "Can I hold Sparky?"

He was kicked twenty feet into the air by Tex the horse and taken to the vet—assumed dead. Upon arrival at the clinic, he opened his eyes, gave a big wink, and was pronounced totally fit by the doctor. He was stuck under a lakefront cabin for a night, stabbed by a porcupine, and lost for a day in the middle of the North Woods. Campers searched high and low as we whistled for him on the intercom. A ten-year-old camper found him just before dinnertime. We then proceeded to march him around the dining hall in conga line fashion as he wore sunglasses and a visor.

Everyone chanted, "Spark, Spark, Spark is out of the dark."

Sparky's last hurrah was a wild wrestling night with the "evil" James. He pinned James to the count of three as the theater erupted in a deafening chant of, "Sparky, Sparky, Sparky!" He thanked James for being a good sport as they hugged at the end. These are just some of the numerous camp adventures of the "Young Man."

I found Sparky in a small cage in a pet shop in Kansas. A lot of people walked by as he hid timidly in the corner. I walked by and he came forward with his tail racing back and forth, almost in a blur. As I left, I watched people walk by him again, and he retreated back into the corner. I came back to the store later that day with Anne B. There he was, sitting lonely in the corner. Anne B walked over, and I stood behind her. The "little man" walked right to the front of

the cage, and there went his racing tail again. Anne B pleaded to have him.

I said, "Anne B, we don't need another dog."

She said, "Let's call him Sparky."

And so began the Little Man's career as a great family dog and camp mascot.

Spark, Spark, is now in the dark. I know he thanks all of you for the hugs, the scratches, the

walks, the caring visits, and warm cuddling. I know he thanks all of you for being his friend and

for your love. I think that on opening day next summer and every summer to come, the Sparkman

will come out of the dark and look down at all of his camp friends. He'll see the campers piling off

the bus and his tail will become a racing blur. So long, Little Man.

We hope all of you have a nice December.

Campingly yours and love,

Mel and The Flash

• • •

"Where is '79?"

So many events, so many happy campers, funny staff members, crying campers, frustrated staff members, tired staff members, and tired directors. I fell off the stage each summer, handed out countless amazing prizes at wake-ups, marveled at Mel turning sad campers into laughing campers, and watched as a thousand little girls transformed into caring counselors.

"I was here in '79, '79, '79, where is '78?

No one was left standing.

ou became ill and faded quickly. I called Renee, and she explained that Lou was fighting hard, but had trouble speaking.

"Hi, Lou," I said when Renee handed him the phone.

He took forever to respond, and I knew he wasn't just putting down his pipe and clearing his throat before he finally said, "Hi, Flash."

When I asked how he was getting along, he said, "Not well."

Renee took the phone, and that was the last time I heard Lou's voice. I flew to Milwaukee for Lou's funeral, and there were former campers from all over the country in attendance. Without realizing it, Lou had put together another boys camp reunion, and it was nice to see everyone for a great reason—to honor the Master of All Campers.

A year later, Renee passed away—prompting another boys camp reunion for another great reason. I thought about the impact that Lou and Renee had had on my life. Their guidance had led me in a positive direction. I only could hope that my acts of guidance would be as meaningful to others as the ones that had been bestowed upon me by Lou and Renee.

As I thought about those two wonderful people, I found myself whispering, "So long, Lou and Renee. Make sure your film breaks, wherever you are. There's still a lot of camping to do."

38

Not All Magical to Me

A **fun night of sports culminated at the basketball court as campers cheered for** their favorite staff members. The entire camp surrounded the court as the final event ended. Just for the heck of it, I took a basketball and stood at half court. I shouted to the campers and staff that if I made a hook shot, the whole camp could go for ice cream. Without much fear of making a half court hook shot, I let the ball go, Globetrotter style— and swish—all net. I was feeling it.

Everyone stormed the court and I felt as if I'd hit a hole-in-one. Actually, it was a better feeling than any hole-in-one! All the campers and staff piled into vans and we shuttled off for ice cream. It cost me over $400, and I couldn't help but think about how much Dad would have complained about the ice cream bill.

Dad remained pretty constant for four years. He considered the nursing facility his home and didn't complain much. He knew me, but had trouble expressing his feelings. He remembered distant events more than recent happenings. He still couldn't remember being married to Mom, which was the toughest part for me.

He remained jovial and often mentioned giving money to people. He loved the casino, so I took him there every day of each visit. Amazingly, he came out a winner more times than not, despite the fact that he couldn't read the numbers on the cards. We went out to dinner each night, and once in a while I'd sneak him a half a beer or glass of wine.

Sometimes Mel would make the trip with me and she'd take Dad walking in the park. That was a beautiful sight, seeing the two of them strolling by a pond and throwing bread to the ducks. Dad lit up whenever Mel walked into the room. He knew she belonged to me.

Once in awhile I'd test Dad's memory. He remembered his original address and phone number and could sing every Frank Sinatra song. One day, I was sitting in the room with Dad and it occurred to me that he'd never told me why he was grinning that day he was being robbed.

"Dad, do you remember the day two guys held you up with knives and I walked in, only to see you grinning?"

He said, "Yeah, Jack Benny."

That's all he said—Jack Benny. Then I realized that he had to be referring to the old "your money or your life" routine!

"Dad, did you know those guys had real knives and could have killed you?"

All he said was "Don't tell your mother."

In one of life's many transformations, we had switched roles and I had become Dad's dad. All those years of wanting to pay Dad back—and I'd finally gotten my chance. Dad needed me like I used to need him, but I wasn't paying Dad back. I didn't need to pay him back. In fact, he wouldn't have expected to be paid back. It made me feel good to help him, and I imagined that it was the same feeling Dad had all those years helping his own two sons. Dad didn't need his son to pay him back. I was Dad's dad, and I wanted to help him—with no payback necessary. Why hadn't I figured that out years earlier?

・ ・ ・

M el and I completed our fifth summer together as directors and she continued to amaze me with her never-ending willingness to be there for the campers and staff members. She became a true friend to the campers and a trusted confidant to the counselors. Every day she taught aerobics, Pilates, and beginning swimming classes. She was also in charge of the kitchen, the infirmary, camp supplies, helping with the older cabin special events, organizing CIT training, and participating in staff evaluations. On top of everything else she was the go-to person for homesick campers and the main contact for parents. She had a way of speaking to campers and staff members—and making them listen.

The girls camp was full, and Mel was the primary reason. She was the most complete camp director I'd ever known. Lou and Renee would have been proud of her; I wish they could have seen her in action.

We were averaging an eighty percent return of staff members and a ninety percent return of campers. The girls loved the camp and we loved them. A few parent complaints didn't bother me, a few cabin problems were normal, now and then a staff member would be unhappy, and sometimes a crisis day would occur—but none of that really bothered me. The girls camp was all magical to me.

Mel and I flew back to camp during the last week in September to enjoy the fall colors. What a serene time it was to walk around the camp. The variations of leaves cast multi-colored reflections on the lake and cobwebs hung on each building, their maker putting on the finishing touches before the harsh winter set in. Two-foot beehives hung by the webs and deer pranced across the fields, playing their own form of touch football. Mel and I sat silently as nature took care of our thoughts. It was all magical to me.

We sat by the lake for an hour with no cares and no outside world bothering us, just a bald eagle soaring toward its nest. We finally strolled back to our house, where I heard a beeping on the answering machine. I pushed the playback button to hear the message I hadn't wanted

Campingly Yours

to hear—the one I had dreaded for four years.

I thought I couldn't listen to that message, but I did. A nurse had called to inform me that Dad had passed away in his sleep that morning. While Mel and I had been enjoying our no-worry peaceful morning at camp, Dad had shed all of his worries. He had quietly left the world to which he'd given so much happiness—without asking for anything in return.

I sat by the lake and thought about the man who had thrown thousands of balls to me; the man who knew his roundhouse curve wasn't so curvy. I thought about the man who cried for his bulldog and laughed at his push button station wagon. I thought about the man who had given up part of his life's desires to stay by Mom's side.

I remembered the man who had thought Lou and Renee were decent people. I thought about the man who had thrown a ball right down the middle to make sure a camper got all the glory. I thought about the man who had grinned at the thought of my brother rescuing a bumbling father from a sailboat. I recalled the man who had once told me to think about Abigail before I dealt with five drinking staff members. I thought about the man who had doubled my savings bonds.

I stared motionless at the lake and remembered the man who had always made me tingle every time he grinned my way. I recalled the man who had told me to go for the camp, even when almost everyone seemed to think it was a bad deal. I thought about the man who would have made a great camp director. I remembered the man who gave me my catcher's mask.

I was never really Dad's dad. I still wanted his approval, even during his four-year illness. Dad grinned every time I walked into his room at the nursing home. I always had his approval. I didn't need to dive to my left to throw someone out or to save the girls camp from condos to earn it.

I hadn't understood that for years, and the first time I realized that I didn't have to fight for Dad's approval was the day he did that cute little dance in the dining hall. It was so cool watching Dad improvise, and equally cool to see the campers take to him. Then, when he threw that pitch right over the plate to the athletic camper, I knew I was like Dad, and he was like me. Dad was king of the junk world, a great father, and an overly devoted husband. Dad would have made a great camp director.

"So long, Dad; don't leave me, Dad. Say hi to Mom and Bulky for me, Dad. Don't leave me, Dad. Tell Charley I'm sorry; don't leave me, Dad. All my life, Dad, you were there for me. Your roundhouse curve always broke my way, Dad, right into my heart. So long, Dad…so long, Dad…so long."

• • •

The following summer, the camp was full, the campers were happy, and the staff was full of girls who had grown up with me. Mel was everywhere, as usual, and the noise level in the dining hall remained at peak level. I woke everyone up with songs and quizzes, and amazing prizes were given out almost daily. Oscar, the paralyzed wiener dog, had done his best to replace Sparky's antics, and Maggie had long been the reincarnation of Ramona.

Counselors frequented my office late every night. The faces were different every few years, but the conversations remained the same. I was lucky to have so many wonderful staff members over the summers. They were the ones who carried on the camp traditions and welcomed all the new campers to their summer home.

However, it wasn't all so magical to me anymore. I'd lost my zest, my zeal, my enthusiasm the day Dad passed away. I never let the campers and staff know and I kept my magic loss to myself. Mom was gone, Dad was gone, and I needed to be gone.

A wonderful young man from the boys camp had worked for Mel and me for several summers. He'd learned every angle of the girls camp except ownership. He planned to own a camp one day, so after some serious thought, I sold him the girls camp.

He agreed to let me stay on as long as I wanted as a guide and mentor. His enthusiasm reminded me of my own—twenty-seven years earlier. I knew that wonderful young man would put his heart and soul into the girls camp, so I wrote a letter to the campers, parents, and staff members, explaining that there was going to be a new owner of the girls camp:

Dear Girls Camp Friends,

Mel and I trust all is well with you and that you're enjoying a nice summer season. Camp is approaching the final days of the summer and it never ceases to amaze me how fast a camping season can sift by. It actually amazes me how fast the past twenty-seven years at the girls camp have breezed by, and with that thought, I send you this letter concerning upcoming changes for Mel and me, and the girls camp.

Mel and I will be turning over the reins to Cliff, and he'll be the new owner at the end of this camping season. For all of you "Mel and Tom" old-timers and followers, please bear with this letter and you'll see this is all very positive for Cliff and us. In fact, I've signed an agreement with Cliff that states that Mel and I will be co-directors for many years to come (maybe indefinitely—some of you might have grandchildren here before we move on). Mel and I will be keeping the property on the south end of camp, including the house and second ski area.

The reason Mel and I would consider this transaction is two-fold. First, we'd be able to remain active directors for at least ten years. Second and equally important, Mel and I needed to find an individual who is totally devoted to not only the girls camp, but to the camping industry as a whole, and there's no doubt in our mind that Cliff is the correct choice. Mel and I have grown quite close with Cliff these past years and we know his concern for each camper and staff member is genuine. His concern that the camping industry remains strong is a vital element to our decision.

Cliff spent his camper and counselor days at my boys camp (twelve summers) and came to us with glowing recommendations from their directors, Sue and Leb. Cliff has been our co-director and head counselor for the past three years. He has visited with new campers and families the past three winters and has headed up new staff hiring, and Cliff has been totally involved with winter mailings and correspondence.

It's of extreme importance to Mel and me that Cliff is dedicated to carrying on the traditions of the girls camp—Tan and White, Friday campfires, key logs, cabin songs, crazy lunch and dinner

Campingly Yours

meals (the spirit will continue), trips, theater, horses, my early morning wake-ups, the fun evening activities, the Creed, and of course all of the fun and rewarding practices we've become accustomed to over the years. But most important is the fact that Cliff truly believes in the welfare and advancement of each camper and staff member. Mel and I believe that Cliff will put his heart and soul into the girls camp, and if we didn't think this, we wouldn't be writing to you at this time.

When I was reaching for my dream (twenty-seven years ago) to own and direct the girls camp, I was told by lawyers, accountants, and friends that it was a bad deal, don't do it. The girls camp was being sold for real estate and there were very few campers. Only three people encouraged me to go for it—Lou (my camp director), and my mom and dad. They knew where my heart was and let me know in simple terms that they had confidence in me, and through the years they remained proud that I was able to build the girls camp into a giant learning ground. I'm forever grateful for their encouragement and will carry their lesson of wonderful guidance with me forever.

Our counselors know that at the weekly staff meetings I like to review the past week and go over upcoming events. I suspect that maybe I've bored them with my ramblings, but I guess that's the way I am, so here's a quick review:

I've been at the girls camp twenty-seven years; I've helped form thousands of relationships and countless best friends; I've fallen off the stage at our camp version of the Academy Awards for twenty-six summers; I've given out punishing demerits in jest, and fleegles, and assistant to the assistant directorships; I've umpired twenty-three leg wrestling championships; I've been shot with archery arrows eleven summers with Sparky on my head; I've been run over by horses and pummeled with tennis balls, only to be dragged away by happy campers; I've listened to 18,312 key log speeches (I kept count); I've taught first period tennis since day one; I've watched twenty-seven song-and-dance shows, forty-two musical productions, and actually "starred" in Bye Bye Birdie; one summer I had staff members named Macho Bob, Jim Bob, Bob Jim, Beth Bob, Regular Bob, and Donna Bob, and I was brought into the fold as Flash Bob; I've watched our sailors beat all the boys camps at the huge boys camp regatta; I've watched our sports teams not lose for nine years to other camps in the 1990s (OK, I suppose I always had a bit of competitiveness in me); I was lucky to watch Abby and Anne B grow up at camp; I was twice murdered in the all-camp murder mystery (most everyone cheered); I've never kept a clean office desk; I've handed out 192 United Nations Day torches to elected captains; I've watched twenty-six Tan and White songfests and interrupted the winning announcement each year (and always got booed off the stage); I've co-hosted twenty-seven parent weekends (thanks to most of you for not complaining); I've not smiled in twenty-seven all-camp photos; I gave out 12,152 prizes at morning wake-up quizzes; I sang such songs at campfires and in the theater as: "Teenager in Love," "Walking," "Garbage Man," "Bye Bye Blue," "When I First Came to This Land I Was Not a Wealthy Man," "Welcome to Girls Camp, Our Ten-Year Girls," "Shanty Town" (in sign language by Sparky and Oscar), "Don't Take Your Guns to Town" (with Doc and Anne B), "Johnny Apple Seed" (and the middle verse), "Keep on the Sunny Side," "Piccolomini," "I Was Here in '79, '79, '79," "Good Evening, Folks, Good Evening, Folks," "Today is Monday," and "Girls Camp You Are Good Enough for Me;" I helped deliver 4,051 graces before the meals; I've ridden up and down the emotional rollercoaster when girls announced, "Flash, your momma called, and she said—;" I had two "extra" grandparents for my children— Grandpa George and Jackie; and finally, I was fortunate enough to meet the love of my life, Mel. I could go on for fifty pages, but I think you get the idea that it's been a really nice ride.

Now the upcoming events (remember, I do this at staff meetings) look very promising. Cliff will take over ownership. Mel and I will stay on as co-directors and continue giving our all to camp. Mel will teach aerobics and swimming and will continue to be a vital part of camper and parent relationships. I'll continue doing all of the above mentioned and will keep bringing in new songs, programs, and fun times. Mel and I will continue to live on the grounds as usual and be here for all of the camp happenings. I think you get the point; Mel and I plan to be co-directors of the girls camp for many, many years.

Thank you for all of your support, and Mel and I look forward to many happy camping experiences with all of you.

Campingly yours,

Mel and The Flash

Campingly Yours

• • •

That night, Mel fell asleep while I lay awake, thinking about my life in camping. I knew I had disappointed Mel; she was a great camp director and camp owner, and I had taken that away from her. She was an even better wife; she never complained about my decision. She was happy to be able to stay on and help as a mentor, an aerobics and swimming teacher, and as an overall guide to the campers and staff members.

"Why did I take that away from Mel?...zzzzz...No, I wasn't that sleepy—do I see a few cobwebs in the corner of the bedroom?...There was always sand in the bed. Did The Bulk shake his blanket on purpose?...zzzzz...The Big Guy looked perturbed when his film broke, but he let my brother fix it...zzzzz...Don't be mad at me, Dad, for selling the camp...zzzzz...I'd give anything for one more roundhouse curve...I'll wear my catcher's mask...zzzzz...You can pick on me all you want, Snarl...zzzzz...my brother told The Vacuum that I'd catch his curveball...Lou was watching...zzzzz...I'm sorry, Mom. Tell Dad not to be mad at me for selling the camp...zzzzz...She said Dad never got mad at me...zzzzz...The Merry Fairy House, up on the camp world's shoulders...zzzzz...Be well, Sherman; stay by the dock, Sherman; Dad will pitch to you, Sherman...at armpit level...zzzzz...Your shoes are untied now, Kid Flash...zzzzz...I don't want to fall asleep...zzzzz...Thanks, Doc, Macho, and Jackie...Grandpa George...zzzzz...Get it? Got it!...Not good...zzzzz...Mom and Dad, say hi to Moose's mom...zzzzz...The last bus has left, Supplecheck, I need to go now... zzzzz...Hudson, make a meal for Mom and Dad...Dad will buy you a leather coat...no need to pay him back...zzzzz...No bad campers, Jack...Renee, take care of the Master of All Campers...zzzzz...Be well, Charley...thanks for listening...zzzzz...Spark, Spark, come out of the dark...zzzzz...I scribbled your name at River Rats, Ramona...This is too hard; I need to sleep...zzzzz...Sorry, Mel; sorry, Mom; sorry, Dad...forgive me...zzzzz... 'This girls camp is your camp, this girls camp is my camp, this girls camp is made for you'...but not for me anymore...zzzzz..."

Epilogue

I awoke early the next morning while Mel was still in a deep slumber. My night's rest had been anything but restful. I quietly put on a pair of jeans, a t-shirt, and a ball cap and headed to the lake. It was overcast and the clouds reflected a multitude of formations in the water. I thought about my life in camping and how magical it had all been to me. I hoped that I had also made it magical for those around me.

I thought about all the girls who returned year after year, all those key logs of praise and thanks, and all the campers and staff members who claimed the girls camp as their summer home—their second home. I thought about all those newsletters I had loved writing, and hoped that the girls had enjoyed reading them. I thought about giving the drinking counselors a second chance and about how each one had returned several summers as even better counselors. I thought about the guidance of Lou and Renee, not just for me, but also for thousands of boys. I thought about hearing Lou tell me that I'd make a good camp director.

I stared at the cloud formations reflected in the lake and framed a vague picture of Mom and Dad. I couldn't quite make it out, but the clouds were slowly swirling into place.

I thought about Supplecheck, The Vacuum, The Bulk, Moose, Farb, Rooster, Leb, and Macho Bob—all great friends for life. I'd made so many great camp friends—for life. I thought about all the guys at the boys camp and all the gals who had attended my girls camp. They too developed into close friendships—for life. Camp friends didn't go away; maybe they lived in different areas, but the friendships remained—undying.

The cloud formations of Mom and Dad were becoming clearer. I still visited The Bulk now and then. I still had all the questions, and he still had all the answers. It was always as if we had never parted.

I still planned to wake the girls up each morning and accidentally fall off the stage each year. Oscar and I would get shot with arrows and campers would continue to win amazing prizes. Mel would remain a solid mentor to all the girls, and so would I.

The cloud formations were becoming quite vivid.

My zest for camp had never left, and it still could be magical. Those cloud formations of Mom and Dad made sense, and I framed them perfectly in my mind. I ran into the camp office, grabbed my catcher's mask, and hustled back to the lake.

I must have looked like a complete nerd to anyone who might have seen me wearing my mask and staring at the lake—but I didn't care. I spoke out loud and announced that I was going to write a book, my memoir about summer camp—containing anything that came to my mind.

Then, with my mask firmly in place and my hat on backwards, I announced that one day, when the book was finished, I'd help start or save another camp.

The clouds had arranged themselves into a vivid picture of Mom and Dad, sitting in their fold-up lawn chairs. Bulky the bulldog was by Dad's side. I knew they'd heard me say I was going to start or save another camp.

I stared at those cloud formations through my catcher's mask and clearly saw Mom clapping happily while Dad stood and looked straight into my eyes—wearing a huge grin.

Author's Note

The purpose of Campingly Yours is to help children from all over the country and world have a chance to attend a summer camp program. The majority of my proceeds will be donated to various camp scholarship funds.

Jennifer Lynn Snyder
1991-2008

The camper every counselor hopes to have.
The counselor every camp director hopes to have
The friend everyone hopes to have.

Jennifer passed away at home suddenly, while playing soccer. She was a seven-year camper/counselor at Chippewa Ranch Camp. I have included her scholarship fund information in her memory and honor. Proceeds sent directly to the Jennifer Lynn Snyder Scholarship Fund will be used to help children from all over the country and world attend a summer camp. The Snyder family and I thank you in advance for your contribution.

> **The Jennifer Lynn Snyder Scholarship Fund**
> P.O Box 475
> Northbrook, Il 60065

Campingly yours,
Thomas C. Adler

. . .

About the Author

Thomas C. Adler cried on his first day at North Star Camp for boys—and got a face full of pudding. He told his parents he did not want to go to camp and hated camp that first day. Forty-five years later, he's still at it, serving as co-director of Chippewa Ranch Camp for girls, in Eagle River, Wisconsin. Thomas owned and operated Chippewa for 27 years.

Thomas was raised in St. Joseph, Missouri, and resides in the "off season" in Tucson, Arizona, with his wife Pamela and dog Oscar. Thomas has two grown daughters, Abigail and Anne B. Each attended Chippewa Ranch Camp for over twenty years.

About the Publisher

Campingly Yours is published by **Five Star Publications**. One of Five Star's missions is to help authors create books that help foster tolerance and acceptance of the differences in others. President **Linda F. Radke**, who started the firm in 1985, has worked with hundreds of authors over the years; some famous, some obscure, but all with the messages they wanted others to hear. She's garnered a long list of publishing awards along the way. Five Star is one of the country's leading small press publishers. Book Publicists of Southern California recently named Linda "Book Marketer of the Year".

5 Five Star Publications, Inc.

Endorsements

"... Campingly Yours is more than a loving memoir of summer camp, it is an enchanting journey through the heartland of one man's life. Written with disarming simplicity and honest emotion, the folksy anecdotes and wry observations entwine like woodsmoke from an evening campfire. The book invites you to sit down and listen in to treasured stories full of laughter and friendship, music and memory, a sense of life's joys and its inescapable sadness.

In addition to being a wonderful read, Campingly Yours asks us to share the author's lifelong desire to preserve and extend the values of a lost American childhood, a more innocent time in which boys and girls were able to experience life more directly, independently, and responsibly. To Adler - and all of us lucky enough to have shared similar summertime adventures - camp is far more than a place or a time; it is a way of looking at the world.

As a writer, Thomas C. Adler is an American original. His prose is distinctively homespun - understated, yet deeply felt; by turns amusing, sweet, and often surprisingly affecting. You know from reading this book that Adler is the guy you want in your canoe on a long day's paddle into the wind.

I recommend reading Campingly Yours to anyone who has been to summer camp or wonders what they missed by not going to camp. And they missed a lot. Beyond that, however, the book will appeal to anyone who wants to know what it was like to grow up in a more innocent age and discover a singular slice of heaven in the forested lakes of northern Wisconsin."

Jeff Melvoin
Television Writer/Producer (Hill Street Blues, Northern Exposure, Alias)

"Campingly Yours is an honest and heartfelt memoir about a lifelong journey of finding a dream and making it come true. It's about dedication, perseverance, family and finding true love. Campingly Yours made me laugh, cry, and want to go back in time; back to the time of being a child and having no worries in the world… except waiting for another season of summer camp to begin.

Thomas C. Adler takes the reader on an exciting ride through the north woods of Wisconsin. He is honest, passionate and devoted from child to adult. Thomas C. shares with us as he fulfills his dreams and the dreams of many others, through a time and place of simplicity, to a time of modern technology. Every person should experience what it's like to have a 'home away from home'. A place that is so special, that it becomes a part of you for life…a place that is 'in you blood'."

Betsy Werbel
Ensemble Member of the National Tour of Wicked, The Musical.

"Campingly Yours is much more than a book about camping. It helps you appreciate how strong families are the core of a strong society. It is full of lessons in life that display how wisdom, loyalty, dignity, and humility are essential qualities that can propel someone to reach his or her goals in life. This book takes you back to your childhood and jogs your memory to help you trace your steps back to the foundation of life that made you the person you have become."

Jerry Hairston Sr.
Former Major League Baseball Player
Hairstons: The only family in Major League History to have five members to play in Majors:
Father Sam Hairston, brother John, sons Jerry, Jr. , and Scott.

"If you have been fortunate enough to have experienced the joy, the memories and the "magic" of camp, this book will resonate as loud and clear as the camp dinner bell! But it's not just for "camp people". It's for everyone that appreciates the joy and magic of family and friends and the great and touching experiences of life. Masterful, on the mark..."

Gary Baier
Camp Birch Knoll for Girls, Eagle River, WI

"Tom Adler's book does a great service to those of of us who believe in the positive power of the camping experience . It provides a humorous and touching personal history that is deeply connected to the best traditions of camping in America--teaching children and young adults about community, responsibility, self-reliance, and respect for the environment. As a former camper and counselor, I recommend this book to anyone who is interested in the best that camping has to offer."

Paul Adelstein
Actor

"If you've attended summer camp before, Tom's book will deluge you with your own camp memories, thoughts, and feelings as you read about his. He recounts details so vividly, you can remember being there yourself. This book clarifies for us that camps need not be about the latest technology on their websites, or the gourmet food coming out of their kitchens, or even the slick ski boats or basketball courts. As Tom's journal of camping makes clear, camps do their greatest good through the people they bring together to live and play for a summer, and learn for a lifetime."

Mike Cohen
Owner and director of Camp Timberlane for Boys

"Campingly Yours is an engaging read with appeal to anyone who has been to summer camp, is considering camp for their children, or is interested in human psychology. It will bring back memories, provide a guide of how camps 'work', and foster understanding and tolerance. Thomas C. Adler is a natural."

Gary Stern
President, Federal Reserve Bank of Minneapolis

"Campingly Yours brought smiles, laughs and a few tears. So many memories came pouring back. Whoa! Tom's stories of his camper and counselor days made me feel as if I had just stepped out of a time machine to relive the important moments of our childhood. Reading of Tom's life as a Camp Director renewed my passion for our chosen profession.

Thanks, Tom, for validating the work of everyone who has been a camp counselor."

Mike "Moose" Jay
Co-Director: Camp Kamaji for Girls
Co-Founder: Camp For All Kids Foundation

"Thank you so very much for allowing us to read an advance copy of Campingly Yours. My husband and I found Tom Adler's book to be one of the most touching and heartwarming stories we have ever read! We laughed, we cried, and we reminisced. Although the characters and events in his book are real, the subject matter is universal. Tom's love of family, passion for camp, and concern and understanding for humanity make this book a must read! It is truly a 'LOVE' story. Thank you for giving us the opportunity to express our feelings about Tom's beautiful and inspirational book of memoirs."

Diane & Jim Levy
Vice Chairman, Levy Entertainment

"No matter how many miles we've traveled away from that fantastic little camp in the corner of northwestern Wisconsin, those of us who were lucky enough to spend our summers there will never forget it - leeches and all. Tommy, the Flash, Adler brings it all hilariously back to life with the warmth and accuracy of his memories. He's done a lot of camping since I first saw him throwing pop-ups to himself on a dusty baseball diamond and, like his mentor Lou, is now a senior pied piper for the joys of living in the woods. So write your name in your underwear, pack that trunk, and go camping with the Flash! You'll have a blast."

Regards,

Chip Zien
Actor - Broadway, Television, Movies

"Campingly Yours is a heartfelt valentine to summer camp. Warm, witty and wise, Campingly Yours demonstrates that traditional values like friendship, compassion and loyalty never go out of style.

Thomas C. Adler is "full of compassion and insight into the lives of kids who find themselves away from home for the first time. He understands as well the feelings of young adults who experience their first taste of leadership and responsibility, and relates it with down-home Missouri wisdom."

Michael Katz
Writer/Producer, Prevalent Films, LLC

"Campingly Yours is a wonderful journal of a boy who attends summer camp, and the effects this experience has on his life. This story is heartwarming and reminds us of the 'old days', when life was much simpler, and relationships were the barometer for personal growth.

Thomas C. Adler is expressive and thoughtful in his presentation. His life experiences are truly heartwarming, and his writing style expresses his commitment to his story. The way he chapters the book gives a fluidity to the story, while a better understanding of this life is understood. Tom's life experiences will bring a tear to your eye, a smile to your face, and an appreciation for those that touch our lives."

Stephanie Moss
Director, Camp Lenox

"Campingly Yours is a warm, vivid picture of how camping can extend and strengthen one's family. These are not just one man's memories-they are a guidebook to keeping alive the flames of friendship and family, both in the shared communal moments themselves and the power those moments can retain over time if they are cherished, understood, and passed on.

Thomas C. Adler's voice is unique. And it should be, considering his varied experiences, his life's intersection with the paths of so many people so important to camping, and-most importantly-his unflinching honesty with his own feelings. A clear, powerful memory makes for a clear, powerful memoir."

Dan Bernstein
CBS Radio, WSCR 670 The Score

"Campingly Yours is an insightful view to a kind and giving soul who has grown from a young camper to a reflective adult. Tom has grown and matured as he witnessed and facilitated the development of his campers and staff.

Thomas C. Adler is as kind and generous in his writing as he has been in his real life-never taking the credit that he is often due. I loved the book and felt disappointed when it concluded."

Beth Paradies
The Paradies Shops

"Campingly Yours is a poignant recap of the memories that were important milestones and building blocks of a life and career in camping. That career was truly a passion and continues in all those campers who were lucky enough to experience a summer with Thomas C. Adler.

Thomas C. Adler is eloquent in his easy style of down to earth poise that makes the book a fast and enjoyable read."

Fritz S. Hirsch
President of Sassy, Inc

"Campingly Yours did not have me from page one. Nope, it wasn't until page three that I was magically transported to Lake Plantagenet in Bemidji, Minnesota, where I spent my formative summers. Tom Adler's evocative memoir is a must read for anyone who has ever hunted for snipe, searched for skyhooks, or skinny-dipped in the north woods."

Steve Fiffer,
Author, former camper at Camp Thunderbird

"Campingly Yours is a heartfelt story about a relationship between a boy and his family that can't help but put a smile on your face. It is a must read for anyone who has ever spent time at summer camp or for anyone thinking of sending their kids. If you have had bug juice, sand in your sheets, or sung songs around the campfire you will love to relive your memories with this book because as you know, that camper is always going to be a part of you throughout your life.

Thomas C. Adler is an amazing camp director and surrogate father to many. He has a place in my memoirs as he provided my home-away-from-home and through camp helped me to become the person I am today. I was happily surprised to see that he is also a gifted and talented writer. I look forward to his next surprise."

Sandra Gordon
Emmy Award-winning producer and published author

"... Campingly Yours is: A loving reflection tracing a young boy's journey from his first years at a summer camp through to his golden years assisting his successors in directing the girls camp he ran in Wisconsin for many years. In frequent anecdotes, Adler gives the reader a solid glimpse at the constant challenges a camp director faces. This book is hard to put down.

As a writer, Thomas C. Adler is able to capture the uncertainties of a 10-year-old boy on through his many years in the magical world of summers at camp to his years as a camp counselor and then a director. His love for his parents, his camp directors, his own campers, his staff, even his dogs who inhabit his Wisconsin summers, shine through on every page.

I recommend reading Campingly Yours to anyone lucky enough to have spent a summer at camp. They will find in Campingly Yours all the fun, growth, tears, and laughter, that is present in a well run camp as well as the depths of love we all can derive from living every day of our lives."

Bernard Stein
Retired Co-Director Camp Nebagamon

"... Campingly Yours is a page-turner. Though I have "been there, done that," Adler's memoir was compelling and transforms his life in camping into a book which will interest anyone who has ever been at a camp-or who has ever been a child!

As a writer, Thomas C. Adler is literate, tender and honest. He has the unusual combination of being able to write like an adult, yet describe from the perspective of a child, then a young adult, then a nostalgic about-to-retire older adult. This is a rare quality, and he has written a rare book!

...I recommend reading Campingly Yours to anyone who wants to hear, for once, about a "functional" family -or to anyone who wants a happy read."

Sally Lorber Stein
Retired Co-Director Camp Nebagamon

"Everyone who loved going to summer camp has had a secret wish to stay there the rest of their life. Tom Adler wished that same wish, and really lived it! Campingly Yours fulfills for so many of us a life of camping that still resonates from the very first canoe we paddled, campfire that we helped build, trails we explored, wildlife we spotted, song we sang, and friends that we made. Open the pages of this book and the secrets pour out, confirming a camper's hunch-if we could only have just stayed at camp, it would have been good."

Steven L. Katz
former camper and author of
Lion Taming; Working Successfully with Leaders, Bosses, and Other Tough Customers.

"Each year millions of children go to summer camp, where they have the benefit of activities, programs, and adventures that would never be available to them in their own hometowns. When children go to camp for the first time, they're only thinking about the fun activities and are totally unaware of the real value and benefit of attending camp—which is as it should be. However, by the end of the session, campers can't wait to return, both to rekindle the bonds of friendship and to renew the sense of belonging to a community of people who truly care. The real beauty is that without knowing it, campers are also being taught life lessons.

Thomas C. Adler's *Campingly Yours* quickly captures his readers with his story of attending camp for the first time as a ten-year-old boy. His memoir is an honest, humorous, and endearing account of the impact summer camp had on his life—and on the lives of thousands of others. By telling his story, Thomas also teaches a new generation of campers the same values he was taught by his parents and camp directors.

As a child, Thomas learned the value of living with other people and making new friends, the concept of compromise and respecting other people, and how to make decisions without mom or dad's help—and we watch him grow and mature as the book progresses. As a young adult, Thomas teaches us about making choices and the consequences that come with decision making. Later, as a camp owner/director, he teaches us that by sticking to our core beliefs, we can have a profound impact on the people around us. All this is done in an unassuming and tongue-in-check manner that is, for those of us who are fortunate enough to know him, totally and undeniably Thomas C. Adler.

His portrayal of camp episodes will rekindle memories for anyone who ever attended camp, and for those that didn't (and this book will make them wish they had), the lessons Thomas learned from his father and mother and camp directors Lou and Renee (and reinforced by countless counselors and staff members) are brought home in a style that's enjoyable and fun to read.

I've been a camp director for twenty-seven years and I can verify that the stories in *Campingly Yours* are true, and more importantly that variations of these episodes still take place in thousands of camps throughout the world every year.

Jack Weiner, our wonderful CIT Director for seventeen years, once said, "The real world is summer camp; the rest of the world should take notice."

Thomas Adler learned his lessons well and anyone who reads *Campingly Yours* will be at the very least entertained—and may even be moved to find out more about the real world of summer camp.

Thomas makes me proud to have chosen camping as a career."

Campingly Yours,

Robert "Leb" Lebby
Owner/Director, North Star Camp for Boys
President, Association of Independent Camps

 **Campingly Yours**